HOW_TO'S GUIDE .... •• *4*

How to Unlock Fast Trave ... *4*

How to Save *4*

How to Use Amiibo *6*

How to Get a Horse *7*

How to Get Rupees Fast *8*

How To Change Outfits *9*

How to Make Drinks (Smoothies) *10*

How To Remove Zelda's Hood *13*

How to Fly (Borrow Some Wings) *14*

How to Dig *16*

How to Break Spider Webs in Faron Wetlands *17*

How to Use the Bow *18*

How to Get & Use Bombs *19*

WALKTHROUGH **23**

Prologue *23*

The Mysterious Rifts *26*

Dungeon - Suthorn Ruins *35*

Searching for Everyone *42*

Searching for Everyone - Gerudo Desert *45*

A Rift in the Gerudo Desert *46*

Southern Oasis Ruins Rift *54*

Southern Gerudo Desert Rift *54*

Ancestor's Cave of Rest Rift *55*

A Rift in the Gerudo Desert - Part 2 .... *56*

Dungeon - Gerudo Sanctum *60*

Gerudo Desert Exploration (Optional) *71*

Searching for Everyone - Jabul Waters *73*

The Jabul Waters Rift *79*

Chaos at the River Zora Village *89*

Rampage in Zora Cove *91*

The Jabul Waters Rift - Part 2 .... *92*

Dungeon - Jabul Ruins *96*

1

Jabul Waters Exploration (Optional) 104

Still Missing 107

Dungeon - Hyrule Castle 110

World Exploration 118

Hyrule Field Exploration (Optional) 121

Lands of the Goddesses 132

Lands of the Goddesses - Eldin Volcano 133

The Rift on Eldin Volcano 134

Lizalfos Burrow 139

Rock-Roast Quarry 143

The Rift on Eldin Volcano - Part 2 145

Dungeon - Eldin Temple 148

Eldin Volcano Exploration (Optional) 155

Lands of the Goddesses - Faron Wetlands 157

A Rift in the Faron Wetlands 159

Dungeon - Faron Temple 179

Faron Wetlands Exploration 192

Lands of the Goddesses - Holy Mount Lanayru 192

Rift on Holy Mount Lanayru 196

Lanayru Temple Walkthrough 214

Mount Lanayru Exploration 226

The Prime Energy and Null 226

Rescuing the Hero Link 231

Null's Body Dungeon Guide 234

SIDE QUESTS **239**

World 239

Suthorn Prarie 239

Gerudo Desert 242

Hyrule Field 249

Hyrule Castle 259

Jabul Waters 267

Lake Hylia 274

Kakariko Village 276

Eldin Volcano *279*

Faron Wetlands *286*

Hebra Mountain & Mount Lanayru *291*

OPTIONAL RIFTS **296**

Stilled Lower Suthorn Forest Rift *296*

Stilled Lake Hylia Rift *297*

Stilled Northern Gerudo Desert Rift *298*

Stilled Eastern Zora River Rift *300*

Stilled Western Eldin Volcano Rift *302*

Stilled Northern Sanctuary Rift *304*

COLLECTIBLE & OTHER USEFUL ITEM LOCATIONS **305**

Pieces of Heart *305*

Accessories *318*

Fairy Bottles *321*

Outfits *321*

Stamps *323*

All Might Crystal Locations *331*

All Echo Locations *348*

HOW_TO'S GUIDE

HOW TO UNLOCK FAST TRAVEL

When Do You Unlock Fast Travel?

Eventually, as part of the main story, you will end up in Suthorn Village after progressing through Suthorn Beach. Leave the village and head east past the sign to find **Echo**es of Wisdom's first fast travel point, called a Waypoint.

These little structures glow yellow and allow Zelda to travel to any other unlocked Waypoints across the map. Of course, as you get through the game, there will be plenty of other ones to activate. To activate these, you just need to approach them and press the A button on the Switch controller.

You'll eventually unlock the second Waypoint in the northeastern section of Suthorn Forest. Once you pass the group of Spear Moblins guarding a **Treasure Chest** containing Grapes, you'll find the waypoint to the right.

How Do You Fast Travel in Zelda: Echoes of Wisdom?

To actually fast travel between Waypoints, just interact with the statue, hover over the Waypoint you want to teleport to, and press 'Warp.' Tri will go on top of Zelda's head, and the game will take you to the chosen location in just a few seconds. Luckily, teleporting between Waypoints does not waste any resources, so you can do it as often as you wish.

HOW TO SAVE

How to Save Your Game in Zelda: Echoes of Wisdom

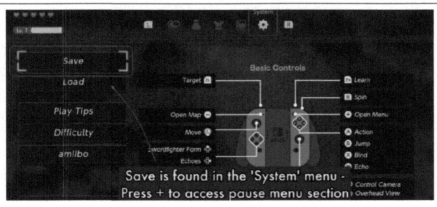

Like most Zelda games, **Echo**es of Wisdom can be a bit overwhelming when you are first released onto the massive open-world map. Before you know it, you'll either be completely absorbed in the classic dungeons, or you'll be off completing one of the many side-quests found through exploration. What you may not be thinking about, is saving your game. It's good for every player then, that **Echo**es of Wisdom has an extremely simple saving process, and a fairly robust autosave mechanic.

Those players who are familiar with modern Zelda games will easily recognize **Echo**es of Wisdom's saving mechanic. Manual saves are done in the System Menu, and as the first option on the list, it's hard to miss. Simply hover over the 'Save' option, press A, and then confirm when the game asks you to. This will complete the manual save process in Zelda: **Echo**es of Wisdom.

❖ *Saving Steps:*

- Press the + button
- Press R or L until you are in the System menu.
- Hover over "Save" and press A
- Select "Yes" and press A

Note: Echoes of Wisdom' s autosave system is very good, so you shouldn't have to worry too much if you go a while without saving. With five autosave slots, you'll also be able to return to multiple points earlier in your game if you feel you missed something, or would simply like to replay an area.

How to Load Your Save Files

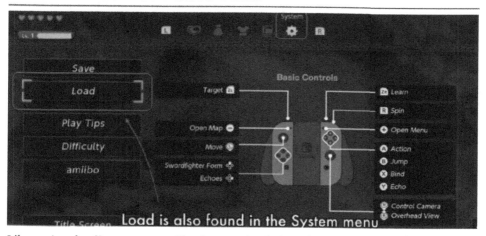

Like saving, loading your save files is very simple in Zelda: **Echo**es of Wisdom. In the System menu, "Load" will be the second option on the list. Selecting this option with the A button will bring up all of your save files, which include one manual save slot and five autosave slots. Highlight the save file you wish to load, then press A.

❖ *Loading Steps:*

- Press + button
- Use L or R to reach the System menu
- Select the "Load" option
- Confirm your choice

Like other modern Zelda games, **Echo**es of Wisdom only has one game file per profile. If you wish to start a brand-new game, you'll have to erase your current save file and start over, or create an entirely new profile.

How to Use Amiibo in Zelda: Echoes of Wisdom

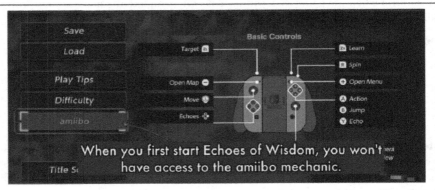

When players first start their **Echo**es of Wisdom playthroughs, they'll likely notice the "amiibo" option in the System menu is greyed-out and cannot be accessed. While it's true that you cannot use Amiibo immediately, you will not have to wait long to gain access to the mechanics.

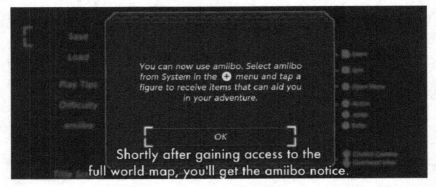

When the time comes, you'll get a message in the pause menu that notifies you when amiibo can be used. There was not a major event that signaled this for us, other than generally being released into the open-world. However, we did not immediately get the notice. Instead, it occurred shortly after exiting Beach Cave. We got access to amiibo just before learning **Echo**es of Wisdom's fast-travel mechanic.

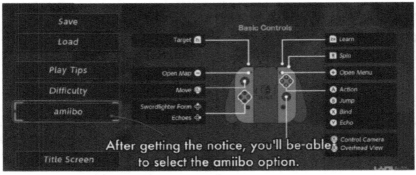

6

Once we received the notice, we were free to use amiibo. However, there are strict limitations on how often you can use amiibo in **Echo**es of Wisdom.

- You can only use amiibo three times a day. After that, you will get a notice stating that you can no longer use amiibo for the day.

Note: It appears that you can only use amiibo figures from The Legend of Zelda. It does not matter which game they represent, only that they are from the Zelda f ranchise . Figures from other franchises are widely reported as coming up incompatible. If we find any non- Zelda figures that do work, we will update this guide to reflect that.

❖ *Amiibo Rewards in Echoes of Wisdom*

During the early game sections, using amiibo appears to only get you Smoothie materials and monster parts. You can get a wide variety of these materials, but only three times a day. Once you complete Hyrule Castle, amiibo will have the chance to drop cosmetic **Outfit**s for Zelda. We do not currently have confirmation on the complete list of **Outfit**s but they will be added as soon as we have it.

HOW TO GET A HORSE

How to Start "Runaway Horse" in Echoes of Wisdom

❖ *Visit Hyrule Ranch:*

To get the first horse in **Echo**es of Wisdom, which is called a Rental Horse, Zelda will have to make her way to Hyrule Ranch in western Hyrule. This can be done any time after completing "The Mysterious Rifts" and the first main dungeon in Suthorn Ruins.

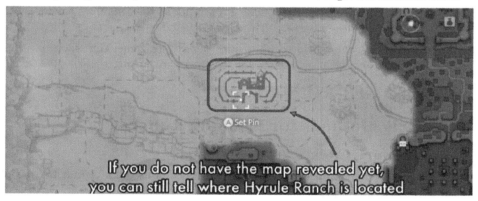

Upon arriving at Hyrule Ranch, make your way into the main courtyard, and you'll find an old man with a quest marker over his head. While speaking to the man, he will reveal that he is not currently loaning out horses because there is a mount missing. He tasks Zelda with helping to find it. Once the horse is returned, Zelda will have access to the horse for herself.

How to Get a Horse in Echoes of Wisdom

❖ *Complete Runaway Horse:*

The old man gives Zelda a hint: the horse likes to graze west of the ranch. With that knowledge, it'll be a quick trip to collect the horse. Make your way west to the small pond shown on the map. You'll find that the horse is stuck on an island in the middle of the pond. Zelda can jump directly to the pond, but you'll have to lay down a bed so the horse can make it across.

Once you are out of the pond, make your way back to Hyrule Ranch. When you arrive, the old man will be overjoyed that the horse is back safe, and he'll agree to let you use any horse you want. From here on out, you can use the ranch's horses as 'rental horses.' This is an important distinction, because this means that Zelda will not yet be able to call the horse back to her should you get separated. For now, the Rental Horse will show up on the map as a horse icon, but that's it.

Make sure to activate the fast-travel marker at the ranch so you can return any time, just in case you lose track of your horse, and it cannot be found on the map.

Zelda will be able to get her beloved white horse later in the game. This will be possible after "Still Missing" has been completed, and the guards are no longer looking for Zelda.

HOW TO GET RUPEES FAST

Best Early Methods for Farming Rupees

❖ *Treasure Chests, Cutting Grass*

Zelda lacks the iconic sword and cap, but she has her own spin attack in **Echo**es of Wisdom. By tapping the R-button, Zelda can spin in a circle and cut down grass. While it doesn't sound exciting on paper, longtime Zelda fans know that cutting grass will sometimes uproot **Rupees**. Thus, you should cut grass and weeds wherever you go. The **Rupees** that drop from grass will normally be Green **Rupees** (value of 1), but if you're lucky, you may get a Blue Rupee (value of 5).

Tip: If you manage to learn the Ignizol **Echo**, you can use it to burn the grass instead. There's an Ignizol in one of the caves you'll find en route to the Still Suthorn Forest . Just be careful Zelda doesn't get caught in the line of fire. If she does, you can put out the flames by spinning (R-button).

Another way to get **Rupees** quickly is to open chests. If you look around, you might find a stray chest out of reach that requires the use of your **Echo**es. There's one on the left side cliff in Suthorn Forest that has 50 **Rupees**. You should also be opening every chest you find in dungeons since most of them have Red or Purple **Rupees**.

Farming Rupees with Crow Echo

❖ *How to Get Crow Echo*

After you've cleared the Suthorn Ruins Dungeon, you'll meet Lueberry, Impa's older brother. From there, you'll need to reach two giant rifts in Gerudo Desert and Jabul Ruins. If you take the left path from Lueberry's house, you'll soon enter a desert/mountainous area with Crows. Defeat a crow using one of your **Echo**es, and then learn the Crow **Echo**. At this point, you'll have 4 "triangles" of Tri's power, allowing you to summon two Crow **Echo**es at a time. One Crow **Echo** requires 2 "triangles."

With the Crow **Echo**, you can target enemies (ZL-button) and tap Y-button to have them attack. Attacking enemies with the Crow **Echo** causes them to drop a handful of Green and Blue **Rupees**. Your Crow **Echo** may sweep down and gather a Rupee for you even if there are enemies nearby.

If you're fighting Crows, be warned that they will try to steal any dropped **Rupees**. You can steal them back by defeating the Crow.

HOW TO CHANGE OUTFITS

When Can You Change Outfits?

Zelda's fashion sense is held back by the narrative in **Echo**es of Wisdom. For several hours, you will be locked into wearing Link's cape and a cute yet inconspicuous number as wanted posters of our heroine litter the landscape.

TIp: Despite taking her disguise off in a way that serves the plot, you can still choose to wear Link's hooded cape if that tickles your fancy.

After completing the Zora, Gerudo, and Castle Town dungeons, you will face Ganon in a hard battle, but after emerging victorious, you will emerge into a reformed world where Zelda is not a wanted criminal but a celebrated hero.

Your father will then gift you the Royal Travel Attire, an **Outfit** which feels like Zelda's iconic dress but with an adventurous twist. You can't exactly move around and complete dungeons in heels, so this is the next best thing.

How To Get New Outfits

Echoes of Wisdom won't allow you to earn new **Outfits** for Zelda to wear until she's allowed to change out of her initial disguise. A wise choice, as it means you won't be finishing quests and earning rewards you can't even use.

Once you have left Castle Town behind and new rifts have appeared in Lanaryu, Eldin, and the Faron Wetlands, you will also be free to tackle a variety of new side missions that reward Zelda with fabulous new costumes.

TIp: Amiibo will have a chance of rewarding you with **Outfits** after this point, instead of a constant stream of smoothie ingredients.

The cat **Outfit**, for example - which allows you to speak to any feline in the open world - can be found in Kakariko Village, while Zelda's original dress can be earned by completing an adorable quest set by a young girl called Romi near the royal castle.

How Do You Change Outfits?

This is simple. Just head into the pause menu and navigate to the **Outfits** tab, and you will be able to select any of your unlocked costumes to wear.

Some **Outfits** have unique abilities, but most are merely cosmetic. Pick whatever appearance you love most or require at the time and go for it.

HOW TO MAKE DRINKS (SMOOTHIES)

How to Make Smoothie Drinks

In several locations through **Echo**es of Wisdom's map of Hyrule, Zelda can encounter the Business Scrub. This unique NPC is the owner of a chain of Smoothie stands, where Zelda can use the unique materials she collects during her travels to make special drinks that can heal or provide healing hearts or special effects like energy for Swordfighter Form or elemental resistance.

Zelda will encounter Busniess Scrubs in multiple locations around Hyrule

There are no special requirements for making drinks in **Echo**es of Wisdom, other than locating your first Smoothie Stand and having at least some materials. Because they are spread throughout the kingdom, Zelda will not have to wait long once she has the freedom to travel around Hyrule.

❖ *Making a Smoothie*

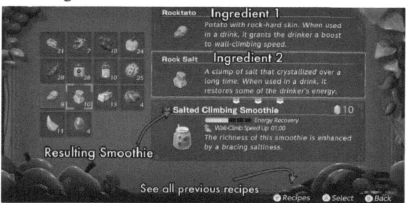

When you find a Smoothie Stand in **Echo**es of Wisdom, making drinks is an incredibly simple process. Smoothies are made from two ingredients. Follow these steps for making a drink:

- Pick Ingredient 1: Decide which ingredient you want as the base of your Smoothie. This should be the key ingredient.

- Pick Ingredient 2: You have several options for your second ingredient. First, you can simply double your first ingredient, making a basic Smoothie. You can also use a second ingredient to create a mixed Smoothie, with multiple effects. Some ingredients will simply bolster the main ingredient. Using trial and error is the best way to find what works, and what doesn't.

- Select Make Smoothie: The Business Scrub will charge you 10 **Rupees** to mix your

11

ingredients.

Note: While you should definitely experiment with all ingredients, keep in mind that mixing two bolstering ingredients will usually get you an Unfortunate Smoothie. These drinks will still provide a small amount of health, as well as a bit of Energy, but they will take up a valuable

❖ *Smoothie Notes:*

- Zelda can carry 20 Smoothies at a time.

- When you first meet the Business Scrub, he will initiate the "Recipes, Please" side quest, which will require a total of 30 unique Smoothie recipes to complete. Check the quest description in the menu to see how many recipes you've completed.

- When mixing ingredients, the menu will let you know whether you've made a particular recipe before, and what the resulting Smoothie will be.

- Ingredients are found in a variety of places: **Treasure Chest**s, in Pots and Plants, Quest Rewards, and even amiibo Rewards.

All Smoothie Shops in Zelda: Echoes of Wisdom

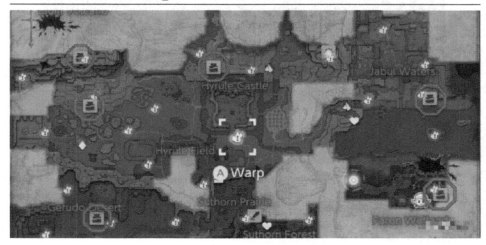

There are six Smoothie Shops in The Legend of Zelda: **Echo**es of Wisdom. They are found in the following locations:

- Gerudo Oasis
- Jabul Waters
- Eldin Volcano
- Faron Wetlands
- Kakariko Village
- Northern Sanctuary

HOW TO REMOVE ZELDA'S HOOD

How To Remove Zelda's Hood in Echoes of Wisdom

To remove Zelda's hood, **Echo**es of Wisdom players have to reinstate the kingdom's trust in her as their princess – our titular heroine is on the run, after all, which is why she is wearing the hood in the first place. But the only way to do that is to rid Hyrule of its impostor King, because then Zelda will be able to prove her innocence and won't have to hide her identity anymore.

The only way to take off Zelda's hood in **Echo**es of Wisdom is to complete the Hyrule Castle dungeon, which is the fourth of the major dungeons in **Echo**es of Wisdom.

You must complete the Suthorn Ruins dungeon at the start of the game, then continue to both Gerudo Desert and Jabul Waters for the dungeons in each of these areas, before you can access Hyrule Castle.

After beating the Hyrule Castle dungeon, and sealing away the Rift that set off her banishment, Zelda will pull down her hood and reveal her identity.

Note: People will now recognize Zelda instantly, too, changing some of the dialogue throughout the game.

❖ *Other Zelda Customizations Unlock At The Same Point*

After Zelda gets back to her bedroom (and after learning the very-high-Heart-restoring Zelda's Bed **Echo**), she will climb out of bed and be summoned to the King once more. Here, you will unlock the Royal Travel Attire, an ancient vestment befitting the heroic priestess of legend. This costume is more regal and gives Zelda a ponytail that whips around when she spins.

While you remain in the castle, before going to the next cutscene, Zelda's hood will remain down on the default Disguise **Outfit**. However, when you are forced to change into the Royal Travel Attire the Disguise goes back to its Hood Up mode.

There isn't a way to permanently remove Zelda's hood with this costume, but you can equip other costumes after reaching this point that do not have a hood at all.

You can also unlock three unique Amiibo costumes in **Echo**es of Wisdom after reaching this point. Before beating Hyrule Castle, Amiibo will only reward Smoothie and Monster materials. Afterward, different Zelda Amiibo can reward the Red Tunic, Blue Attire, and Black Cat Costume.

Though there are a handful of costumes that you can unlock without finishing Hyrule Castle, the majority of them are locked behind progressing here and unlocking the rest of the game world up for exploration.

HOW TO FLY (BORROW SOME WINGS)

How to Fly in Zelda: Echoes of Wisdom

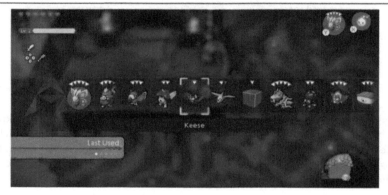

The first step towards flying is creating a flying **Echo** in The Legend of Zelda: **Echo**es of Wisdom, and there are many suitable options. Indeed, any winged **Echo** can facilitate flight, and players should look at the birds, bats, and moths that they have collected.

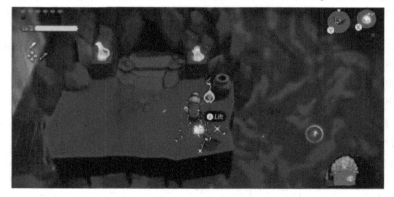

After summoning a flying **Echo**, **Echo**es of Wisdom players should approach the creature and press "A" to lift it. Notably, fans should try to grab onto their winged **Echo**es very quickly after creating one, as they will not be able to lift the creature after it gains some elevation.

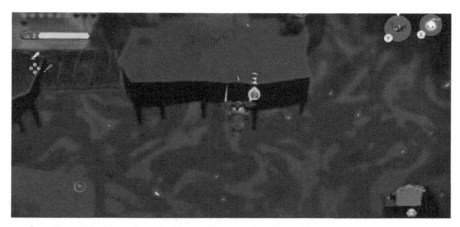

Once the winged **Echo** is lifted, players have completed all the preparatory work that is required for flying, and they should simply run off any ledge to take flight. Fans should resist the urge to jump from the ledge, though, as pressing "B" will cause Zelda to release the **Echo** and put a premature end to things.

Zelda: Echoes of Wisdom Flying Tips

Players should now have a solid understanding of how to fly in The Legend of Zelda: **Echo**es of Wisdom. That said, the flying mechanic has some quirks of which fans should be aware.

The first quirk is that winged **Echo**es will continually lose elevation once a flight has been initiated. This means that the flying mechanic is typically used to cross gaps and fly over obstacles, and it is not usually a tool for increasing Zelda's vertical position. Fortunately, there are a variety of **Echo**s that are great at facilitating vertical movement, such as Water Blocks and Strandtulas.

Note: There are vertical air streams that can be used to combat a flying **Echo**'s elevation loss. Indeed, entering one of those air streams will send the **Echo** upward, and their presence generally indicates that the player should take flight in the area.

The other thing to know is that winged **Echo**es will drop Zelda after flying for approximately three seconds, and the size of the monster in **Echo**es of Wisdom does not seem to impact that duration. This limitation means that even if a player starts their flight at a very high elevation, and with a very large **Echo**, they will not be able to use the mechanic to cover vast distances.

HOW TO DIG

Where to Find Holmill Echo

❖ *Holmill Location in Echoes of Wisdom*

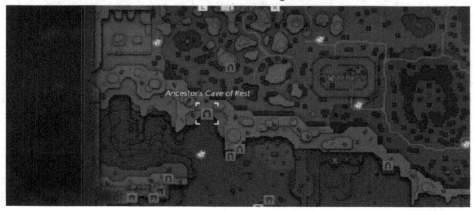

Ancestor's Cave of Rest

After clearing the Stilled Suthorn Forest, you're given the choice to go to Gerudo Desert or Jabul Waters. The choice itself won't matter since you'll need to fix the rifts in both areas. However, the Gerudo Desert has a few **Echo**es that will make platforming easier, such as the Flying Tile and Platboom. If you work through the Gerudo Desert/"A Rift in Gerudo Desert," you'll eventually find the Ancestor's Cave of Rest.

The Ancestor's Cave of Rest is located north of Gerudo Town, specifically north of the red Lanmola spawn point. There's a Waypoint statue in front of the Ancestor's Cave of Rest. If you haven't defeated the Lanmola, you'll know you're close to the Ancestor's Cave of Rest if a sandstorm obscures your map.

Tip: After rescuing Dohna and speaking to her at the Oasis , the Ancestor's Cave of Rest will be marked on your map , making it easier to find it if you have not already done so.

Inside the Ancestor's Cave of Rest, you'll see a large rift cutting you off from the ancestor's tomb. Go left, and use Tri's Bind ability to remove the giant boulder. Enter the room that was hidden by the boulder, and you'll find two Holmills.

Holmills are mole-like creatures that burrow in the sand/dirt. They'll dive back into hiding if you get too close, so use the Bind ability to pull them out. Then, summon an **Echo** to defeat it and learn the Holmill **Echo**.

How to Use Holmill

❖ *Where Should You Dig?*

Summon Holmill just as you would with any other **Echo**. As soon as it's summoned, Holmill will try to burrow in the dirt. If you summon Holmill over a spot that it can't dig, it will leave itself vulnerable to enemy attacks.

Zelda can jump into the holes that Holmill digs. Certain caves have floors of sand that lead to suspended platforms you wouldn't be able to reach normally. However, when used in Hyrule/3D map, jumping into a Holmill hole will make Zelda respawn.

You'll want to use Holmill to dig small squares of dirt. There's usually a **Might Crystal** hidden in these patches of dirt. In other cases, the patches may lead into a cave with a Heart Piece, such as the one east of Kakariko Village. You'll need Holmill if you want to get every Heart Piece in **Echo**es of Wisdom.

HOW TO BREAK SPIDER WEBS IN FARON WETLANDS

How to Break Faron Wetlands Spider Webs

To break the spider webs in the Faron Wetlands, **Echo**es of Wisdom players need to burn them. This burning can be done by putting a flame into contact with the web, and the fire on top of an Ignizol works perfectly for this approach.

Note: After creating an Ignizol, players may want to use Tri to grab the creature and then move it next to the web that is to be burned.

While this is the basic method for breaking webs in the Faron Wetlands, there is an issue that can arise. Specifically, the rain that can appear in the area will prevent Ignizols from igniting, rendering them useless against webs. Fortunately, players can easily put an end to the rain in the Faron Wetlands if they understand its source.

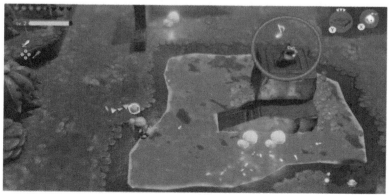

With respect to that source, the rain in the Faron Wetlands is created by singing frogs, and players will know that one of those enemies is nearby if it is raining. When that situation arises, fans should simply focus on locating the nearby singing frog, and the rain will stop as soon as that **Echo**es of Wisdom monster is defeated.

It is expected that many readers will be interested in breaking a web that blocks a chest on the west side of the Faron Wetlands. Players can find the frog that is making it rain in that area to the right of the chest.

What is in the Spider-Web-Blocked Chest in Faron Wetlands?

The aforementioned spider-web-blocked chest holds five Electro Apples, items that can be used to make Smoothies in The Legend of Zelda: **Echo**es of Wisdom. As the name of this item suggests, Smoothies that contain Electro Apples provide resistance to electricity, and players may find that effect useful in some situations.

HOW TO USE THE BOW

How to Get the Bow in Echoes of Wisdom

The only way to get the Bow in **Echo**es of Wisdom is during the main story quest, A Rift in the Gerudo Desert, which is also part of the overarching storyline of the 'Searching for Everyone' quest. Once you reach the Gerudo Desert and complete the objectives, you will eventually face the final challenge: the Gerudo Sanctum dungeon.

In the first part of the dungeon, you will have to face off against Shadow Link, but this time, he has a bow to shoot arrows at you with. In order to get the bow for yourself, you just need to beat Link in this dungeon. He will drop the bow upon his defeat.

How to Use the Bow in Echoes of Wisdom

Right when Zelda picks up Shadow Link's Bow of Might, you'll learn that you can only use it in Swordfighter form (up button on the d-pad). Once you're in the form, you can press X to shoot arrows at baddies and switches.

How to Upgrade the Bow in Echoes of Wisdom

Once you get through a good chunk of the intro, you'll learn about Lueburry; visiting him with **Might Crystals** will let you upgrade your Swordfighter form, like its Energy Gauge and attack power. You can also upgrade your Bow here (and Bombs later).

HOW TO GET & USE BOMBS

How to Get Bombs in Echoes of Wisdom

Thanks to **Echo**es of Wisdom's new **Echo** mechanic, Bombs come in several different forms. Before Zelda gets her hands on the more traditional form of Bombs, she will likely discover two important **Echo**es: the Bombfish, and Zirro. Of these two, the Bombfish has the most practical applications, so we will focus on finding them first.

❖ *How to get Bombfish*

Bombfish can be found at several locations in Jabul Waters, the eastern-Hyrule home of both the River and Sea Zora. For a guaranteed location, you can go to the cave that sits directly south of the "Zora River" title on the map, which sits south of the Zora River Village in northern Jabul Waters.

19

A Bombfish is the first enemy you'll encounter in the cave. Learn it after defeating it.

After you complete **Echo**es of Wisdom's first major dungeon, Suthorn Ruins, you'll have the option to go to Jabul Waters or Gerudo Desert. You can either wait until this point to get the Bombfish, or you can head there as soon as you get access to the open-world. If you plan to explore early in the game, then having the Bombfish **Echo** will be hugely beneficial.

❖ *How to Get the Zirro Echo*

Zirro are found all along this brdige are in Eldin Volcano

The Zirro is another enemy that produces bombs, though in this instance it is not as practical as the Bombfish. The Zirro is a floating mushroom that drops bombs. Zelda can pick up the bombs that are dropped and then use them as she sees fit. The timing of the explosion is pretty fast, so you have to move quickly.

Zirro drop bombs that Zelda can pick up and use

Zirro are found in Eldin Volcano, not far west of the entrance to Goron City and the nearby Smoothie Shop. Look for bombs hitting the ground, and you'll know you are in the right area. These **Echo**es can be fun, but the Bombfish has far more uses.

20

❖ *How to Get Traditional Bombs*

Just like acquiring **Echo**es of Wisdom's Bow and Sword, Zelda will have to face Link's evil doppelgänger to acquire the more traditional style of bombs. In this case, Zelda will encounter Dark Link as she makes her way through Eldin Temple, the final dungeon in the Eldin Volcano region.

This door leads to Dark Link's chamber in Eldin Temple

Once you reach his chamber, Link will try to defeat you with bombs exclusively. First, you will stand below as he throws bombs down to your level. There is a layer of cracked blocks that make up the floor and some smaller walls on the side. As they break, you can access climbing walls that allow you to reach Link.

Dark Link will throw bombs down at Zelda - she can pick them up and throw them back

You can climb up and attack Link from the high ground, using arrows or any other weapon you choose. In Phase 2, Link becomes much more aggressive, throwing multiple bombs at once. When he is defeated, he will reward you with permanent access to Bombs.

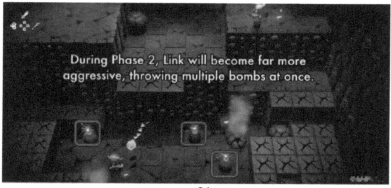

During Phase 2, Link will become far more aggressive, throwing multiple bombs at once.

How to Use Bombs in Echoes of Wisdom

❖ Echo Bombs:

Bombfish can be a bit tricky to use, as they flop around like the fish they are. Your best option when using them to destroy objects is to pick them up. The explosions will not hurt you, so there is no need to run and hide after summoning the Bombfish or Zirro.

❖ Swordfighter Form Bombs:

Once you defeat Dark Link in Eldin Temple, and unlock traditional Bombs, they will only be accessible in Swordfighter Form. Once you switch forms and are using the main Energy bar for combat, Bombs can be thrown by pressing A.

Tip: Once you unlock traditional Bombs, you can return to Lueberry's house to upgrade them , just like the Bow and Sword.

❖ Exploration:

In **Echo**es of Wisdom, Bombs help with exploration in largely the same way they have in past games. When you see a cracked wall or block, you'll know that this signifies a surface that can be destroyed by Bombs. These areas commonly hide secrets, or special items, like Heart Pieces or **Might Crystal**s.

Bombfish are the best tool to use in these instances because they are limitless. They do not rely on energy, and can be summoned anytime as an **Echo**. They also work underwater, though their movements can be less predictable. If you are having trouble getting them to destroy a specific object, use Bind once their timers have been triggered.

WALKTHROUGH

PROLOGUE

Prologue Dungeon

We will begin the game in control of Link. We will have some action buttons located in the top, right of the screen controlling the Sword , Bow and Bombs so try out each of these before heading onwards. Use the elevator at the end of the hallway.

Upon exiting the elevator climb the stairs and then hop over the rubble on the right to continue upward. After hopping over the next collection of rubble, you will encounter a couple of Darknut enemies.

These fellows are equipped with 2-handed axe and are armored. Use Link's Shield to block incoming attacks before following up with attacks of your own. Continue to the right and up the next set of stairs. Another three Darknuts await you in the room at the top. Again, take them all out to unlock the door leading onwards.

At the top of the next stairs, you will encounter some Keese. These are bat-like creatures that love swooping attacks. Wait for their attack, and then attack them once they are in sword range.

Continue to the left, and navigate across the gaps in the path, dispatching more Keese as you go. At the far end of the room, use the collection of rubble as a path up to the ledge with the door above.

Defeat the pair of Keese here and then continue to the north. There is another group of three Darknuts here, one of which is a blue variant and a little tougher. After dispatching the group, continue up the stairs for a scene.

❖ *Boss: Ganon*

The first boss of the game is Link's arch-nemesis Ganon. Fortunately, we have a ton of health and the boss himself only has two real attacks that we need to watch out for.

Our goal is to avoid the attacks and then quickly run over and swat Ganon a couple of times with your sword whilst he recovers.

The first attack has him wind up backwards before lunging quickly forwards with a jabbing attack using his spear. Simply running to the side should give you enough time to avoid this. The second attack has the boss summon a slow-moving fireball which he will throw at you. We can either run past this, or hit it with the sword to deflect it back towards the boss.

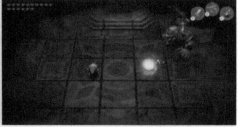

Each time you damage Ganon enough, he will power up a little. All that really happens though is that he speeds up a little. This will happen two times before the fight draws to a close with another scene.

Following the scene, we will take control of Zelda. She is currently trapped in a purple crystal, so wiggle the movement stick to break loose. Work your way around the rift on the floor and pick up the Swordsman's Cloak from the floor.

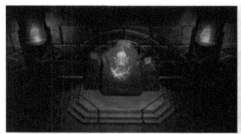

Approach the stairs and the rift will start to expand behind you. At this point we simply need to keep running all the way through the area until we reach the exit. Avoid the falling blocks, and jump any gaps or obstacles that get in your path as you go.

After safely exiting the area, a scene will play.

Hyrule Castle Town

When you regain control of Zelda, we will find ourselves in Hyrule Castle town. You can speak with the villagers here and have a bit of a wander around if you like. To continue however, you will need to head for the castle.

Upon entering the castle, continue north where you will meet Impa. After a brief chat, you can also check out the open door on the right to find Zelda's bedroom (there is a bed and a cat we can interact with here). To continue however, you need to head through the door behind Impa to reach the throne room.

Approach and speak with the king and his advisers, General Wright, and Minister Lefte. After a short chat here, another scene will play.

Hyrule Castle Dungeon

Following the scene, we will find ourselves in a prison cell. Soon after we arrive we will be greeted by a Tri, a glowing yellow creature who will accompany us for the rest of the adventure. After a chat, you will be given the Tri Rod.

Note: After acquiring the Tri Rod, you will find things shimmering in the environment. If you go up to this and press ZR, you can learn an **Echo** of the object. This allows you to essentially create a clone of the object.

Head on over and interact with the table to learn **Echo** – Table.

Use the Tri Rod to create a table next to the wooden ledge on the left side of the cell. Jump atop the table and then up to the shelf. Drop down inside the adjacent cell and continue out the open door.

Once outside, the right path leads to a dead end, so enter the door on the left. We will now need to do a bit of a stealth section here to get past the patrolling guards. Note that if we get caught, we will end up back in the starting cell and we will need to escape all over.

Use some tables to create a path up to the top of the shelf here so that you can run past the first guard. Drop down to ground level and check out the boxes here for **Echo** – Wooden Box.

25

The next section has two guards patrolling around a central shelf. Wait for one to pass and follow them along their route until you can continue to the left. Continue past the next two guards. Climb the ladder here and at the top you can examine the pots on the left for **Echo** – Hyrule Castle Pot.

Note that we can use these pots to distract enemies. Throwing a pot will have them go and investigate the source of the noise. If you look to the left, there is a guard watching the area ahead. Toss a pot to distract him before dropping down and quickly running past his initial location.

The final guard is another patroller. Watch his patrol route and make a break for the exit when it is safe to do so.

In the next room, a scene will play where we will encounter Impa once again. After a short chat, Zelda will get changed behind a statue. Speak with Impa once again for another scene during which we will be given a map and journal.

Note: The map is accessible by pressing (-). This will show your current location on the world map and will be slowly filled in as you explore new areas. Additionally, you will see objective markers and can drop pins to track quests and other objects of interest. The journal on the other hand allows you to track quests - both main and side-quests. Nice!

THE MYSTERIOUS RIFTS

Hyrule Castle Prison

As soon as you arrive in the new area, you can examine the plant in the lower, right for **Echo** – Decorative Shrub. Climb the nearby ladder and use the shrubs here as a path. Create a couple of decorative shrubs to fill the gap in the path and continue across.

On the far side, climb down the ladder to find a bed we can examine for **Echo** – Old Bed
Climb back up the ladder and use bed **Echo**es to work your way across the gaps to the
left and to the next doorway.

We will find ourselves outside. Here, head for the well along the left-hand wall and jump
down inside. We will arrive in our first side-scrolling area.

Royal Family Shortcut

In this area, dive under the water and grab the **Rupees** in the lower left. Climb up out of
the water and continue left. When you reach the ledge that is too high, spawn a
table/bed to reach it. Continue onwards until you find a rock blocking the path. Scan this
for **Echo** – Boulder.

We can walk into the boulder to push it. Keep going until it drops into the water. Jump
into the water after it and grab the **Rupees**.

Climb up and jump onto the box floating on the surface. Create a bed or two to reach the
next ledge on the left. Once across, you will reach a platform made of floating wooden
boxes. Spawn a boulder onto one of the boxes to make it sink.

Jump into the water and swim upwards and to the left to exit the side scrolling area.

After climbing out of the water here, a rift will appear again and begin expanding. Jump down into the flowing river below for a scene.

Suthorn Beach

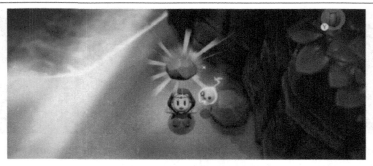

When you regain control, you will find yourself waking up on a beach at the very southern end of the map. Once up, head on over and inspect a nearby rock for the **Echo** – Rock.

Head over to the right and then through the opening to the south to reach Suthorn Beach. Tri will encourage you to look at the map at this point. If you do so, you will see that a section of it has now been uncovered. This will continue to expand as you explore the map.

After a short jog, a few Zol will appear. These little green blobs will jump at you and damage you if they make contact, but do not really present a threat otherwise. Now, we do not have anything in the way of weapons, however we can defeat this by throwing rocks or crates at it. Once dead, you can examine it for the **Echo** – Zol.

Note: As Zelda does not have any weapons (at least for the moment) we can spawn
***Echo**es of monsters to fight for us. This is done in the same way as spawning regular*
items using the Tri Rod. To get them to target a specific enemy, lock them on!

Continue to the right and use a rock to hit some Sea Urchins. Again, examine one of these once defeated for the **Echo** – Sea Urchin. Note that these **Echo**es are a good defensive option because although they cannot move, you can spawn them in front of Zelda and any enemy approaching to attack will take damage from the spikes. Handy!

In the area just left of the first Sea Urchins, head to the northern wall to see a ledge above. Use your beds and tables to create a path up here. There is a **Treasure Chest** here containing a Red Rupee (20 **Rupees**).

Proceed into the water in the lower, right section of the area. You can dive below and grab some **Rupees** between some Sea Urchins. We want to climb up onto the central island here. From this location, use some beds to the left to reach a ledge with a **Piece of Heart**.

Note: Pieces of Heart are handy collectibles to track down. Finding four of these will expand Zelda's health by a single heart.

Return to the previous island and this time use beds to reach the island to the north and then use them to cross the broken bridge to the north. Use the rocks here to clear out the Sea Urchins and then proceed into the cave.

Suthorn Prairie

After exiting the cave, look along the right wall just behind some trees there is a ledge we can jump up to. Follow this around the corner and then create a set of stairs using beds/tables to reach the ledge above with a **Treasure Chest**. It contains a Purple Rupee (50 **Rupees**).

Return to the main path and follow it to reach Suthorn Village.

When you arrive in Suthorn Village, you will find a few people around that we can speak with and houses to explore. There are a couple of **Echo**es here that we can acquire. You can find them in the following locations:

- The house in the lower, left has **Echo** – Meat in the fireplace
- The house in the lower, centre has **Echo** – Pot.
- Outside the shop, you will find **Echo** – Trampoline.

After nabbing the **Echo**es, you can also jump down the well. There is a **Treasure Chest** here with Floral Nectar x5. This can be consumed to restore hearts, but the game mentions that it is more effective when mixed into a drink... I guess we will be learning how to do that at some point.

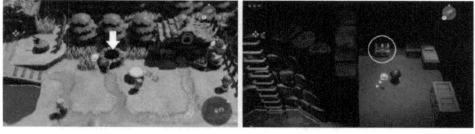

Additionally, if you check out the shop in the upper, right of the village you will find that there is a **Piece of Heart** for sale for 80 **Rupees**. If you grabbed the **Treasure Chest**s on the way here, you should have enough **Rupees** to purchase

To continue, head to the east from the village. There will be a sign we can examine for **Echo** – Sign. If you head north you will encounter a Rift blocking the path forward. As such, we will need to take the path leading to the east instead. You will encounter your first **Waypoint Stone** here.

Note: After interacting with and activating a Waypoint, you will be able to use them as fast travel points from the map. Nice! As such, be sure to activate them whenever you see them.

Suthorn Forest

Continue to the east until you see some water north of the path. Cross this and defeat the Zols on the far side. There is a **Treasure Chest** here with Electro Apple x5.

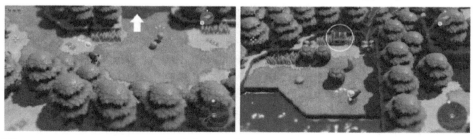

When you come across a cave, look just to the left of this for a ledge we can climb. Once up, use a collection of beds/tables to reach the next ledge above. There is another **Treasure Chest** up here with a Red Rupee.

31

Head back to the path and proceed into the cave here. Fight your way through the Zols until you reach the area with an Ignizol. This is a Zol that is on fire – be careful because it can set grass and boxes alight. Use your **Echo** monsters to defeat it and then examine it for **Echo** – Ignizol.

Proceed into the next room. There are a bunch of Zols in here. Take them out one at a time or pop your Ignizol into the grass to burn them all alive (and mop up any survivors) After clearing the enemies, head to the northern end of the room. Set an Ignizol into the brazier on the right to unlock the door. Inside you will find a **Treasure Chest** with a Fairy Bottle.

Note: Fairy Bottles are useful as they allow you to capture Fairies inside. If you have a Fairy Bottle and lose all of your hearts, the fairy in the bottle will revive you with full health. Its essentially an extra life.

Exit the cave and continue to the east. You will come across a grass area where several snake-like enemies called Ropes are hiding in the tall grass. Again, send your Ignizol into the grass to deal with them. After dispatching one, examine the body for **Echo** – Rope.

Head north from this area and you will find another cave. Head on inside.

We will be side-scrolling again here. Climb down the first two ladders to the bottom to encounter a new enemy type a Caromadillo. After dispatching it, be sure to grab **Echo** - Caromadillo.These enemies are handy as **Echo**es because they can they curl into a ball and launch at enemies at high speed. Nice for hitting things from range!

Proceed to the right and send out a Caromadillo to burst through the line of crates ahead Climb the climbable walls at the end, whilst avoiding the second Caromadillo. At the top you will find a **Piece of Heart**.

After leaving the cave, continue to the left. Defeat the Moblin here (it is a good opportunity to try out your Caromadillo!). Examine it after defeating it for **Echo** – Spear Moblin. Just past this enemy in a pool of water is a Fairy. Swim into it to capture it in the Fairy Bottle.

Continue onwards and you will arrive at the objective marker on the map... only to discover that the house we want to enter has been half-eaten by a rift and we cannot enter.

Follow the path leading upwards and to the right. We will soon come across a Moblin camp with three Moblins patrolling. There is some meat here that we can use to distract the enemies if needed. Once they are all dead, the **Treasure Chest** in the middle of the camp will unlock. Climb up to it for Refreshing Grapes x10.

From the camp, continue to the right to find another **Waypoint Stone**.

Before continuing, head south from the Waypoint to find a lower path we can drop down to. Defeat the Spear Moblin here and you will find a cave. Examine the torches either side of the door for **Echo** – Brazier.

Enter the cave here. Continue upwards and you will encounter a Peahat. These plant enemies have thorns around their base and will spin at high speed whilst converging on your position. Wait for their spikes to retract and they stop for a moment before sending out your **Echo**es to attack. Defeat this and then examine it for **Echo** - Peahat.

Return to the Waypoint. Head up the slope behind this and approach the rift. A scene will play and afterwards we will be able to jump inside.

Stilled Suthorn Forest

After arriving in the Still World, climb up the stairs for a scene. After the scene, follow the set path, being sure to use beds/tables to construct bridges across gaps as you go. At the top of the first slope, you will be attacked by a Keese and Moblin. Fend them off.

Hop across the trees on the right to reach the entrance to a cave. Continue inside.

In the first room, on the right side of the pit there is a pressure plate. Stepping on this will unlock the door to the next room. Use some beds/tables to create bridges across to the pressure plate (and kill the Keese if they get on your nerves). Continue through the now open door.

The next room has four Zol enemies in it. Again, use your **Echo**es to take them all out. Defeating them all will unlock the next door. Continue through here to find yourself back outside.

Continue up the nearby ramp and defeat the Zol and Spear Moblin at the top. This area has several different areas to explore branching off from it. The two main optional paths include some ledges in the upper right there where you will find a Blue Rupee and a more involved are in the lower left.

The lower left path has an island with a ladder we can descend to reach a side-scroller area. Defeat the Spear Moblin inside and open the **Treasure Chest** it guards for a Purple Rupee.

Exit the side-scroll area and climb onto the tree here. From the top, create a stairway up to the ledge above and to the left. There is another **Treasure Chest** here to loot for a Red Rupee.

With all the optional stuff done, return to the larger platform. When you are ready to continue, take the upper, left path. Here we will bump into Minister Lefte (who we met in the presence of the king earlier) and just past her location, the entrance to the game's first dungeon, Dungeon - Suthorn Ruins.

DUNGEON - SUTHORN RUINS

Suthorn Ruins

As you enter the Suthorn Ruins, you will find a **Waypoint Stone** here. Go ahead and activate this. When you are ready to get started, proceed inside.

The first room has a locked door in the back, right and a pressure plate in the back, left. The pressure plate is blocked by a giant boulder on one side and a chasm on the other. We need to reach the pressure plate to open the door.

If you approach the rock, Tri will chime in and reveal a new power – Bind. Using this we can press ⊗ to bind objects into the environment to us so that we can move them about In this case we can move the giant boulder. Position this on the pressure plate to open the door.

In the next room, there is a giant boulder in a recess in the floor. Again, use Tri to move this to the side, revealing a ladder leading downwards. We can also maneuver the boulder out of the pit and into the water where we can place it beside the ramp to create a path upwards.

 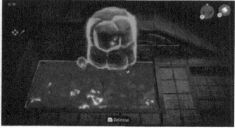

35

Climb the ramp first. In the room at the top, you will find a half-buried **Treasure Chest** Use bind on this to yank it out of the ground so that you can loot it. It contains Radiant Butter x5.

Head back to the previous room and down the ladder. Here you will need to jump across strands of spider's webs, past the first spider and then drop to the floor. We can use an enemy (I used Caromadillo) to kill a second, low hanging spider to claim the **Echo - Strandtula**.

Use the Strandtula to create a rope to reach the floating platform here and then use it again to climb up through the opening in the ledge above to reach the **Treasure Chest**. This contains the Dungeon Map.

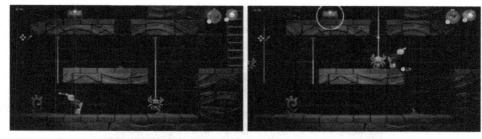

Note: The Dungeon Map will show you the layout of the dungeon and the area surrounding the dungeon in the Still World. You can switch between maps on the map screen by pressing ⯈ *or* ◀.

Use the Strandula to reach the ladder on the far, right side of the side scrolling area. Climb up to reach the next room.

This room has a door high up on a ledge on the western side. The easiest way to reach this is to use a Strandula to create a web that we can climb and jump to the upper ledge.

In the next room, you will find an Ignizol to the south (and not much else of interest) and to the north an elevator platform. Ride this up to the floor above.

Once up, climb the nearby stairs and defeat the Darknut at the top (Sea Urchins work well here) for **Echo** - Darknut.

Use a bed/table to climb up to the stairs on the left and enter the door at the top. Continue down the ladder here.

We will arrive in another side-scroller area. Here the exit is locked and to open it we need to light the two non-lit braziers. There is one in the lower left, summon an Ignizol to light it and another up the ladder beside the locked gate. At the top, there is another brazier behind a stack of crates. Either use bind to move the crates (boring) or throw an Ignizol at them to light them all on fire, lighting the brazier in the process.

Head up the ladder to escape the side-scrolly area. At the top, you will find another **Waypoint Stone**. Go ahead and activate that.

The door ahead is locked, but if you look along the walls either side of it, you should be able to see a series of statues. One of these has a gold shield. Create a bridge out to its location and then use bind on the shield. Pull the shield away from the statue and once it breaks free, the door will pop open for us.

In the subsequent room, there is a pair of Keese waiting for us in the initial area and a pair of Darknuts further north. Try to pick off the enemies one at a time and eliminate them.

After clearing the enemies, look in the southwestern side of the room for a sloped dirt ramp and a pile of fallen bricks. We can use the Strandtula to climb up on top of this. On the far side there is a **Treasure Chest** with a Purple Rupee.

Return to the main section of the room and proceed up the stairs at the northern end. At the top you will get a mini-boss fight.

❖ *Boss: Shadow Link*

*Shadow Link is armed with a sword and shield and can do a significant amount of damage with the weapon if you get too close to him. Fortunately, to win we will not need to do that! Instead, our goal is to stay out of sight and get our **Echoes** to attack him. Note that when approached by an **Echo** front-on he will use his shield and block any incoming attacks, so we need to find way around it. We can use the two walls on either side of the main area and the ledges around the perimeter of the room to outmaneuver him.*

*I had success in luring him behind one of the walls and have him follow around it until he loses sight of you. At this point he will stand still, and his head will move from side to side, looking for you. At this point, you can sneak up and summon an **Echo** behind him (Darknut is a good one) and have them attack him in the rear. They should land a couple of blows before Link recovers and finishes them off. Repeat this process.*

*After he takes enough damage, a scene will play, and Shadow Link will start glowing purple. At this stage he moves a little faster and his attacks do a little extra damage. The good news is that we can use the same tactics here to fight and defeat him. Continue to have your **Echo**es damage hm from, behind until he is defeated.*

Following the fight, claim the Mysterious Sword from the ground nearby.

Note: The Mysterious Sword will enable you to transform into swordfighter mode by pressing ▐▲▐*. Once transformed, you can use* ⬤ *to attack, hold down* ⬤ *for a charge attack and use* ⬤ *to block using a shield.*

In swordfighter form, a blue gauge will appear in the upper-left corner of the screen. This will deplete rapidly and when it is empty, you will transform back to regular Zelda. You will need to gather Energy to replenish the gauge.

Activate Swordfighter mode and slice up the purply goop blocking the door here. Continue down the ladder behind it. We are back in side scroll mode.

As you descend the ladder here, hop to the highest ledge on the right. Drop down from the far end. Use a Strasndtula on the ledge below and then climb up so you can jump to the area with the **Treasure Chest** on the right. It contains Heart Pin.

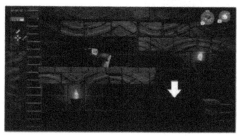 

Drop down to the lower area. There is a giant rock here. Bind this and carry it back to the left and leave it in the impression in the floor. Climb the ladder on the left, then jump onto the giant rock and then drop down past it to continue onwards. Descend the ladder to return to the dungeon proper.

The next room has three doors and a **Waypoint Stone**. The northern door leads to the dungeon's boss room and the right-hand door is currently locked, both of these need keys to enter, so that leaves us left hand door as our only option for exploration.

As you enter the left room you will encounter a Deku Baba. These things are carnivorous plants that will lunge at you and try to bite you. Note however that we can use the bind ability to pull their 'head' section right off without too much hassle. After dispatching this first one, check it out for **Echo** – Deku Baba.

There is two more Deku Babas to deal with in this room, one on the left behind a purple goop wall (use Swordsman's mode to slice though this) and another on a raised ledge along the right-hand wall. Defeat the pair to open the two doors.

The left-hand door leads to a small puzzle room. Grab the statue with bind and then walk to the southern wall. Climb up the ramp and this will position the statue on the upper ledge at the rear of the room. Walk it over to the right and then position it on the pressure plate. This will lower the fence here, allowing you to access the **Treasure Chest**. It contains a Purple Rupee.

39

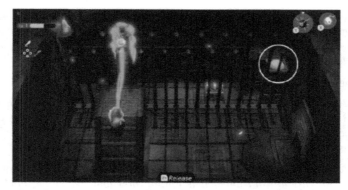

The northern door leads to a room with another Deku Baba behind a fence. Use bind to grab and kill this. Doing so will have a **Treasure Chest** appear. We can loot this for a Small Key.

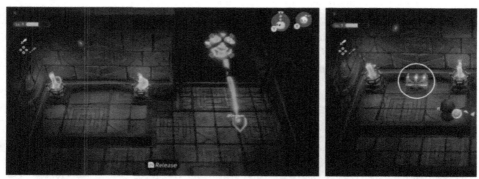

Return to the room with the boss door and use the Small Key to open the door along the right-hand wall.

In this room there is a fence running the length of the area. Behind the fence, on the right you will see a statue that you can bind. We need to move it onto the green tile on the floor nearby. Doing so will open the gate.

Continue down the ladder here to enter another side-scrolling area.

Use the first moving platform to cross the gap and head to the right. Upon reaching the next screen, Tri will chime in to tell you about another ability associated with bind.

Note: If you use Bind on an object, and hold the R button, Zelda will copy the bonded objects movements, rather than it copying Zelda's movements.

Use Bind on the platform above, and have Zelda copy its movements – it will transport us across the gap here. Once across, climb the ladder and ride the platform back to the left. You will find that the next moving platform we reach will not go all the way across the next gap. Here you want to ride it all the way right and then look upwards and bind the lift platform above. This will take us all the way to the right.

Ride this platform back to the left once you are on top of it. Atop the next ladder, you will see a **Treasure Chest** across a gap. Bind to the platform above and ride it over. Loot the chest for a Red Rupee.

Make your way to the ladder in the upper left of this area to exit the room.

In the next room there is a fence, behind which you can see the big fancy chest containing the boss key. There is a pressure plate in here and a statue. We need to move the statue onto the pressure plate by creating a set of stairs using beds/tables and then binding the statue and hopping up to the correct height. Doing so will lower the fence, allowing you to loot the chest for the Big Key.

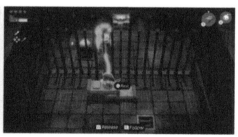

Head through the now open door and backtrack to the room with the boss door. Use the Big Key on this door to continue inside to challenge the dungeon's final boss.

❖ *Boss: Seismic Talus*

*The Seismic Talus is a large rock monster with a number of different damaging abilities. Our goal is to target and attack its weak point using our **Echoes**. This weak spot is a glowing, purple rock which will change locations as the fight progresses. Each time you damage the boss enough, the purple rock will fall to the ground. When this occurs, you want to transition to Swordfighter mode and attack it until the boss re-forms.*

The boss can perform a punch attack, where his fist will fly towards you as a projectile. He can also perform a slamming attack, where he will bring both hands down on the ground in front of his location. After damaging its core for the first time and the weak spot changes position, it gets a new attack where it holds its hands out and spins around.

During the first part of the fight, the weak spot will be at the boss's base, making it relatively easy to target – a Darknut or Caromadillo can get the job done here. Wait until the boss performs a slam attack, then move behind it and summon your enemies to get a solid attack window.

The weak spot will then move to the boss's right shoulder (our left). This one is a bit trickier to target by a melee enemy, so wait for it to perform an attack and then send a Caromadillo at it. In the final part of the fight, the weak spot moves to the boss's head. We will need to wait until it performs the slam attack and then throw objects at his head to damage it.

After smashing the purple core for the third time, the fight will end.

For defeating the boss, you will receive a full Heart Container. Once the scene here runs its course, you will be able to claim it. Additionally, Tri will level up, giving it four-charges rather than three and hand over Unusual Crystal x5.

Speak with Tri by the glowing section of ground at the back of the room to teleport out of the dungeon.

Suthorn Forest

We will end up back outside in the 'real' world. Here Minister Lefte will appear for a chat After an initial conversation, she will bid you to follow her. Do so and she will lead you to the house that we wanted to enter previously but could not because of the rift blocking it.

Continue inside to meet a new character, Lueburry. After another chat here, our objectives will update, and we will get a new main quest - Searching for Everyone.

SEARCHING FOR EVERYONE

Suthorn Prairie

After acquiring this quest from Minister Lefte and Lueburry you will find that there are two objective markers on your map, both pointing towards new rifts that Tri wants us to investigate. Each of these will lead to a new quest chain.

Note: *At this point, you are able to explore a good portion of the world map, where you will find new abilities, **Echoes**, and other collectibles. Alternatively, you can just*

For now, exit Lueburry's house and head up the slope to the left. There is a **Waypoint Stone** here to activate.

From this location we can head north or south. Head to the south first to Suthorn Village where we can pick up a new side quest:

❖ *Finding the Flying Plant*

We can also head to the north from the **Waypoint Stone** and into the open area in the northern part of Suthorn Prairie. In this immediate area there are a few points of interest that we want to check out whilst we are here.

At the top of the ramp, move north and a little to the right. You will come across a series of stone pillars and ruins on the ground. IN amongst these ruins are quite a few Spear Moblins. Of particular interest however is the black and red spider baddie. We want to kil lone of these to unlock the **Echo** – Crawltula.

There is a square pool of water at the centre of the columns here with another large stone column at its centre. Atop this, there is a **Piece of Heart**. To grab this, you can place a bed/table bridge at its base and then summon a Crawltula. Bind yourself to this and have it carry you up to the top of the pillar to claim your prize.

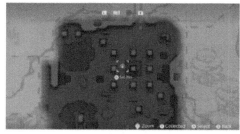 

In the upper, tight corner of this area, you will find Verley and a side-quest:

❖ *Up a Wall*

In the upper, left part of the area there is a small lake where there are several Octorok enemies. Use a flying enemy such as a Keese or Peahat to take them out and examine one of them for **Echo** – Octorok. In the centre of this lake, there is a circle of seaweed on the lakebed (it's a bit hard to see, but its there). Dive down and perform a spin on the central piece of seaweed to receive a Might Stone.

To the north of this lake, you will find the entrance to a cave. Head on inside. Inside the cave there is a Crawltula on the back wall. Defeat this and then summon and bind a Crawltula of your own and have it walk you up the wall. There is a midway ledge with a Red Rupee and an upper ledge with a **Treasure Chest**. This contains a Purple Rupee.

 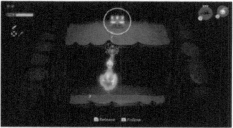

Exit the cave and head west from the lake, looking for the large red cliffs. Here we want to find a small path leading to the north. There is a fellow here who will give you a side-quest.

❖ *The Blocked Road*

Head south from the previous lake to find a second, smaller lake surrounding a ruin. Agan, there are multiple Octoroks in the water here. Clear them out and check the section of the ruins surrounded by water. Pop a couple of beds down with a trampoline on top to bounce up to the top of the ruin (or just use your Crawltula). There is a **Treasure Chest** here with Rock Salt x10.

...and that is all there is to find in this area. To continue, we are going to head onwards and to the regions where we will undertake the next portion of the main quest, of which there are two options.

SEARCHING FOR EVERYONE - GERUDO DESERT

Suthorn Prarie

In the Suthorn Prairie area just north of Lueburry's house, we want to head all the way to the west to find an orange/red cliff. This is the edge of the Gerudo area. Follow this wall to the south to find a path leading to the left.

As you enter this area, you are likely going to be attacked by a Crow enemy (there are a couple around). These things will swoop at you, and if they damage you they can also steal some of your **Rupees**, and drop them to the ground. Kill one of these and then learn the **Echo** – Crow.

Look along the southern part of this area just inside the entry area to find a tree stump with a **Treasure Chest** on top. Drop a trampoline in front of it and hop up onto the stump to open the chest for a Purple Rupee. Continue to the west until you find a **Waypoint Stone**. Just north of this there is a tree stump with a rock on top of it. Again, trampoline up and bind the rock to move it. Beneath the rock there is a **Might Crystal**.

If you continue to the left/west from this **Waypoint Stone**, you will trigger a new main quest - A Rift in the Gerudo Desert.

A RIFT IN THE GERUDO DESERT

Gerudo Desert, East

From the **Waypoint Stone** on the eastern side of Gerudo Desert (on the path leading back to Suthorn Prairie) we want to head a short distance to the west until we see some Gerudo nearby. Approach them for a brief chat about the current situation in the area.

Continue north from their location. Note that as you go you are likely to be attacked by a scorpion-like Aruroda enemy. These will bury into the sand and emerge again close to you before attacking with their tails. Kill one to learn the **Echo** – Aruroda.

When you reach the northern cliffs of the desert, follow it to the east a little to find a half-buried **Treasure Chest**. Defeat the Arurodas here and then use bind to pull it out of the sand. It contains a Red Rupee. Just west of the chest, you will find a section of cliff with some ledges we can climb. At the top you will find a cave we can explore.

Inside the cave you will find a Caromadillo, but this one is a yellow variant. This is a powered-up version of the critter. Defeat it and you can learn the **Echo** – Caromadillo Lv. 2. Head through the door at the northern end of the room to reach a sandy area with two Caromadillos. Defeat the pair to have **Treasure Chest** appear. This contains Chilly Cactus x10.

 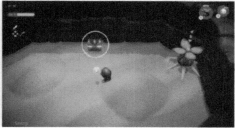

Return outside and continue to the west. There is a ruin here with a Rift on it that we cannot do anything with just yet (we will be back as part of the main quest in a bit). As such keep heading to the west until you reach another, larger section of desert.

As you arrive, you should see a small oasis nearby.

Oasis

In this oasis area there are a few NPCs about that we can speak with.

There is a Business Scrub who can make Smoothies for us (we can finally combine those ingredients we have been finding into a drink) and if this is the first Business Scrub you have spoken with, he will give you a new side-quest. Behind him there is a **Treasure Chest** with Chilly Cactus x5, there is also an NPC named Tormali we can speak with for another side-quest:

❖ *The Flying Tile*

The pink tent here contains a bed we can examine for **Echo** – Soft Bed. This is in essence the same as a regular Old Bed, but if you are sleeping in it to regain hearts, the process will be quicker.

Note: If you head north from the oasis, a sandstorm will kick up and it will knock out your map and reduce visibility significantly. This will remain in place until we defeat a nearby mini-boss enemy, the Lanmola which we will deal with in a bit.

Gerudo Desert, West

Make your way south from the Oasis to find some ruins overrun by rifts, including a large one (this is where the area dungeon will be, once we have progressed the story a little further.

Around these ruins you will encounter Sand Piranhas, which bury below the sand and jump up to bite at you and Redeads, which emit a scream to stun you (and any summoned **Echoes**) and melee attacks – use Ignizols to set them on fire or use a Caromadillo to hit them from range to speed up the fights... because the stunlocking is not fun. Be sure to kill one of each for **Echo** – Sand Piranha and **Echo** - Redead.

There are also some smaller Rifts around, if you get too close to them, they will spawn rift clones of enemies, so approach with caution.

In this southern area you will find a half-buried **Treasure Chest** with Chilly Cactus x10 Just north of this, there is also a cave that we can enter.

Inside the cave, you will encounter wind cannons. These shoot jets of wind that will push you off platforms if you run through them. Drop boulders in front of them to block them. Pass the first row of wind cannons to find **Echo** – Gerudo Pot just past them.

Climb the ramp to see a wind cannon ahead. Use beds/tables to create a bridge beside it and then approach it to learn **Echo** – Wind Cannon. These are particularly handy at blowing away piles of sand. Handy in a desert!

In the next room, spawn a wind cannon and use it to clear away the piles of sand. There are a few **Rupees** to be found, along with a pair of doorways and a pressure plate. Note that you will probably disturb an Aruroda so dispatch that if required. Standing on the pressure plate will open the door on the righthand wall. There is a **Treasure Chest** inside with **Might Crystal** x2.

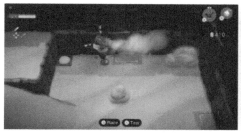 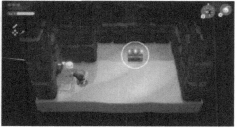

Make your way through the door leading north. You will reach a small room with a pair of Tornado enemies. These frog-like creatures can fly and charge at you at high speed. Create a wall of Sea Urchins though, and they will dispatch themselves for you. Be sure to check out one of them after death for **Echo** – Tornado. Defeating the pair will also have a **Treasure Chest** appear. Loot this for Rocktatoes x3.

We are all done here so go ahead and exit the cave.

Upon exiting the cave, head to the east until you hit the cliff. Climb up here using a trampoline and continue north to find a Stamp platform. Interact with this to meet the Stamp Guy, a fellow who will encourage you to find these stamps platforms around the world map. He will also give you a Stamp Rally Card. Filling this in will net you some cool rewards, so it is worth doing!

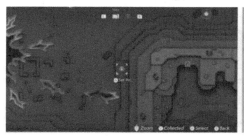 

Follow this ledge to the south to find a pile of sand. Summon a wind cannon to blow this away to reveal a **Might Crystal**.

Drop down and continue to the west to find another buried **Treasure Chest**. This one houses a Red Rupee. Directly north of this chest, you will find a square section of ruins with a **Waypoint Stone** at their centre. Go ahead and activate that for the fast-travelly goodness.

Keep moving west along the southern side of the large Rift until Tri stops for a chat. Afterwards continue to the west until you find an entrance guarded by a Gerudo. Speak with her here. She will not let you through.

Following the chat, head back to the east to find another Gerudo under attack by rift monsters. Fight them all off and then chat with her. She will mention that her name is Dohna and that if we want to clear the Rift, we will need to chat with the boss lady in Gerudo Town.

Now that we have our marching orders, return to the Oasis.

From the pink tent at the Oasis, we can travel directly west to reach Gerudo Town. However, there are some goodies to round up along the way. Around halfway to Gerudo Town, you will come across a pair of rocky pillars. There is another Stamp to collect here for your Stamp Rally.

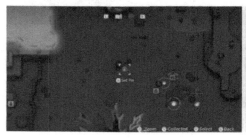 

From this location, head a short distance to the northwest to spot a small bubbling fountain of sand. Approach this to trigger a boss fight against the Lanmola.

❖ Boss: Lanmola

The Lanmola is a large, centipede like enemy that will initially cover the ground in quicksand, leaving only four, small islands made out of regular sand for you to stand on. The boss will bury under the ground, move towards you, and then emerge from the ground, throwing a collection of boulders about the area before diving back underground again.

50

To defeat it, take note of the hook-like tail that it has, this is the key to victory. As Lanmola moves away from you, you want to grab its tail with bind and then pull backwards. This will pluck it out of the ground and have it collapse on its side. Use this opportunity to run in and wail on it using Swordfighter mode.

We essentially need to repeat this process until it dies.

Defeating the Lanmola will have it drop a bunch of **Rupees**. It will also remove the sandstorm that had been plaguing the northern part of the Gerudo Desert region, allowing us to explore with both visibility and our map uncovered. Nice!

We are going to make a quick detour to the northern part of the desert now to round up some more goodies (although you can zip right to Gerudo Town if that is more your style).

Gerudo Desert, North

Following the fight, head north to find a cave entrance and a small Boarblin camp to the right. Clear out the Boarblin camp (they are essentially Moblins, but more piggy) and be sure to kill one of each for **Echo** – Boomerang Boarblin and **Echo** – Club Boarblin. Defeating all these enemies will unlock the **Treasure Chest** in the camp which we can loot for Warm Pepper x7.

To the west of the Boarblin camp, you can find a pool of quicksand with a number of stone pillars in it. The large, central stone pillar has a **Piece of Heart** atop it.

There are a couple of different ways to get to this. Initially, I used a collection of beds to keep making higher ledges until I could jump to it, however you can also use the stone pillars to the north of the quicksand to reach the large ledge facing the heart piece. From here you can simply create a bridge across. Much easier!

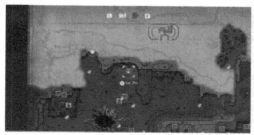

Return to the Boarblin camp and enter the cave just west of it.

Inside the cave, you will encounter Beetles. These things will pour out of the Beetle Mounds nearby and will continue to do so until you remove them. Pull out an **Echo** or two to hold them back (Peahat is good). Head up and destroy the nests. Afterwards you can learn both **Echo** – Beetle and **Echo** – Beetle Mound.

Continue through the nearby door to find yourself outside again and on a ledge atop the cave. There is a **Treasure Chest** here with a **Might Crystal**.

Drop down and continue to the west to find a **Waypoint Stone**. Activate this to unlock the location for fast travel.

Directly north of the **Waypoint Stone** you will find the entrance to a cave called Ancestor's Cave of Rest, leave that be for now as we will need to visit it as part of a quest shortly. To the west of the **Waypoint Stone**, you will find the entrance to a higher level Boarblin Camp. Let us leave that alone for now too – you can clear it if you like, but to get everything there, you will need to come back later after acquiring some more **Echo**es... best to hold off and get it all at once.

For now, head to the southwest until you reach the walls of Gerudo Town.

When you reach the walls of Gerudo Town, follow them south and then to the east to find the entrance. There is a **Waypoint Stone** here to activate.

Before exploring the town, head to the south from the entrance until you find a small recess in the ground with a pile of sand in it. If you use the wind cannon here, removing the sand will reveal a **Treasure Chest** containing a Purple Rupee. On some ledges just south of this, you will find a collection of sand piles. Again, use your wind cannon. There are several Arurodas hiding here along with a **Piece of Heart**.

Gerudo Town

Make your way into Gerudo Town. There are a few different buildings about to explore and people around that we can speak with, along with a shop. The shop sells a new Accessory – Gerudo Sandals for 400 **Rupees**. This one is quite handy as it stops you sinking in quicksand.

Around the area you can also find three side-quests to attempt:

- Elusive Tumbleweeds
- Gerudo Tag Training
- Tornado Ghost?

To continue, you want to head to the northern end of town and enter the large building here. Once inside, head up the stairs to meet Donha and a pair of new characters tied into the main region in this quest – Facette and Seera.

Following a brief chat here, Donha will run off and we will need to go and speak with her once again.

Gerudo Desert

To find Donha, you will want to head back to the oasis. Here you will find her talking with some of the other Gerudo. Speak with her here and she will tell you about three small rifts located in the Gerudo Desert that she wants us to try and deal with.

SOUTHERN OASIS RUINS RIFT

Gerudo Desert

We will receive this short main quest from Dohna at the oasis in central Gerudo Desert during the A Rift in the Gerudo Desert main quest.

After getting the task, make your way to the ruins south of the oasis. Here you will find a pair of tired Gerudo guard here. Approach their position for a short conversation and a scene.

Immediately following the scene, a group of monsters will emerge from the nearby rift. Use your **Echoes** to help fight them off. Defeating all of them will trigger another brief scene and the quest will end.

SOUTHERN GERUDO DESERT RIFT

Gerudo Desert

We will receive this short main quest from Dohna at the oasis in central Gerudo Desert during the A Rift in the Gerudo Desert main quest.

To acquire this quest, we want to run to the south from the **Waypoint Stone** at the entrance to Gerudo Town. Here you will find a collection of exhausted Gerudo fighters. As you speak with them, Donha will show up and ask you to get them a drink before handing over Chilly Cactus x2.

Fast travel to the oasis and speak with the Business Scrub here. We want to make a Cactus Smoothie. To do so combine a Chilly Cactus with... a Chilly Cactus. The resulting smoothie will be what you are after!

Once you have the Cactus Smoothie, return to the group of guards south of Gerudo Town and hand it over to Donha. This will trigger another short cut-scene and the quest will be completed.

ANCESTOR'S CAVE OF REST RIFT

We will receive this short main quest from Dohna at the oasis in central Gerudo Desert during the A Rift in the Gerudo Desert main quest.

To reach the Ancestor's Cave of Rest, we want to exit Gerudo Town and follow its eastern wall to the north. Activate the **Waypoint Stone** here (if you have not already). Continue directly north from here to reach the cave – you will know when you are in the right place as it will be flanked by lit torches.

Once inside, speak with the Gerudo sentry here, she will tell you that the torches have gone out, and that we need to light them once again.

Head to the left side of the room and bind the giant rock here, and pull it away from the wall to reveal a hidden door. Inside you will encounter some Holmill enemies. These will dig underground before popping up to throw rocks at you repeatedly. Kill them to learn **Echo** – Holmill.

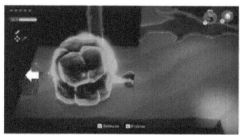

Bind the boulder at the northern end of the room and move it to reveal a ladder we can descend. Do so to enter a side-scroll area.

In this area you will see large ledges made out of sand. These appear solid, however if we use our new Holmill **Echo** on them, it will bury through them, allowing us to drop down through the ledges. Do so at the very, left side of the first ledge and drop down to find a **Treasure Chest** holding Gold Egg.

Use the Holmill to dig through once again to reach the area below. Continue to the right, defeating an ignizol as you go. Note you can climb back up to the area above and dig back through the sand to grab a Blue Rupee and a Green Rupee if you like. To continue though, we want to climb up the ladder on the far left and exit the area.

After exiting the underground area, you will find yourself next to the unlit braziers. Use an Ignizol and toss it into both to light them once more. Upon doing so, a scene will play followed by a couple of chats. These will end the quest.

A RIFT IN THE GERUDO DESERT - PART 2

Gerudo Town

After completing the three above mini main quests, you will next be required to head back to Gerudo Town to speak with Donha and the chief once again. We will learn that the ruin with the rift we saw in the eastern part of the desert has now expanded and everyone will rush off to check it out.

Fast travel to the oasis and head to the east to reach the ruin that we spotted earlier. Approach the crowd of Gerudo here. Inspect the yellow ripple in the rift here for a scene. We can now explore this.

Stilled Desert Temple Ruins

We are now in the still world and this time around we have a goal – to find and rescue Tri's friends. There are five glowing orbs hidden around this area and we will need to find and collect them all to complete the area.

From the start hop across the floating islands here until you see a ladder leading downwards. Ignore this for now and head to the left side of the platform. There is a pillar here we can climb down. At the bottom, there is a pool of quicksand with a stone column at its centre. The first orb is atop the pillar. To get on top, we can summon a Crawltula and bind to it before letting it carry us up the pillar. At the top we can grab the Glowing Orb.

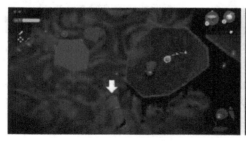 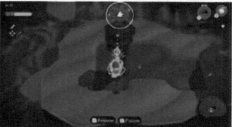

Head back up to the ladder we saw earlier and head on inside to reach a side-scrolling area.

As you enter this area, you will encounter a new type of enemy a Platboom. These resemble thwomps in the Mario games and will slam the ground beneath them periodically. We can destroy these ones however. To do so summon an **Echo** and then bind the Platboom when it is at ground level – this will hold it in place allow your **Echo** to attack it. Kill one to learn **Echo** – Platboom.

At the far left of this area you will see two Platbooms, one atop the other. There is a second Glowing Orb just past them. We need to get rid of one of these – either kill one, or bind and drag one out. When there is one remaining, you can jump atop it and then up to the ledge with the orb. If you kill both, you can summon your very own Platboom to do the same!

Exit the side-scrolling area. Once back outside, you can climb the ledges behind until you reach the larger ledge at the top. Here we can go one of two ways – left or right.

Head to the right first and make your way across the various platforms and floating debris until you can climb on top of the main structure you just ascended. Here, continue all the way to the right to spot a floating island. Create a bridge across to find a glowing rock. Push this out of the way to find the third Glowing Orb.

Return across the major platform to the left and continue your ascent upwards using the next set of ledges and debris. As you go, you will come across the fourth Glowing Orb.

Now make your way all the way back down to the area immediately above the ladder. We now want to head to the left from this upper ledge. Jump to the next ledge and clear out the rift enemies that appear.

At the rear wall here, summon a Platboom (and trampoline to jump onto it). Ride this up to the ledge above and then repeat the process here to get to the top. We can then find the last Glowing Orb atop a tree stump.

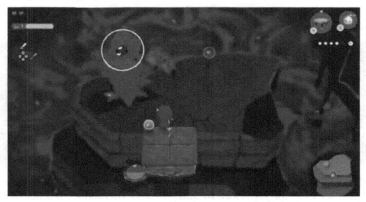

Finding all five will trigger a few scenes in which Tri and her friends will cleanse the rift. Tri will also gain a bit of XP, but not enough for a new level and will hand over **Might Crystal** x2. We will also find ourselves back outside where the Gerudo questline will progress further.

At this point, the chief will allow us to venture into the Gerudo Sanctum, which is the next dungeon. This happens to be south of the oasis beneath the large rift in the desert. Remember the guard we spoke to earlier that would not let us in? Well, she will now!

Cryptic Cavern

As you enter this area, you will spot a blue object over against the left-hand wall. This is a switch. Summon a flying enemy and get it o attack the switch to have it open the nearby door.

In the next room you will see a locked door ahead. There are two other open doorways off to the right, one on the northern wall and another on the eastern wall. Both of these will essentially lead to the same area, although the eastern room includes an extra fight (and a Red Rupee) before rejoining the other door in the main puzzle room. Either way you decide to go, you can get there by using boulders to block the wind cannons.

When you reach the main puzzle room, we want to head all the way to the left first. You will encounter a series of Pathblades here. These are in essence bladed Roombas that patrol along a set route and damage you if you touch them. They can be destroyed, or if you have trouble with that, blocked by boulders. Dispatch one so you can learn **Echo** – **Pathblade**.

At the end of the Pathblade path, there is a switch, have an **Echo** hit this to trigger a **Treasure Chest** to appear on the far, right corner of the room.

As you arrive in this area, you will encounter a pair of Gibdos. These are similar to the Redeads we fought outside, but without the screeching. Again, use fire to take them down quickly. Be sure to kill them to learn **Echo** – Gibdo. Loot the **Treasure Chest** for a Small Key.

Backtrack to the previous room with the wind cannons and open the locked door using the Small Key. Head down the ladder to reach a side-scrolling area.

Head down the ladder on the left to reach a platform with a Pathblade. Summon your own Pathblade to take it out. Descend the next ladder on the right and you will see a **Treasure Chest** across a gap with a wind cannon beneath it. To grab this, look down and bind to the Pathblade below, allowing Zelda to follow its path across the gap. The chest contains a Red Rupee.

Continue to the next screen to the right. We need to climb this area. As you do, use a Wind Cannon to clear the sand piles, and Pathblades to clear the Pathblade enemies. After climbing the second ladder, spawn a Wind Cannon, pick it up and throw it to the left to clear the sand pile on the ledge opposite, then bind a pathblade below (spawn one if you killed the existing one) and ride it across to the far ledge.

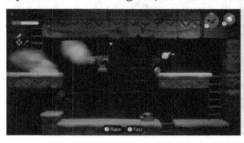 

At the top of the next ladder, you can climb a second on the left to open a shortcut back to the start. To continue though, you want to go right. There is an upgraded Gibdo enemy here. Be sure to kill it for **Echo** – Gibdo Lv. 2.

Proceed to the right to find a large plug. Bind this and pull it backwards to remove it. Doing so will remove the sand from the dungeon entrance outside.

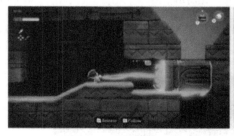 

At this point, we can exit the Cryptic Cave and make for the dungeon entrance. Head on inside to begin the Dungeon - Gerudo Sanctum.

DUNGEON - GERUDO SANCTUM

After entering the Gerudo Sanctum, approach the rift and interact with it so that Tri creates an opening. Hop down inside to begin. As you land, you will see a shadowy version of Link run off... looks like we will be fighting him again here at some point by the looks of it.

Climb the ladder here to reach a side-scroller area. Here we need to climb the rock walls on the right. Push a boulder along the floor to block the lowest wind cannon and climb up and over the second. When you reach the upper ledge, push the next boulder left to block the third wind cannon. We can now climb out of the area.

Upon arriving in the dungeon, there will be a room with three doors and a **Waypoint Stone** to activate. The northern door is locked, but we will be able to explore both the left and the right.

Check the left room first. As you enter, you will see that the floor tiles are sparkling. Quickly run over and inspect one for **Echo** – Flying Tile. These will rise off the ground and launch themselves at you before breaking. Avoid all the tiles to have a **Treasure Chest** appear. It contains a Red Rupee.

Return to the previous room and this time head right.

In this puzzle room, there is a handle just inside the door. Pulling this will open a door on the northern wall. After letting go of the handle, the door will slowly close. The trickiness here comes in the fact that we need to navigate a conveyor. We will need to use a trampoline on the conveyor to reach the ledge with the door and head through it before it closes... oh and there are Keese, so you may want to take them out first if you think they are going to be an issue.

In the next room you will see a pair of handles on the far wall. Grab one of these with bind and pull backwards until the door opens, allowing you to pas through it. Behind it you will find a **Treasure Chest** with a Small Key.

Return to the room with the locked door (and **Waypoint Stone**) and use the key to open it. We will arrive in a room with four purple snake statues. Head up and examine these for **Echo** – Snake Statue. This will come in handy later on. Continue through the next door.

At this point we reach a room with a pair of Mothulas. These flying creatures will charge up and launch at you at high speed. Nothing a few Sea Urchins or a flying **Echo** cannot handle. Be sure to learn **Echo** – Mothula. You will see the door to the boss room half buried in sand at the rear of this room. We will not be able to access it yet, but his is where we will need to go come boss time. As there are no other options, head through the door on the left.

You will see a **Treasure Chest** on the other side of a wall here which is inaccessible for the moment (if you know how to get this one please let me know!). Continue south into the next room.

In this area, you will again need to navigate some conveyor platforms to reach the far side of the room. This time around, the next ledge is blocked by some crates. As such, spawn an Ignizol and throw it at the boxes. Once they burn away use a trampoline or a bed on the far-left conveyor as a steppingstone to reach the ledge. Continue down the ladder here.

We be side-scrolling again! Climb down the first ladder and dispatch the patrolling Caromadillo. After doing so, jump the gap and spawn a Holmill to dig through the sand, allowing us to reach the **Treasure Chest** below. It houses a Golden Egg.

Dig through the sand again to reach the area below. Kill another Caromadillo here. Use the ladder on the left to exit the area.

We will arrive in a room with four doors and a **Waypoint Stone** to activate.

Outside of the door we came from, there is an ornate door on the northern wall. There is a tablet in front of this with the inscription "Seek two distinct tributes. Clues to the desired tributes are recorded somewhere on this floor." There is also an open door to the left and a spinny door we can bind and pull open on the right.

Head through the right door first and dispatch the Holmill. Use a Wind Cannon to remove all the sand in here. Defeat the Aruroda you will undoubtedly upset in the process. With the sand clear, read the tablet I the upper, right for the inscription "It stands quietly in the sanctum. It is blue in color, with large tusks and a long nose" and loot the **Treasure Chest** nearby for Rock Salt x10.

Proceed through the door on the left to encounter a Poe enemy. These things are particularly annoying because they will constantly move away from you (or your **Echo**es and leave a tail of fire behind them. Flying enemies have better luck against these fellows Note that it is also possible to get them to run into their own fire to damage themselves. Defeating this will enable you to learn **Echo** – Poe. A **Treasure Chest** will also appear holding the Dungeon Map.

Mosey on through the door to the south and you will find yourself outside the sanctum. Note the small, square opening on the wall nearby. Use a Platboom here and ride it up. Jump into the opening to find a small room filled with **Rupees**. Back outside, we need to follow the set path along the fragmented platforms here. Pass by a rift monster and a collection of Sand Piranhas and look for a **Treasure Chest** on a raised ledge to the left. It houses a Red Rupee.

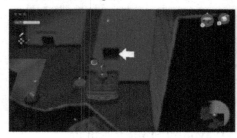 

Hop up to the next ledge to find a large, cylindrical structure. There is a ladder midway up and handles on the lower section. Pull the handles with a bind until they rotate and complete the ladder. Climb up to find a **Treasure Chest** with a Purple Rupee.

 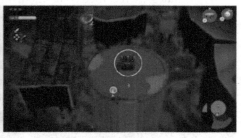

Follow the route along the floating objects here (its fairly linear) but watch out for the Tornado enemies – be sure to use Sea Urchins to stop them in their tracks or they will knock you off ledges fairly easily. Eventually you will reach a pool of quicksand.

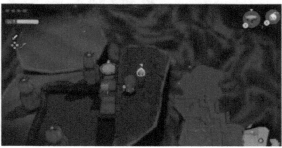

Either build a path up either side of the pool itself, or quickly build a staircase of beds with a trampoline on top to jump up to the ledge above. Once up, continue to reach the top of the sanctum building. There is a **Waypoint Stone** here to activate.

On this rooftop you will find some rift enemies and a Mothula. Take the lot of them out before checking the southern end of the roof for a sand pile hiding a **Treasure Chest** with a Monster Stone.

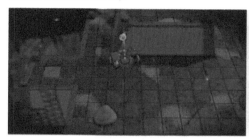 

Climb down the wall on the right side of the rooftop to ground level. There is a door leading back inside here. Before venturing in though, let us explore to the right first.

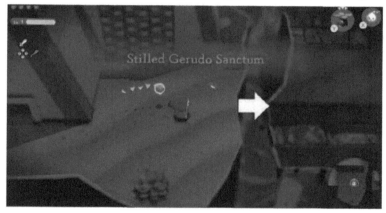

Hop across the gap and scale the wall on the far left. You can use a Platboom to make it quick, or do what I did and make a makeshift set of stairs. At the top, across the gap to the northwest is a long, sandy platform occupied by three Redeads. Eliminate them all from afar.

Once the platform is clear, head to the far end to find another cylindrical structure. Again, use bind to rotate the lower segment to complete the ladder before climbing up. At the top is a statue we can inspect for an **Echo** – Hawk Statue, much like the snake statue, this bad boy will come in handy later.

Make your way back to the Gerudo Sanctum building and head back inside using the door we spotted earlier.

We will arrive in a room with a large quicksand pit on the left, a raised ledge above it with a locked door on the right wall and another door controlled by pulling a lever on the left wall. We need to create a path using **Echoes** (I used trampolines and beds) leading to the upper ledge before yanking the handle and then quickly moving up to and through the door before it closes again.

The room to the north has a lot going on. There are two Gibdos and a Redead to address as soon as we get into the area. After dispatching them, check out the statues for **Echo –** Cat Statue. Move the cat statue by the northern door out of the way and continue through it.

Next up is a hallway. There is a **Waypoint Stone** here. Activate this before continuing into the next door. As you enter, a scene will play followed by a mini-boss fight.

❖ *Boss: Shadow Link*

*This time around, Shadow Link is armed with a bow with which he will shoot at you from range. He has a standard single arrow shot, or a charged up magical arrow which fires a spread of three pinkish arrows. Again, the goal here is to stay out of his line of sight as much as possible and get our **Echoes** to tackle him. Note that he is very quick and when approached by Zelda or an **Echo** front-on he will usually run away, take up position form range and begin firing again.*

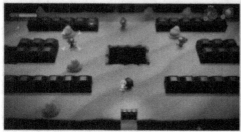

I used the Caromadillo to constantly send a rolling projectile his way. You can angle it off the ramps lining the pits around the room. Alternatively, you can use Sand Piranhas or Arurodas. Both of these Echoes are pretty handy as Link will be unable to target them when they go beneath the sand. If you can get in close to him, you can also use Swordfighter mode, but you probably will not get too many chances.

After he takes enough damage, a scene will play, and Shadow Link will start glowing purple. He will also duplicate so that there are now three of him. At this stage each of the clones will also moves a little faster. The good news is that we can use the same tactics here to fight and defeat him.

Try to focus on eliminating one clone at a time, but keep your eyes on the other two – you do not want to start taking fire from an unexpected location! Continue to have your Echoes damage and destroy all three clones as once they are pushing up daisies, the fight will end.

Following the fight, claim the Bow of Might from the ground nearby.

Note: The bow can be used in Swordfighter mode by pressing X. This will allow you to target objects in the distance. Nice!

To continue, head through the door at the rear of the room to enter a side-scrolly area.

As you enter, you will see a Beetle Mount on a platform to the right. Use Swordfighter mode and shoot it with your arrow. Easy! Across the next gap, you will see another of those purple webbed walls. We cannot reach this with the sword, so you will need to shoot it with arrows until it dissipates.

After crossing the gap, climb up and out of the area. Upon entering the next room, you will find another **Waypoint Stone** ahead.

To progress through this room, you will need to use the conveyors, however these are being exposed to jets of flame from some statues situated nearby. We want to use boulders to shield us from the fire. Drop a boulder and stand behind it to pass by safely. Note that the second and third flame jets are on opposing side so either use bind to move a boulder to the opposite side or spawn a new one to get by.

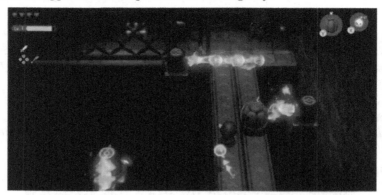

At the end of the second conveyor, check out the statues here for **Echo** – Elephant Statue and loot the **Treasure Chest** for a Small Key. Climb the nearby ladder and maneuver past one final flame jet to return to the entrance.

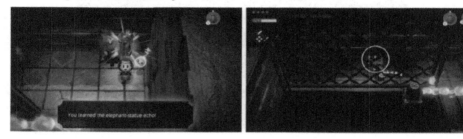

Use the **Waypoint Stone** to warp to the previous **Waypoint Stone** (the one just after re-entering the sanctum from the outdoor area). Backtrack to the rom with the quicksand pit and the handle-controlled door.

We can now open the locked door to the right of this. Inside, the room looks empty, however there are scuff marks on the floor by the northern wall indicating another spinny door. Use bind to pull this out. Head through to another puzzle room.

In this area, there is a flame jet at the centre of a pit with three unlit braziers around it. There is a wind cannon in the back, left corner aimed at one of the braziers.

The first thing we need to do here is get rid of the wind cannon. To do so, create a bridge leading towards it and then use bind to grab it and drop it into the abyss. Next, we can toss an Ignizol at the two braziers closest to the edge. Finally, grab the handle on the flamethrower and pull it, so that it rotates and lights the third brazier.

Doing this will have a tablet appear, read this for an inscription "It rests its wings atop a tower. It bears sharp eyes and a strong beak." This is our second clue. We are all done here.

To continue, we want to fast travel back to the room with the fancy ornate door and the tablet. With all four statues and both clue inscriptions, we now can solve the puzzle here.

You will notice two red tiles in front of the door. Place an Elephant Statue on one and a Hawk Statue on the other. Doing so should open the door. Inside, there is a handle on the right-hand wall that we can grab. Pull this all the way out to trigger a scene.

When you regain control, head through the opening the plug had been in. We will reach a room with a circular mechanism at its centre with a **Treasure Chest** held inside. First use the wheel in the lower left to rotate the blue section of the mechanism so that the black line on it lines up with the line on the red, outer segment.

Next, you will need to use bind to rotate the inner, green circle until the black line is facing to the southeast. We can then use the wheel in the lower left to turn it so that it lines up with the red and the blue segments. With all three aligned, the **Treasure Chest** will be accessible. Loot it for the Big Key.

Use the stairs in the back, right corner to leave the area. We will arrive n a small ledge right in front of the now uncovered boss door. Activate the **Waypoint Stone** beside it.

When you are ready to continue, use the Big Key on this door to continue inside to challenge the dungeon's final boss.

❖ *Boss: Mogryph*

Mogryph is a large mole-like creature with wings, yep you read that correctly – a mole with wings... anyway, here is how you can beat him.

Attack wise, the boss will often bury under the ground before emerging and performing one of his attacks. These include a swipe attack which sends out a damaging wave of sand as a projectile in front of it and a charge attack with which he will lunge at you from across the room. Additionally, the boss can let out a roar, this will cause sand to fall from the roof and create a new sand pile at random.

To damage this guy, we want to make use of the statues – note that all four of them are in the corners of the room to start with, how convenient! When the boss comes up to perform a charge attack, quickly position yourself behind a statue. The boss will charge into said statue and be stunned. Take this opportunity to shift to swordfighter mode and smack him up until he recovers.

Initially the sand in the room is safe to run around in but after damaging him enough, the boss will change the arena to quicksand, leaving only a few, small islands of safe sand to position yourself on and the statues will vanish. At this point, the boss becomes more aggressive. He will now use his sand swipe attack up to three times in a row and gains a new attack in which, the boss summons sandy vortexes which will slowly move across the room in a straight line. If you see these coming, quickly shift to a different island to avoid the drama.

*The good news is that despite the statues vanishing, we learned the **Echo**es earlier, so summon them on the sand islands. Here we simply need to repeat the process of luring the boss's charge into the statues and wailing on him when he does so until he runs out of health.*

For defeating the boss, you will receive a full Heart Container. Once the scene here runs its course, you will be able to claim it. Additionally, Tri will level up again, unlocking a new ability – we can now create **Echo**es at range (hold down Y to do this). Tri will also hand over **Might Crystal** x5.

Speak with Tri by the glowing section of ground at the back of the room to teleport out of the dungeon.

GERUDO DESERT EXPLORATION (OPTIONAL)

Gerudo Town

When you regain control of Zelda, following the previous dungeon, we will find ourselves back in Gerudo Town. We will be on the upper level of the Gerudo palace, an area that was previously inaccessible. Use a Platboom against the back wall and ride it up to the ledge above to find a set of stairs we can descend.

We will reach a side-scroll area. Move past the first Platboom here and then use the second as a lift to reach a ledge above. You will see some stacks of crates in the next vertical shaft. Spawn a Platboom on top to crush them all. Jump down after it.

You will find a giant boulder blocking the path. We want to bind this and then jump back onto the previous Platboom. Ride this up and carry the boulder with you. At the top, walk to the right to place it on an upper ledge. Return down the shaft and continue to the right to find a **Piece of Heart**.

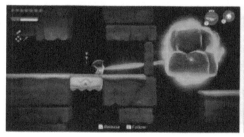

Next, head to the western side of Gerudo Town. On the cliff overlooking the settlement, you should be able to spot another Stamp platform. Spawn and ride a Platboom up to it to add it to your Stamp Rally.

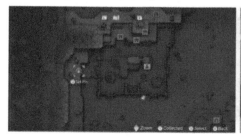

71

Gerudo Desert

Next, from the **Waypoint Stone** south of the entrance to Ancestor's Cave of Rest Rift, enter the canyon to the left. This is a larger, and higher levelled Boarblin camp (we avoided this earlier if you have been following along).

Continue through this area and you will encounter three small camps (these are part of the larger overall camp). The first camp is guarded by three Club Boarblins and two Boomerang Boarblins. Some Arurodas patrol the path between the first and second camps.

The second camp is occupied by a Club Boarblin, Boomerang Boarblin and some Arurodas. There is a **Treasure Chest** here to loot for Warm Pepper x5.

The final camp is guarded by a pair of upgraded Boarblins (one Boomerang, one Club). Note that the Club Boarblin is now equipped with a shield. A Darknut **Echo** is handy against the shielded enemy. Defeat them both to learn **Echo** – Club Boarblin Lv 2 and **Echo** - Boomerang Boarblin Lv. 2. If you killed everything else along the way, defeating this pair will also unlock the Tresure Chest here for Accessory – Energy Glove.

 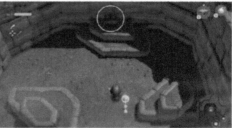

In this location, use a Platboom to reach the ledges to the north overlooking this area. Once up, head north to find a cave to explore.

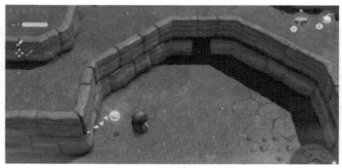

As you enter, the first room will be occupied by Flying Tiles. Avoid those that come to life and proceed into the next room. This time around there will be more Flying Tiles to avoid. Keep moving to avoid them and once they stop coming the door leading onwards will open.

In the next room there is a **Treasure Chest** behind a gate ahead. Off to the right are some ledges along with an Otctorok and Keese. Eliminate the enemies first before traversing the gap using the ledges for a makeshift bridge.

At the top of the stairs on the far side, there is a switch across a gap. Have an **Echo** hit this (or use your bow in swordfighter mode). Doing so will unlock the gate. Loot the **Treasure Chest** for a Silver Rupee (100 **Rupees**).

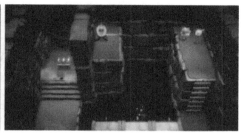

Exit the cave and head a short distance to the east. You will see another Stamp platform above. Use a Platboom to reach it and add it to your Stamp Rally collection.

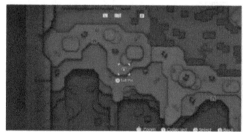

...and with that we are done here, to continue head onwards to the next main quest, Searching for Everyone - Jabul Waters

SEARCHING FOR EVERYONE - JABUL WATERS

Suthorn Prairie

In the Suthorn Prairie area just north of Lueburry's house, we need to head to the north to find the path leading to the Jabul Waters area. Note that there is a second, less obvious path leading to the north on the far, western side of this area and this can be accessed by completing a side quest:

- The Blocked Road.

Get that done and let us use this path to grab some extra goodies (and the ability for Zelda to ride horses!) before continuing. After clearing the road, head north to find a **Waypoint Stone**.

Hyrule Field, South

From this waypoint, follow the road leading to the west and you should come across a Moblin camp to the south of the road. Defeat the enemies here for **Echo** – Sword Moblin and loot the **Treasure Chest** they had been guarding for Fresh Milk x10.

Head directly north from the Moblin Camp and continue through the wooded area here, avoiding the Rope enemies in the grass. You will eventually reach a clearing with a **Piece of Heart** on a stump at its centre. Clear the nearby Peahat and then claim your prize.

 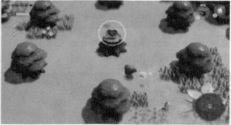

Return to the road and follow it to the west/northwest. As you go, you will likely encounter Zols, Ropes and a new, pink bird enemy. Be sure to knock one of these out to learn **Echo** – Guay.

When you reach the fork in the road, head to the west. Here you will find a **Waypoint Stone** and the entrance to Hyrule Ranch.

Hyrule Ranch

By the entrance to Hyrule Ranch, you will find another Stamp platform which we can interact with to continue our Stamp Rally. If you opted to do the Jabul Waters route first interacting with this will let you meet the Stamp Guy, a fellow who will encourage you to find these stamps platforms around the world map. He will also give you a Stamp Rally Card. Filling this in will net you some cool rewards, so it is worth doing!

Completing this quest will allow you to borrow and ride horses from Hyrule Ranch, making getting around a lot quicker. Very handy.

Hyrule Field, South

From Hyrule Ranch, head southwest to find a small, raised ledge with a single shrub on top. Suspicious, no? Spin through the shrub to find a **Might Crystal**.

Continue to the west, past the pool of water where the horse had been stranded (if you completed the side quest Runaway Horse). Just northwest of here there is a cave we can explore. Inside are three Sword Moblins guarding a **Treasure Chest**. We can loot this for **Might Crystal** x3.

Exit the cave and directly west of the pool where the horse had been, there is a collection of tall grass on the ground in the shape of an arrow. Spin through the shrub that this is pointing to in order to find another **Might Crystal**.

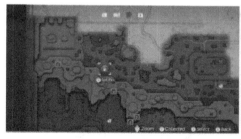 

Head north from his location to find a larger body of water. There are numerous Octoroks here along with some fish called Tanglers, which will swimm at you at high speed to attack and, if you are unlucky a divebombing Guay might join the party too.

Use your **Echo**es to clear the area and learn the **Echo** – Tangler here. In the middle of this lake is a tall stone pillar with a **Piece of Heart** on top. Spawn a bed by the base of the pillar and then a Crawltula. Bind yourself to this and have it carry you up to the top to claim the **Piece of Heart**.

With that, let us stop our exploration here. Further to the north is Kakariko Village and more areas to explore, but we will come here as part of the main questline in a bit, so let us not double dip!

Fast travel back to Lueburry's house and from the Suthorn Prairie area to its north, take the obvious path leading north. We will again reach Hyrule Field.

You should see a pair of soldiers talking ahead. After their chat, look to the left of their position to find a **Treasure Chest** we can pull out of the ground with Bind. It contains Floral Nectar x5. Just northwest of this is a raised ledge we can jump up to with a rock hiding a **Might Crystal**.

From this location, head to the north to reach the bridge leading into Hyrule Castle. Activate the **Waypoint Stone** here.

Hyrule Castle

After crossing the bridge, before entering the town itself, follow the narrow strip of land around the outside of the walls. When you reach the area north of the castle, you will find a **Piece of Heart** to snaffle. Nice!

Make your way into Hyrule Castle Town. There are a few different buildings about to explore and people around that we can speak with, along with a shop. The shop sells a new Accessory – Stone Anklet for 400 **Rupees**. This one is quite handy as it reduces the knockback effect inflicted on Zelda when hit during combat.

Around the area you can also find a new side-quest to attempt:

- A Curious Child

Also in this area, just north of the house with the rift on it, you will find a bird-shaped statue. Bind this and pull it to the side to reveal a set of stairs leading downwards. There is a **Treasure Chest** here with **Might Crystal** x2.

There is a well beside the house with the rift that we can jump down, but other than a guard, there is nothing down here. The Castle itself is off limits for now as well. As such, head back out the main gate.

Lake Hylia

Head across the bridge and follow the path until you reach a split. Here we want to continue to the east. Eventually you will reach another fork in the road with the path leading to a bridge to the north or to the lake to the south.

Instead of sticking to the road here, continue to the east to find a woman standing on a ledge here who informs you that there is a Great Fairy on the like nearby. Checking this out is most definitely worth your time, so let us make a quick detour to do so.

Head south and enter the large lake here. We want to swim out to the large, central island here. There is a **Waypoint Stone** here and a cave. Proceed inside to meet the Great Fairy.

*Note: The Great Fairy can upgrade Zelda by improving her style. We can purchase these upgrades which increase in price incrementally and each upgrade will give Zelda another accessory slot. The first upgrade is 100 **Rupees**, so if you have been rounding up chests and **Rupees** relentlessly, you should have enough for at least one.*

Just south and east of the fairy island, you will find some Tanglers and Tektites around. The latter is a new creature type that skates around on the surface of the water and love doing jump attacks. Eliminate one of them to learn **Echo** – Tektite.

To the west of the Great Fairy's Island is a rift that we can enter to level up Tri slightly, if that is your kind of thing... although its probably best to do so after completing the Jabul Waters area and dungeon so you have some good water-based **Echo**es (we will be back for it later if you don;t do it now!). South of here, beneath the water there is a large boulder on the lakebed. Grab this with bind and move it to find a **Might Crystal** beneath it.

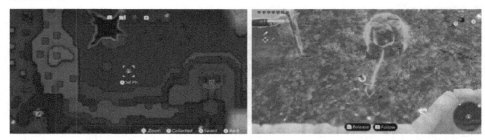

Head to the southeastern corner of the lake to find a ledge that we can climb out on. Here there is another Stamp platform to keep your Stamp Rally going.

With all that sorted, head back to the main road and continue across the bridge to the north.

Hyrule Field, East

After crossing the bridge, there is a path leading north and another to the east. We want to head east. As you go, watch out for a Crow that will likely attack. Defeat it. Before continuing, look by the tree the Crow had been on initially to find a boulder. Move this with bind to reveal a **Might Crystal**.

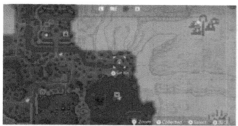

The path will soon come to a four-way intersection with roads leading off in all four cardinal directions. Continue to the east. You will proceed through a fairly lengthy canyon like area occupied by several Ropes and Caromadillos. By the entrance to this canyon, if you climb up to the ledges to the north, you can find a stone we can pick up that is hiding a **Might Crystal**.

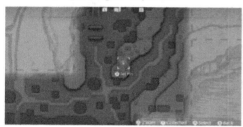

Drop down and continue along the canyon to the east. When you reach the end you will arrive at the start of a beach area. Here you will encounter Sand Crabs. These things essentially patrol from side to side and damage you if you touch them. Other than that, they are fairly harmless. Kill one to learn the **Echo** – Sand Crab.

Move across the next pool of water, avoiding the Sand Crabs and Sea urchins to reach another, larger beach. Approach and interact with the **Waypoint Stone** here. This is the start of Jabul Waters.

From this location proceed to the right and you will trigger a new main quest - The Jabul Waters Rift.

THE JABUL WATERS RIFT

Seesyde Village

After entering this area, you will find a couple of villagers on the beach nearby talking about Lord Jabu-Jabu and rifts. Once they have finished talking, you will be able to explore the rest of the area. Just beside this pair is another Stamp platform. Go ahead and add to your Stamp Rally collection.

At this point, we can explore the village here. There is not a whole lot to it, but check out the docks on which it is built to chat with the locals. There is a shop her and a couple of boats that we can enter.

On the eastern side of the docks, you can find a woman to speak with who will give you a side quest. After chatting with her you can learn **Echo** – Grilled Fish.

- Deliver the Grilled Fish!

Off the left side of the village in the water there is a half-buried **Treasure Chest** with a Red Rupee. At the very southern end of the docks, you can find a **Might Crystal** below.

Exit the village via the dirt ramp to the north. When you reach the river, cross the fallen stone pillar here. Clear out the Moblin camp on the far side and loot the **Treasure Chest** they had been guarding for Riverhorse x10.

Cross back over the stone pillar and you will see a bridge to the east. This leads to the Crossflows Plaza, but this is vacant for the moment. Follow the stairs down to the beach and you will find a **Waypoint Stone** and nearby, Business Scrub. He will give you a new side quest:

- Out of Bubble Kelp

Note that if you want to use his services to create smoothies, you will need to finish his side quest first.

To continue, head up the slope behind the Business Scrub to reach the Zora River.

Zora River

After reaching the river, continue north until you bump into a group of Tektite enemies. Defeat them before proceeding. Note the trees and stone pillars in the area. If we use these with **Echoes**, we can make a path up to a ledge to the north overlooking the area where a dude will be standing. Speak with him to try the Acorn Gathering minigame.

Conitinue up the river and you will soon come across several platforms with log bridges between them. Activate the **Waypoint Stone** here and continue to the left to find the entrance to Lord Jabu-Jabu's Den.

Continue inside until a scene plays and Tri and a pair of River Zora that show up, give you an idea as to what to do next – we will need to pay a visit to the leaders of both the River Zora and Sea Zora clans. The Sea Zora can be found down in Zora Cove south of Seesyde Village, whereas the River Zora clan is located further up the river. Since we are already halfway there, let us go and check out the River Zora village first.

Exit Jabu-Jabu's Den and continue to the east to reach the next section of water. Before following it to the north, look on the far, eastern side of this stretch of river to find a Stamp platform to notch another entry in your Stamp Rally.

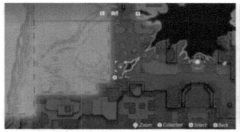

Proceed to the north, dealing with Tanglers and Octoroks as you go. Look out for a cave on the right side of the river. Continue inside here.

As you enter the cave, you will be able to see a Bombfish in the water below. These will spot a target, approach it and then blow themselves up. Send an **Echo** out to meet it and once it explodes, check it out for **Echo** – Bombfish.

*Note: Bombfish are one of the more useful **Echoes** in the game, and in essence replace bombs that Link usually carries around in his adventures. You can use these to destroy/damage enemies, and weak items/walls in the environment. Handy!*

Swim to the next platform to spot some Tanglers and Sea Urchins below. Drop a Bombfish or two into the water to deal with that quick smart. There will be some additional Tanglers ahead and a ladder leading down to a side-scrolly area.

Swim down the first shaft and use a Bombfish to break the weak block. Note that you can perform a spin with Zelda to trigger the explosion faster. Avoid the patrolling Bombfish here and blow open the next block as well. As you enter the next segment, you will immediately be spotted by a large group of Bombfish. Quickly spawn a few aqua critters (Tangler, Octorok) so that the Bombfish target them instead.

Upon exiting the water, you will see a **Treasure Chest** in a small alcove above, with a weak wooden platform beneath it. Unfortunately, we cannot throw a Bombfish. We can, however, summon one, quickly bind it and then climb the nearby ladder so that it is close enough to the wooden platform to destroy it. The chest contains a Golden Egg.

Climb the ladder here and continue through the nearby door to find yourself back at the cave entrance.

Back outside, head to the west and then to the north when you can. Continue up the ramp. At the top, you will see a bridge leading way to the left and another cave on your right. Head to the right first and defeat the small dragonfly enemies to the south of it for **Echo** – Needlefly. Head on into the cave for more puzzly goodness.

In the first room of the cave, you will see a crate floating around the water here following a current. We need to hop on top of this. Ride it to the rear wall and use bind to grab the crate behind the fence. Pull this to the right until it comes to a stop atop the pressure plate here. This will unlock the next door.

The second room has a similar puzzle. Again, we need to ride a crate, bind a second crate and place it on a pressure plate, but this time around, there are tiered levels behind the fence, meaning you will need to keep jumping whilst standing on the crate to move it upwards and into position.

In the third and final room, we will be behind a fence, and we will need to position a crate on a pressure plate behind a second fence. To do this, drop one of the crates into the water. When it is all the way to the left, bind it and then hold R so that Zelda follows it. The fence will prevent that form happening, but it will extend the length of the bind. When it stops moving, walk to the right and then back towards the screen to place it onto the pressure plate. This will spawn a **Treasure Chest** containing a Silver Rupee.

Return outside and follow the bridges to the west and then north. Activate the **Waypoint Stone** when you reach it. We can now proceed into the River Zora Village.

Zora River Village

At this point, we can explore the village here. There is not a whole lot to it, but check out the various houses on offer and chat with the NPCs that call it home. There is a shop here with Accessory – Zora's Flippers for 350 **Rupees**. This is a very useful trinket as it will increase your swim speed... and there will be a lot of swimming in our near future.

After climbing the first ramp, to reach the middle level of the village, look below the waterfalls to the right to see a sunken **Treasure Chest**. We can loot this for a Red Rupee. Continue up the slope on the western side to reach the top of the village and Dradd's hut. Below the waterfall beside this, there is a Blue Rupee.

Head into Dradd's hut to have a chat. After a short conversation, he will head off to the Crossflows Plaza leaving us alone.

At this point, we will need to go and meet the leader of the Sea Zora. To do this, we want to fast travel back to Seesyde Village.

Zora Cove

The most important area of Zora Cove is the Sea Zora Village. This can be found by swimming to the southeast from Seesyde Village. The village is situated below an island with a large fish tail sticking out of the top of it. There is a **Waypoint Stone** on the island. You will see several Zora in the water around this area. They will point out the entrance to the village below the water.

Swim on down and head inside. This village is a bit smaller than the River Zora village, but there are still NPCs to speak with and a general story to peruse. Our goal here though is to head to the northern end of the village and speak with the leader, Kushara.

After a short chat, she will run off too, letting you know she is on the way to Crossflows Plaza. Now that both chiefs are there, we can progress the quest. Before doing so however, we can do a bit of looting around Zora Cove... there are plenty of goodies to be had.

To the west of the Sea Zora island, you can find a cracked rock on the seabed. Use a Bombfish to blow this up to find a recess beneath it housing a **Might Crystal**.

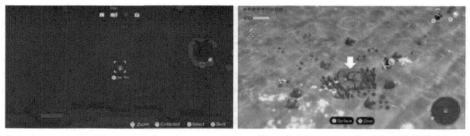

Directly south of the Sea Zora Village island, there is a **Treasure Chest** on the ocean floor surrounded by Sea Urchins. Use bind to remove them and loot the chest for a Red Rupee. A short distance to the east from here, there is another **Treasure Chest** guarded by a Tangler. It holds Bubble Kelp x5.

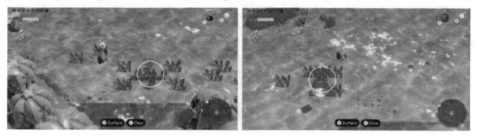

Make your way all the way to the eastern side of the water to find a small island with a Stamp platform. Go ahead and activate this to add another stamp to your collection.

On the seabed just to the right of the Stamp platform, you will find a large, cracked boulder. Swim down and blow this up with a Bombfish for a sneakily placed **Piece of Heart**.

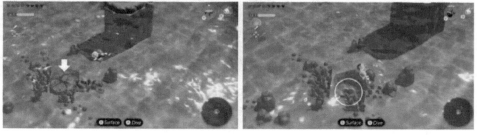

In this general area you will encounter some electrified jellyfish creatures. Use your

Echoes to destroy one of these so that you can learn **Echo** – Biri. To the north you will find an island with two cave entrances (one on land on in the water), they both lead to the same area.

Enter the upper cave first. Inside, enter the water and dive down to reach a side-scrolling area.

In this side-scroll area, we will be underwater for quite a long time. As such, be sure to stop by the bubbles along the way to top up Zelda's oxygen. As you descend through the area, you will also find that the area gets darker. If you swim through the clumps of crystals, they will light up, allowing you a little visibility. You will need to deal with Tanglers as you go as well. Fun!

As you descend, you should come across a **Treasure Chest** along the left-hand wall. This contains Bubble Kelp x10. As you begin descending to the lower, right, you will encounter an upgraded Tangler. Create a wall of Sea urchins for him to throw himself against and then once he is dead, you can learn **Echo** – Tangler Lv 2.

Following the supercharged fish, follow the set path through the tunnels leading to the right. Eventually they will start angling upwards, allowing you to reach the surface. Use the ladder to exit the area and then continue back outside.

Northeast of the Zora island, there is a circular clump of seaweed on the seabed. Dive down and twirl through the plant at its centre to find a **Might Crystal**.

Note that you will likely encounter some Albatrawls here as well, defeat one for the

Echo - Albatrawl. These birds are handy because unlike other birds, their swoop attack can also hit things underwater. Just northwest of the Zora island, there is a smaller island. In the water to the east of this there is another sunken **Treasure Chest**. This contains a Purple Rupee.

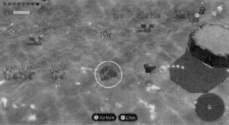

Finally, swim all the way to the west. When you reach the end of the cove, follow the cliff wall south until you find a ledge we can climb up on. There is a cave here to explore.

Upon entering this cave, you will find the first area is occupied with Zols. You will find both regular Zols and Ignizols, however there is also a new type here – a Hydrozol. Be sure to learn **Echo** – Hydrozol here. These are useful for putting out fires!

Continue down the ladder into a side-scroll area.

Here we will encounter what happens when Hydrozols are put in water – they grow giant! Use some of your aquatic **Echo**es to eliminate the pair of Hydrozols here and then climb the ladder on the right to exit. We will arrive in another room. Here there are lots of Ignizols about along with some boxes and grass... so lots of flammables! Eliminate them all.

Once the room is safe, note the four braziers around the room. We need to summon a Hydrozol and throw it into each of the lit braziers to douse the flames. Once thy are all out, both doors will open. The left-hand door leads back to the cave entrance, but the northern door leads to a **Piece of Heart**. Sweet!

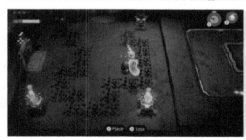

Finally we can fast travel to the **Waypoint Stone** at Seesyde Village. Right beside this there is a weak section of wall. Use a Bombfish to knock this down. Inside is a **Treasure Chest** with a Red Rupee.

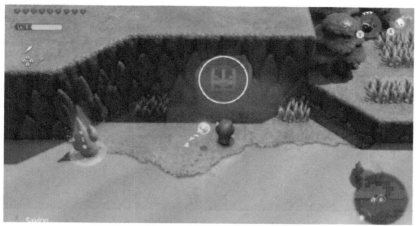

With that, our looting is done, and we can continue.

Crossflows Plaza

Once both Kushara of the Sea Zora and Dradd of the River Zora have made their way to Crossflows Plaza, we should head on over to join them. Watch the scenes that play out here.

Eventually, Jabu Jabu will take off and the two chiefs will run off after it. To continue, you will want to fast travel to the **Waypoint Stone** by the entrance to the River Zora Village.

CHAOS AT THE RIVER ZORA VILLAGE

River Zora Village

After beginning this quest, we will need to check out the River Zora Village. Specifically, the middle section of the village up the first ramp. Here you will find that some of the houses have been broken, and the locals are out of sorts.

Enter the cave behind these houses and walk to the right to find a hidden ramp leading up to a small watery area above. Swim over to the island with the rift here to find Kushara and a River Zora waiting for you.

After a brief chat, approach the rift and interact with it to continue inside.

Stilled Upper Zora River

In this fragment of the Still World, we will be required to find and collect five Glowing Orbs containing Tri's friends to free them. As per usual, you will find them scattered all over the area, so we need to be thorough to find them all.

From the entry point, head across the ledges to the left first. Follow the platforms and pools here along the set path to find the first Glowing Orb at the end.

 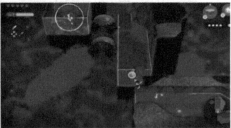

Return to the entry point and this time head to the right. After the first gap you should see a floating stone pillar below. Follow this down and then to the right to find the second Glowing Orb across a gap.

Note the patches of water on the vertical cliffs here. We can jump into these and swim upwards, neat! When you reach the top, hop out and defeat the nearby Octoroks. Proceed to the far, right and use the tree as a stepping stone to reach the ledge above. There is a cave here we want to explore – there are two Glowing Orbs inside it.

The cave contains a side-scrolling area. Swim downwards and to the left, avoiding the Bombfish and Tangler, and breaking open the weak blocks using Bombfish **Echo**es. The first Glowing Orb is behind a weak block. The second Glowing Orb in this cave can be found in the upper, left corner of this area and is dropped by the powerful rift Tektite enemy.

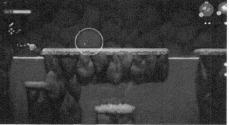

Once you have both Glowing Orbs, exit the cave.

Use some trampolines, a Platboom or furniture pile to get onto the ledge above the cave. Continue to the left, after a pair of gaps you will reach the top of a structure where you will find the fifth and final Glowing Orb.

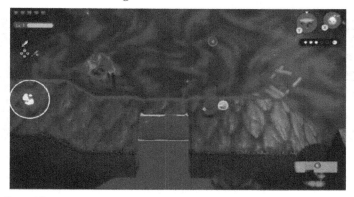

Finding all five will trigger a few scenes in which Tri and her friends will cleanse the rift. Tri will also gain a bit of XP, but not enough for a new level and will hand over **Might Crystal** x2. We will also find ourselves back outside where the Zora questline will progress further.

At this point, the chiefs will chat a little before a Sea Zora shows up with another sighting of Lord Jabu-Jabu down at Zora Cove. Predictably both chiefs will immediately run off, leaving us behind once again.

At this point, the quest will be complete. Before leaving the village however, you can find a new side quest has appeared near the destroyed houses. Its worth picking up and completing this now as it rewards you with Accessory – Zora Scale, which will increase your lung capacity underwater. Handy!

RAMPAGE IN ZORA COVE

After starting the quest, you will find Dradd and another Zora trying to get into a now sealed cave on an island in the eastern part of Zora Cove to find a missing child and Kushara. Now, if you have been following along, you will recognize this cave as we explored it earlier and the unique thing about it is that there are two entrances.

Following the chat, jump into the water and use the underwater entrance to enter the cave. Head down the ladder and through the side-scrolling dark underwater area here, watching out for Tanglers hiding in the dark. Remember that the crystals along the path will illuminate areas around them. Use the bubbles to re-charge Zelda's breath gauge.

If you have not visited this cave previously, you will find an upgraded Tangler we can kill for **Echo** – Tangler Lv. 2 near our stating point and a **Treasure Chest** around 2/3 of the way through it that contains Bubble Kelp x10.

After moving through the underwater section to the far end, we can exit into the sealed cave where we will meet Kushara and the missing child. Following another brief chat here, we can use bind to move the large boulder by the entrance out of the way. Doing so will trigger another scene to end the side quest.

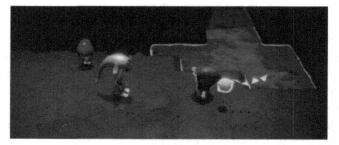

At this point, both of the smaller side-quests have been resolved, allowing us to continue with The Jabul Waters Rift - Part 2.

THE JABUL WATERS RIFT - PART 2

Jabu-Jabu's Den

In order to continue with this quest, we will next need to head for Jabu-Jabu's Den where both Kushara and Dradd are waiting for us. As you arrive, they will tell you that Jabu-Jabu was on a bit of a rampage and wrecked up the place a little bit. We will need to restore it in order for the pair to open the door for us.

To do this, use bind to remove the rubble from atop the two golden platforms here. You will also need to re-assemble the left-hand platform. To do so, look around the room for the fragments and use bind to place them into the correct position. One is to the left of the left-hand platform and the other fragment is at the bottom of the pool on the left side of the room.

 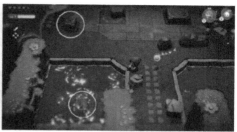

To get the fragment out of the pool, you will need to bind it and then build a set of stairs to raise Zelda off the floor. Once she is high enough, jump away from the pile to yank the fragment out of the water.

With both platforms back in working order, you will be treated to a short scene (and a bit of music) before the door ahead opens. Follow the two chiefs inside. Another short scene later, jump into the water for a boss fight.

❖ *Boss: Lord Jabu-Jabu*

Lord Jabu-Jabu is a large, angry fish monster but despite his size and scary looks he is not too tough as he only has a couple of moves at his disposal. He will also essentially repeat the same basic pattern over and over again, which helps us out.

Initially he will appear at the centre of the room and shoot out a gush of water, sending out lots of debris including boxes, boats, and wooden planks. Mixed in amongst the debris there will also be a few monsters. Note that as the fight progresses, increasingly harder monsters will appear after this attack. Initially, you will encounter Tanglers, but will also have to deal with Octoroks, and Biri.

After distributing his lunch around the arena, he will then appear and begin chomping repeatedly as he swims around the area. Avoid him here and focus on using **Echo**es to deal with the smaller monsters. Albatrawl **Echo**es are a good option here as they can attack the seaborne creatures whilst staying out of Jabu-Jabu's reach.

Once the boss's little journey around the area concludes, he will appear in the middle of the area once again. At this point he will open his mouth wide and begin sucking everything nearby inside. This is our opening to attack him. At this point, you want to spawn a Bombfish. The boss will suck it up and it will explode, stunning him briefly.

Whilst the boss is stunned, swim over and use swordfighter mode to wail on him (see what I did there?) to inflict as much damage as possible until he recovers. At this point, we simply need to repeat the same process, just dealing with slightly harder enemies as you do so.

When he has been damaged enough, the fight will end.

Another short scene will play here and once it has finished, we can swim over to the rift at the rear of the room and interact with it to continue inside.

Stilled Jabul Waters

Exit the water and follow the set path here until you reach some of those vertical water areas we experienced earlier. Swim into this first one and exit onto one of the columns sticking out of it. Use this as a platform to reach the next section of water above. From here we can swim to the very top of the area.

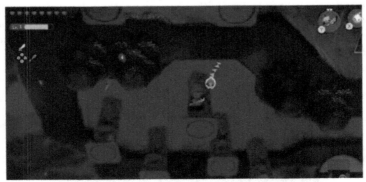

Continue to the right and dispatch the rift Tanglers in the next pool. At the far end of this platform, you will see some floating water in cube form. Examine this to learn **Echo** –

Water Block. Water Blocks are super handy as we can create stacks, both horizontally or vertically, that will allow us to swim through them.

After crossing the gap, we will reach a couple of walls covered in water blocks. We need to use our **Echoes** to complete paths up these walls to reach the top. There are two paths up, but both will lead you to the same place on top.

Continue to the left and then to the north across the platforms here, using the water blocks (or other means) to progress and be sure to deal with the annoying rift Biri creatures as you do so.

Note: *On the far, left side of the area, there is a rather suspicious collection of circular platforms with a pool at the bottom. I am convinced there is something sneaky there but could not find anything (let me know if I missed something good!).*

Head towards the larger vertical platform in the distance and use your water blocks to scale this to the top. As you are working you your way up, we should see a platform off to the right with a couple of boats just north of it. Head over to this platform and climb the boats to reach a floating island with a Tresure Chest. It contains Riverhorse x10.

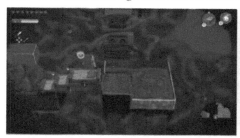

Return to the main platform and swim as high up as you can. We will need to emerge from the water here and use the trees as platforms to reach the next section of water nearby. Swim through here and this will take you all the way to the top.

At the top, you want to head to the left first. You should see a floating platform off to the side here. Head on over to find a **Treasure Chest** with a Purple Rupee.

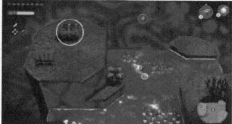

Return across the gap to the top of the main structure. Here you will find a bridge made out of Lord Jabu-Jabu himself leading to the north. Enter the building here.

At this point, you will have arrived at the next dungeon. Head on over to the next page - Dungeon - Jabul Ruins to continue.

DUNGEON - JABUL RUINS

As you enter this dungeon, go ahead, and activate the nearby **Waypoint Stone**. Continue past this and before you get too far, the floor will collapse beneath you sending you down into a watery side-scrolling area below.

Move the large boulder ahead using bind and continue to the left. Bind the next boulder heading downwards and lift it up and place it on a ledge to the right. Continue down the vertical shaft and then to the right when you are able. As you move through this area, a scene will play.

We will now have a giant whirlpool chasing us! We want to swim to the right as quickly as possible whilst avoiding the obstacles ahead. Take the lower path at the two splits (its more direct, and faster). At the second, there are some wooden boxes - at this point, we can take the upper path (or quickly bind and move the boxes). Continue to the right past some Biri and Sea Urchins to reach another large boulder. Bind this and push it forwards until it can drop into the area below.

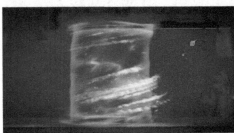 

At this point, we simply need to swim upwards to escape.

Upon exiting the side scroll area, we will be in a small room occupied by Tanglers, Sand Crabs and Octoroks. Defeat them all (Albatrawl is good!) or simply run past them and into the door in the upper, left corner.

At this point we will arrive back by the entrance, but on the other side of the large hole that opened up in the floor. Activate the **Waypoint Stone** here. Enter the next door to continue.

The next room is the main 'hub' room for this dungeon. If you step on the purple plate here a segment on the back wall will light up. Note that there are four other colored segments on the wall - these represent four other plates hidden around the dungeon that we need to step on, all four of which are at the end of little puzzle areas accessible from this hub room.

Either side of the purple plate you will find passages leading to new areas. We can hit them in any order, but we decided to go left first.

After heading down the stairs we will be in another underwater side-scrolling area. As with the dark cave we explored previously, this area will be dark too – do not forget to hit the crystals to illuminate the area and the bubbles to replenish your air supply.

Swim down and to the left, avoiding or killing Tanglers as you go. Be careful as you approach the second crystal as there is a Bio Deku hiding in the dark off to the left. Send some **Echo**es to kill it so you can learn **Echo** – Bio Deku.

Continue to follow the set path through this area. As you go, watch out for more Bio Dekus along with some Biri and Tanglers. When you reach the final shaft leading upwards, head to the very bottom first to find a **Treasure Chest** with a Silver Rupee.

Swim up the far-left vertical shaft to reach the exit.

We will arrive in a room with a locked door and a pool of water at the centre. There are three braziers located around the room and a fourth in the water. To unlock the door, we need to bind the brazier in the water and pull it out of the water. We then want to place it in the upper, left corner of the room and then set all four of them on fire.

After solving the puzzle, cruise on through to the next room where you will find the blue plate. Step on this to activate another of the wall panels back in the hub area.

The hatch in the upper, right corner will open afterwards. Drop down here to return to the start of the side-scrolling area. Here we can backtrack to the hub room. From the hub room, we now want to head to the right and explore the next entrance. Again, we will find ourselves in a water-filled side-scroll area.

Proceed to the right and cross the first pool of water (watch out for the Bombfish!). When you reach the second pool of water, there will be a Needlefly overhead – take this out. Hop across the ledges to the right to reach a **Treasure Chest** holding the Dungeon Map.

Head down into the water and continue to the right, and then upwards avoiding the Bombfish as you go. Once you reach the surface, use the ladder to exit the area.

We will arrive in a large, flooded room with several rocky pillars sticking up above the water with Octoroks positioned atop several of them. In the water itself, there is a group of three Chompfins. These shark-like creatures will charge at you and bite, or perform a spin attack. They will also do a ton of damage.

Lure the first Chompfin back to the entry point and stand atop the small island here. Summon **Echo**es (again Albatrawls are a good option) to take it out. We can now learn **Echo** – Chompfin.

Return to the larger room and climb up atop one of the pillars – take out the Octoroks and then use **Echo**es to take out the remaining Chompfins. When it is safe to do so we can explore the room.

Rather than faffing around with the pillars, jump down into the water and swim to the northern section of fence. Use bind to remove the box in the fence here to reveal an opening. Head on through and climb the ledges on the left to find a **Treasure Chest** holding a Purple Rupee.

From this upper ledge, look back to the right to spot a wooden platform. Use your **Echo**es to reach it. Once here, Use the ropes here to create a bridge (yes beds will balance on them perfectly!) over to the left.

Enter the door here. The next room that we enter will have the doors lock behind us. To get them open again, you will need to defeat all the Sand Crabs here. Do so and continue onwards once the way opens.

The subsequent room is home to the red plate. Step on this to activate another of the wall panels back in the hub area. The hatch in the upper, left corner of the room will open afterwards. Drop down here to return to the start of the side-scrolling area. Here we can backtrack to the hub room.

Upon returning to the hub room, you will find that there is a geyser of water along the northern wall. With three panels active, this is strong enough to get you up to another pair of ledges midway up the wall – one to the right and another to the left. Again, both options lead to puzzle rooms for the remaining two panels.

Let us tackle the left side first.

As you enter this room you will be on a small platform beside a fast-flowing river. There will be numerous pieces of wooden debris flowing down the river and we will need to ride them. As you go, watch out for the Octoroks positioned on other ledges here – keep some Albatrawls out to deal with the pesky critters.

When you reach the southern end of the river, there is a waterfall, so you will want to jump to the ledge on the left. We will then find a second river. This time however we will need to make our way to the north, jumping between the wooden platforms to do so. Again, there will be Octoroks about, but also a Tektite both of whom will try their best to ruin your day, so keep your **Echo**es handy.

After navigating upriver, enter the door on the left.

We will arrive in a large room with five glowing blue switches dotted around it. These are located on platforms and rocky pillars. The base of the room is made up of a giant pool of water with a current that will drag you in a square pattern clockwise around the room. We will need to make our way around the room and hit all the switches to open the door.

The first switch is just inside the door. The second is on an island at the centre of the room, whilst a third is located just south of the central island under the water, surrounded by Sea Urchins.

 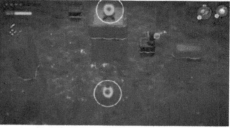

A fourth switch is located on a ledge high up on the room's left-hand wall. You will need to build some stairs off a nearby pillar (or use a Platboom **Echo**) to reach it. The final switch is located to the left of the exit door behind some stacks of crates. Light these on fire with a Ignizol and once they burn, the switch will be activated too.

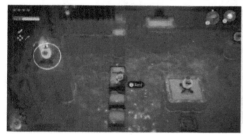 

Enter the door here. The next room that we enter will have the doors lock behind us. To get them open again, you will need to defeat all the Tektites here. I absolutely hate these things, but found if you build a perimeter of Sea Urchins around Zelda, it will usually keep them away and kill them at the same time. Do so and continue onwards once the way opens.

The next room houses the yellow plate. Step on this to activate another of the wall panels back in the hub area. The hatch in the upper, right corner of the room will open afterwards. Drop down here to return to the start of the side-scrolling area. Here we can backtrack to the hub room.

Back in the hub room, use the water geyser to reach the upper, right-hand ledge. Continue into the opening here to reach a side-scrolling underwater area.

Form the entry point, swim downwards until you see a pair of wooden blocks over gaps in the floor. Blow open the first one with a Bombfish and swim through the new opening to find a **Treasure Chest** with a Golden Egg.

Return up the shaft and blow open the second wooden blocker. Break through another couple of wooden planks and a weak concrete block as you continue downwards. At the very bottom of this room, you will find a large **Treasure Chest** holding the Big Key.

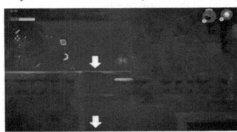

From the chest, swim upwards and take the path leading to the left with you can. You will reach another vertical shaft. Work your way up here and through the wooden crates on the right to reach the exit. Make sure you avoid the Biri and Bombfish as you go!

Upon exiting the side-scroll area you will be in a flooded room with some rift enemies including Tanglers and Biri. The door on the left side of the room will remain sealed until you take care of all the monsters. Summon some **Echo**es of your own to take them all out (try a Chompfin, it will sort the room out real quick!). Head through the door when you are able.

At this point we will find the white plate. It is flanked by a pair of Bio Dekus, so have some **Echo**es dispatch them. To activate the plate, we want to spawn a boulder on top of it. The hatch in the upper, left corner of the room will open afterwards. Swim down here to return to the start of the previous underwater side-scrolling area. Here we can backtrack to the hub room.

Once you are back in the hub room, you will find that the geyser we used previously can now reach the platform at the very top of the room. At the top, the Big Door is located leading to the dungeon boss.

Head on through the boss door and when you are ready to challenge it, drop down the pit at the centre of the room.

❖ Boss: Vocavor

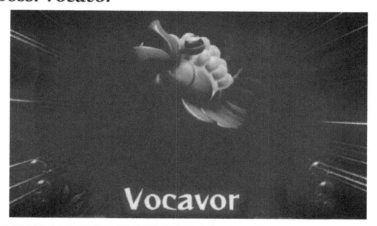

If this boss looks familiar to you, it should! It is the monster that chased use with the giant whirlpool at the start of the dungeon. Its back again with more whirlpool themed tomfoolery along with some new attacks to keep us on our toes.

Initially the boss will swim to one side of the area and summon small whirlpools that you will need to swim around, these can vary a little bit in terms of location – so make sure that you swim under/over as needed. As the fight progresses, the boss will also spawn more and more of these during its attack. Alternatively, the boss can use its tail to shoot off homing barbed projectiles at your location. To avoid these, you can summon some Tanglers or other expendable water Echoes to act as blockers for you.

Note that after using an attack or two, the boss will then swim to the opposite side of the room and do the same thing, but in the opposite direction.

To defeat this boss, you will need to exploit its weak spot, represented by the glowing blue orbs on its back. It is a good idea to line yourself up with the weak spot unleash a couple of Tanglers in the boss's direction whilst you focus on avoiding the whirlpools. Tanglers are good because you can summon two of them, their charge attack is pretty direct and should hit.

Once you have destroyed all the orbs on the boss's back, it will be stunned. Quickly

103

swim over to it, assume swordfighter mode, and attack it to inflict as much damage as possible before it recovers. Be careful as it will perform a powerful tail whip attack as it regains composure, so be sure to move out of range before it happens.

After damaging the boss a few times, the arena will change. Two large, water free patches will appear at the centre of the room with water surrounding each of them on three sides. The boss will enter an air pocket and use its attacks before entering the water and swimming in a U-shape before entering the opposite air pocket to attack again.

Note that during this second stage of the fight, the boss can also summon a giant whirlpool, so watch out for that!

As the boss only attacks from the air pockets, the Tanglers and Chompfins will not work here, as such switch things up and summon Albatrawls. You can summon these from the edge of the water, and they can fly around the boss and keep swooping it.

As before, once the boss's weak spots have all been destroyed, it will be stunned. Keep damaging it until it stops being alive.

For defeating the boss, you will receive a full Heart Container. Once the scene here runs its course, you will be able to claim it. Additionally, Tri will level up again, unlocking a new ability – certain **Echo**es will now cost less to summon. Tri will also hand over **Might Crystal** x5.

Speak with Tri by the glowing section of ground on the left side of the room to teleport out of the dungeon.

We will end up back outside in the 'real' world. After a few scenes with the Zora and Jabu-Jabu General Wright will appear for a chat. After a brief initial conversation, he will run off in the direction of Lueburry's house.

Following this chat, our objectives will update, and we will get a new main quest - Still Missing.

JABUL WATERS EXPLORATION (OPTIONAL)

Zora Cove

After completing the Jabul Ruins dungeon and removing the rift from the Jabul Waters area, you will find that there are quite a few new areas up the Zora River that we can explore for some new goodies. Before doing that however, you can make a brief visit to the Sea Zora Village to find a newly available side quest we can pick up:

● Precious Treasure

That is all there is here for now, so let us proceed to the **Waypoint Stone** by the Crossflows Plaza and head up the ramp to re-explore the Zora River.

Zora River

At the top of the ramp, you should be able to see a **Treasure Chest** in a ledge above to the east. Use some water blocks to stack up and swim up to this ledge. Loot the chest for Riverhorse x10.

Once you reach Jabu-Jabu's Den, you will find that it is free of the rift that covered it earlier. Head around to the right side of the building and you will spot a **Piece of Heart** sitting on a pillar. Use some water blocks to swim right up to it.

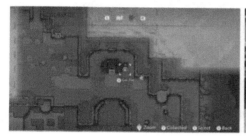 

Head to the west from Jabu-Jabu's Den until you reach the Stamp platform nearby. From here, head south until you reach a section of shallow river with trees surrounding it. Use a trampoline to jump onto the trees here and then follow the treetop path to the west until you can drop down.

We will be in a relatively large open area that is in essence a large Moblin camp. Slowly work your way north, dispatching the Needleflies, Spear Moblins and Sword Moblins as you go. Note one of these Spear Moblins is a more powerful variant. After killing it you can learn **Echo** – Spear Moblin Lv. 2. Defeating them all will unlock the **Treasure Chest** here which holds **Might Crystal** x3.

Now fast travel to the River Zora Village.

River Zora Village

From the entrance by the **Waypoint Stone**, head to the left and just past the houses here, you can use water blocks to swim up and jump onto the trees above. Drop down and use a Bombfish to blow open the weak wall here. There is a **Treasure Chest** inside that contains Accessory – Silver Brooch.

Next, climb up to Dradd's hut at the top of the village. There is a Stamp platform on the ledge above and to the west of this. You can use water blocks to climb the nearby waterfall and then follow the path on top around to reach it. Add to that Stamp Rally!

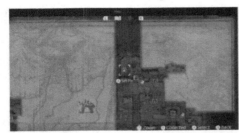

Return to the top of the waterfall behind Dradd's hut. Here we can use water blocks to climb the eastern wall. At the top, head to the east until you see another waterfall. Again, use water clocks to climb this. At the top, you will find a Fairy and a **Piece of Heart**.

Drop down and continue to the east. After reaching some Sand Crabs, look along the rear wall for a weak section we can destroy with a Bombfish. Inside you will find a **Treasure Chest** with a Purple Rupee.

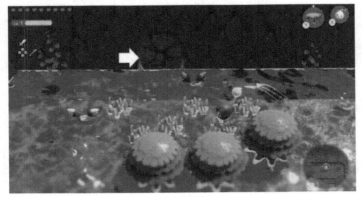

Head for the destroyed huts midway up the River Zora Village and head east from them and then follow the ledge here south and then around the corner to the east. Along the eastern wall you can create a stack of water blocks to reach the area above.

We will land in another large, open Moblin camp occupied by Spear Moblins, Sword Moblins and Needleflies. In the lower, left section of this area you will find a **Treasure Chest** with **Might Crystal** x3, and for defeating all the enemies, you can unlock the **Treasure Chest** they were guarding for Golden Egg.

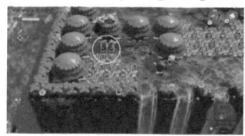

...and with that we are done here, to continue head onwards to the next main quest, Still Missing.

STILL MISSING

Suthorn Forest

Once you have completed both A Rift in the Gerudo Desert and The Jabul Waters Rift and rescued Minister Lefte and General Wright, we can continue our journey.

The first thing we will need to do is to head for Lueburry's house in Suthorn Forest. Upon entering you will find our two rescues here chatting away with Lueburry. After a brief discussion, they will go barreling off, leaving us behind.

Take the opportunity to upgrade your Sword, Bow and Energy level using the **Might Crystal**s we have gathered. If you have not already, speak to Lueburry about upgrading them and he will give you access to the upgrade machine in the corner.

When you are ready to continue, we want to fast travel to Hyrule Castle Town.

Hyrule Castle Town

As you arrive in Hyrule Castle Village, you will see General Wright and Minister Lefte speaking with guards at the entrance. As this conversation proceeds, the rift at the castle will expand and a good chunk of the town will get gobbled up.

Following the scene, we will need to proceed onwards. As you enter the town, you will find a bunch of rift clones of enemies here including Sword Moblins, Spear Moblins and Darknuts. To the left, you will find some more Spear Moblins along with Keese as well.

Note that there is not much to do here other than kill enemies, so if you would rather not we can run by them.

Our goal is the well on the western side of the town. We need to create a trampoline and jump down the well to get to the underground area beneath the village. In this location you will find the entrance to the rift.

Head on inside to continue.

Stilled Hyrule Castle Town

Exit the first building and you will see that many of the buildings and structures we saw in town earlier have made it into the rift as well. Beside the first building you will see the bird statue. Use bind to move this, revealing some stairs. Head on down to find a **Treasure Chest** with Warm Pepper x3.

Follow the main path to the east until you reach the General Store. Defeat the Spear Moblin outside and the Darknut behind it. Note that you can enter the store as well, but you will only find enemies inside which will ambush you (two Spear Moblins and a Redead), nothing good. So, you know, go in and give their noggins a floggin' if you like... or just leave them be.

Continue past the houses north of the general store and look for a section of the city wall that you need to cross. From here there is a hidden island to the northeast. Create a path out to this using beds and then use a stack of water blocks to reach another small island above. There is a **Treasure Chest** here with Monster Fang x5.

Return to the main road and start heading west until you reach a floating island with the fountain. There will be more rift generated monsters here.

North of this is another, larger island with a section of water flowing through it. There is a half-buried **Treasure Chest** on the left side we can yank out of the ground with bind for Radiant Butter x7. There is also a **Waypoint Stone** here to activate.

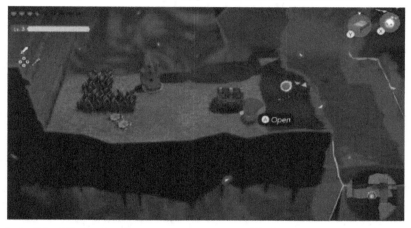

To the left of the **Waypoint Stone**, use some water blocks to get on top of the wall here. At the top, you can create a set of stairs using beds to cross the gap to the west. Jump from the top to reach another ledge. There is a **Treasure Chest** here with a Red Rupee.

From the **Waypoint Stone**, enter the water and swim up the vertical wall. At the top, use the trees as platforms to reach a second pool of water on the right. Swim to the top of this.

At the top, work your way across the next series of islands and water blocks until you reach the entrance to Hyrule Castle.

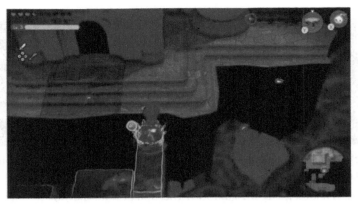

Head on inside to start the next major dungeon, Dungeon - Hyrule Castle.

DUNGEON - HYRULE CASTLE

Upon entering the Hyrule Castle dungeon, head on over and activate the nearby **Waypoint Stone**. Follow the path up the stairs and through the door here. You will encounter a Blue Darknut here. These things are a bit tougher than the standard variety, but will fall easy enough with a few Bombfish thrown their way. After defeating it, you can learn **Echo** - Darknut Lv. 2.

Continue to the north and into the throne room to find the king suspended in the rift. To continue, you will want to walk up to the throne and use bind to move it to the side, revealing a hidden staircase beneath it. Proceed down here to the area below.

When you arrive, activate the **Waypoint Stone**. Use bind on the rear wall to open the hidden path and continue into the next room.

Remember that stealth section we had to do in the intro? Well, we will get to do it again now but in reverse. Additionally, the guards here are rift-versions so rather than sending you to a cell, getting caught will have them send you to a small, void room where you will need to defeat an assortment of random rift enemies before you can escape. If this happens, you will find yourself back at the start of the room once again.

The first guard will be at the top of the screen and will alternate between looking downwards and at the back wall. Wait until it faces away before running by. Use a trampoline to get atop the square-shaped shelf here. The second guard will patrol in a square patten below. Wait until he looks away and drop down and head to the bottom of the screen and to the right.

Again, bounce up onto the shelf here with a trampoline. Drop down behind the boxes here so the middle guard will not spot you. Move up to the next bookshelf and wait for the guard in the upper right to look away before running across the area he watches.

Use bind to move the crates blocking the path here. There will next be a guard patrolling form left to right along the base of the screen. Wait until he walks away before moving the tree here away from the ladder. Climb up to the shelf above. Follow this all the way to the right.

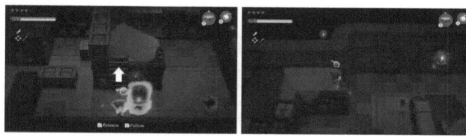

From the end of this shelf, you should see a pair of soldiers patrolling around a central shelf below. Drop down behind one of them and follow behind them. Continue onwards to the right and quickly run to the right when possible. Here, bind and push the tree forwards ASAP and then walk upwards into the opening before the second guard appears.

Use a trampoline to get onto the next shelf and head all the way right, past the next guard. There will be one final guard below. Spawn an **Echo** of a pot and throw it towards the bottom of the screen to distract him. As he goes to investigate, drop down behind him and continue to the right and through the door.

We will arrive back at what is left of the prison cells. Make your way over the half wall here and into the right-hand cell. We will find Impa here. We can also read her journal on the nearby table to learn a bit more about what happened after we escaped.

Follow the path to the right to find a **Waypoint Stone** and a set of stairs leading onwards.

At this point, we will be in a side-scroll area... and it is a pretty big one. Head left first to find a Darknut, use a couple of Bombfish to sort him out – note that you can bind these fellows and throw Bombfish at them at the same time! A second Darknut can be found down the ladders here and an upgraded Darknut on the floor below this. Defeating all three will unlock the door on the left. Head on through.

Proceed to the right until a group of rift enemies spawn. After defeating them, continue down the ladder. Look to the left to spot another, lower ledge with a **Treasure Chest** holding a Monster Stone. Defeat the rift enemies and loot it. Climb back up the ladder and continue down the ladder to the right for another wave of rift enemies and two more **Treasure Chests** with Twisted Pumpkin x3 and Floral Nectar x5.

Head down the next two ladders to leave the room.

In the next room, you will want to first clear out the Keese. Afterwards you will find four unlit braziers around the room. We will need to set them all ablaze to open the door.

For the first brazier just by the entrance, it is behind a fence. We want to spawn an Ignizol **Echo** at range (hold down Y) to spawn it next to the brazier. For the second, look for a fence in the lower, right corner. Again, spawn an Ignizol at range. Afterwards, we want to bind it and then walk north until it reaches the second brazier.

The third brazier is atop the ladder on the right side of the room by the exit. No tricks to this one, just light it. The final brazier is on a raised ledge opposite the last. To light this, spawn an Ignizol just south of the ledge, bind it and then climb the ladder on the right. We can then position the Ignizol by the brazier to set it alight.

We will reach a room with a Gustmaster ahead. These critters will periodically create gusts of wind which can knock you backwards, and make running by them tricky, especially on narrow paths like the one ahead. Send out some **Echo**es to destroy it and then jump to its platform to learn **Echo** – Gustmaster.

Continue to the north, taking out two more Gustmasters as you go and then build a set of stairs to reach the ledge above. Continue to the north until you reach a platform with some Ignizols. Take them all out.

From the Ignizol platform you will have two options, a door on the right, or more of the room to the north. Head through the door on the right first. You will reach a small, sandy room with a couple of Arurodas. After dispatching them, pull out a wind cannon and clear the sand piles to find a **Treasure Chest** containing the Dungeon Map.

 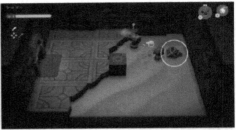

Return to the Ignizol platform and continue north. Build a staircase to get over the gap. Proceed through the door here to reach a larger room with the dungeon's boss door and a **Waypoint Stone** to activate.

From the boss door room, you can go left or right. We will need to explore both areas regardless, but its more efficient to go to the left path first... so let us make it so!

Through the left-hand door is a water filled room occupied by a group of rift Tektites. The water will flow off an edge to the bottom of the screen, which makes fighting the Tektites (or avoiding them) slow and tricky. Try to use flying **Echo**es to take them out from afar. After doing so, swim out to the central island and head down the stairs here.

We will end up in a side-scrolling section here. This one is quite large and the majority of it is under water. It is dark and a bit maze-like so be sure to hit those crystals and make use of your map to re-orient yourself if you get lost.

From the start head straight down to the crystal below. Kill the Bio Deku just to the left of this. Head past where the Bio Deku had been and look downwards to find a **Treasure Chest** with a Red Rupee.

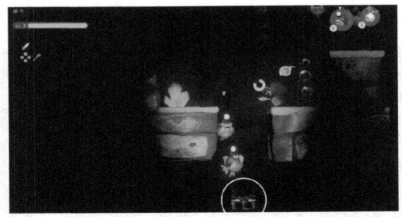

From the chest, head down and to the left. Destroy the pair of purply goop walls with swordfighter mode and continue downwards. There is a crystal and a bubble supply here At this point we can head to the left, or downwards. Head down first, past a Bio Deku to find a **Treasure Chest** with a Silver Rupee.

Return to the previous crystal (below the goop walls) and head to the left. Follow this all the way upwards to find the path leading out of the room.

The next room is another stealth area. The same rules apply as the previous stealth section – if you get caught by one of the rift guards, you will need to kill a few rift monsters before you can escape... and then have to start the area from the beginning. Mercifully, its much shorter (and easier) than the previous one.

From the start, you will see the first soldier patrolling around a pillar at the top of the screen. Follow him around the pillar and then continue to the right, along the back wall. You will come across another soldier patrolling a pillar in the upper right of the room. Wait for him to look away and quickly run down to the lower, right corner to find some stairs.

At the top of the stairs, create a bridge to the top of the pillar nearby with the pressure plate on top. Stepping on this will spawn a **Treasure Chest** at the centre of the room. Drop down when it is safe to do so and head back to the upper, central part of the room. Here create a trampoline and hop over the wall to reach it. It contains a Small Key.

Make your way back to the stairs and head through the door at the top. We will be back in the water filled room with the Tektites from earlier. Head to the right to reach the room with the boss door once again.

From the boss door room, we now want to explore the room to the right.

This room is a sandy one in which a couple of Arurodas are lurking. Take them all out.

The door on the right is locked, however if you look along the back wall to the left of the door you will find a crack. Create a ledge below this and use a Bombfish to blow it up. Inside, there is a **Treasure Chest** with a Purple Rupee.

At the southern end of the sandy room, there is a door that we can open using the Small Key. This leads to another side-scrolling area.

Eliminate the Gustmaster and continue down the ladder to the right. You will see another Gustmaster on a column ahead. I suspect you can probably eliminate it and build a bridge to the column and then to the ladder on the far right, but I ventured downwards instead.

After climbing down the rock wall, you will reach a sheer cliff on the left. Use a Strandtula to create a rope we can climb down. Jump to the next web and then spawn Strandtulas, moving from rope to rope as you move across the lower area to the far side.

Once across, smash to the pot here for a Fairy. climb the rock wall to the top and you will be on the far side of the Gustmaster we saw earlier. Climb the ladder here to exit the area.

After exiting the side-scroll area, continue into the room to the north. The doors will lock behind you and you will need to clear the enemies here to open them again.

You will need to fight a pair of Darknuts and a Ball and Chain Trooper. All of these can be taken down with a Darknut Lv. 2 **Echo** or swordfighter mode. Note that the Ball and Chain guys is a bit tougher than the other two. It can swing its weapon round in circles when you are close to it, but can also launch his chain forwards as a projectile. This latter attack takes him a bit of time to recover from. Defeat it to learn **Echo** - Ball and Chain Trooper.

 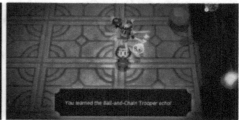

With the room cleared, the doors will open. Head north first to find a collection of three **Treasure Chest**s, two regular ones containing Accessory – Frog Ring (this lets you jump higher, handy!) and a Golden Egg and the large, ornate chest with the Big Key to unlock the boss door.

Now that we have gotten all that sorted, all that is left to do is rest up, return to the boss door, and mosey on through to take on the dungeon's boss.

❖ *Boss: Ganon*

It has been a while since we fought the big blue piggy in the prologue and this time around you will find that he is a bit tougher as he will have a few additional attacks at his disposal, and he can take a lot more damage before we can finally put him down. Each time we damage him sufficiently, he will pick up a new attack and become more aggressive. This will happen three times across the course of the fight (so four mini-phases in total).

Initially, Ganon will use one of the attacks that we will recognize from the intro. The first attack has him wind up backwards before lunging quickly forwards with a jabbing attack using his spear. Simply running to the side should give you enough time to avoid this. He will stay here for a short moment before vanishing and re-appearing nearby to attack once again. Avoid the attack, switch to swordfighter mode, and hit him a few times whilst he is recovering. Rinse and repeat.

After he roars, the second phase of the fight will begin. This time he picks up a new attack where he with throw his spear, which will spin as it flies towards you. He will vanish and re-appear elsewhere and then the spear will fly back to him. He will alternate using this attack and another where he will stand in one location and summon a series of six flaming Keese which will be launched at your position – keep running to avoid these.

Note that the flaming Keese will explode when they hit the walls and will drop Energy, allowing you to run around and gather it up to replenish your energy gauge. Handy!

During this phase, focus on avoiding the Keese (they do a lot of damage) and do not bother attacking during the Keese attack (although if you can get close, you can hit him at the very end). Instead, we want to exploit the staff throwing attack. We want to dodge the spear when it is thrown and run to his position immediately after he reappears as he will be completely defenseless, whack him a few times in swordfighter mode before the spear returns.

After damaging him enough, he will roar again, kicking off a third phase. During this phase, the boss will continue to use the rapid fire flaming Keese attack, but will alternate if with a second that he used during the prologue. This attack has the boss summon a slow-moving fireball which he will throw at you. We can either run past this or hit it with the sword to deflect it back towards the boss. When the boss throws the fireball he will stand still and watch it for quite a while, giving you a perfect opportunity to hit him a few times.

The final phase of the boss fight has him using all of the attacks described above. Again, you will want to avoid the flaming Keese, but we can exploit the openings in his other three attacks to land blows in swordfighter mode.

For defeating the boss, you will receive a full Heart Container. Once the scene here runs its course, you will be able to claim it. Additionally, Tri will level up again, unlocking a new ability – a larger range of **Echo**es will now cost less to summon. Tri will also hand over **Might Crystal** x5.

Speak with Tri by the glowing section of ground on the left side of the room to teleport out of the dungeon.

We will end up back outside in the 'real' world in the throne room of Hyrule Castle. Here we can enjoy a few story scenes with the king and Impa. After a brief nap, make your way back to the throne room for some additional dialogue... and a fancy pants new **Outfit**.

Following this chat, our objectives will update, and we will get a new main quest - Lands of the Goddesses.

WORLD EXPLORATION

Hyrule Castle Town

With the first half of the game sorted and Hyrule Castle and the surrounding town now free of the rift's clutches we can re-visit some of the areas we have previously visited to find some new content waiting for us including – characters, side quests, optional rifts, and other goodies. So, let us go and wrap up some of that before continuing.

In the throne room, you can speak with General Wright who will give you clues where you can go to challenge slightly harder monsters – these are often mini-boss creatures tied into side quests... he won't give you the side quest, but he will tell you where to look for it. We can also speak with Impa for a new side quest:

- Impa's Gift

Head back to Zelda's bedroom and you will find that you can interact with the bed to learn **Echo** – Zelda's Bed. Exit the castle. With our newfound abilities, you can climb up to the roof of the castle itself to find a Might Stone.

Elsewhere in and around the castle town, you will find the fellow with the Acorn Gathering mini-game is now located by the western moat, and you can try a new variant of his mini-game. At the front gate, you can find another side quest:

- One Soldier Too Many

...and that is all for Hyrule Castle Town for now. Next up, lets head for the Suthorn Prairie.

Suthorn Forest

There is not a whole lot to do in Suthorn Forest but there are a couple of new things about! Firstly, if you head back into Suthorn Village here you can pick up a new side quest:

- What is Snow... Really?

Gerudo Desert

There are a couple of new things to do in Gerudo Desert as well. First we want to fast travel to the **Waypoint Stone** on the far, eastern side of the desert (by the path leading to Suthorn Prairie).

From this location, head to the north to find another small bubbling geyser of sand. Approach this to trigger a fight against a Lanmola. This is the source of the dust storm that has knocked out your map.

❖ *Boss: Lanmola*

The Lanmola is a large, centipede like enemy that will initially cover the ground in quicksand, leaving only two small islands made out of regular sand for you to stand on safely (down from one in the initial encounter in the western desert earlier). The boss will bury under the ground, move towards you, and then emerge from the ground, throwing a collection of boulders about the area before diving back underground again.

To defeat it, take note of the hook-like tail that it has, this is the key to victory. As Lanmola moves away from you, you want to grab its tail with bind and then pull backwards. This will pluck it out of the ground and have it collapse on its side. Use this opportunity to run in and wail on it using Swordfighter mode.

We essentially need to repeat this process until it dies.

For defeating this Lanmola, you will be rewarded with a bunch of **Rupees** and some Monster Stones. Defeating this (providing you also killed the other earlier as we suggested) will unlock a side quest.

Now we want to head for Gerudo Town. There are two new side quests out in the open here that we can pick up, and a third in the barracks of the chief's palace. Go ahead and pick them up:

- Beetle Ballyhoo
- Dohna's Challenge
- Wild Sandstorms (this one required you defeat both Lanmolas)

In addition to the new side quests, if you re-visit the oasis and pop into the pink tent, you will also be able to attempt a new difficulty level of the Mango Rush minigame. Yay, I guess.

Jabul Waters

Just like the other regions we have made a quick trip to, Jabul Waters also has some fresh content for us to check out. First we want to for Seesyde Village and Zora Cove. Here we can pick up three new side quests:

- Big Shot
- Secret Chief Talks
- The Zappy Shipwreck

Whilst you are here, you can also pay a visit to the nearby optional rift that has appeared southeast of town to track down some of Tri's friends and level Tri up a little:

- Stilled Eastern Zora River Rift

Lake Hylia

We can also head on back to Lake Hylia. By now you should have enough **Rupees** to purchase another Accessory Slot or two from the Great Fairy. Additionally, if you have not done so already, now that we have plenty of water-based **Echo**es we can easily tackle the optional rift in the southwestern part of the lake that we took note of earlier.

- Stilled Lake Hylia Rift

With all that sorted, let's go and poke around Hyrule Field Exploration (Optional) or continue onwards with the main questline – with main quest Lands of the Goddesses.

HYRULE FIELD EXPLORATION (OPTIONAL)

Before continuing on with the main questline, lets spend some time exploring the Hyrule Field region, gathering up a few more Pieces of Heart, Might Stones and side-quests before pressing onwards.

During this time, we strongly encourage you to complete two specific side-quests which should be done to unlock Zelda's mount and Automatons, both things that will make your life easier. These include:

- Impa's Gift
- Automaton Engineer Dampe

We will be incorporating both of these into the walkthrough below as well, so we will get them done! Let's start at Hyrule Ranch.

Hyrule Field

After receiving the Impa's Gift side quest, you will learn that Impa has been training a horse for you over at the Hyrule Ranch. It is time to go claim it! When you arrive and speak with the little girl in the upper, left corner you will find that the horse has run off.

Head out of Hyrule Ranch to the north and follow the path to the right. If you haven't explored this area previously, you should come across a fellow named Dampe fighting with a Crow. Kill the Crow for him to start his new side-quest:

- Automaton Engineer Dampe

Continue to follow the dirt path here to the east until you reach a pit in the ground northeast of the road. There will be several Ignizols and regular Zols in here. Cut down the plant on the rocky pillar at the centre of this pit for a **Might Crystal**.

Directly north of here, on the other side of a grassy field filled with Ropes and Zols, you will find a collection of ruins. There are a few areas of interest here.

The first is a set of stairs leading downwards. This will take you to a small underground area that we visited briefly during the prologue. There is a **Might Crystal** here... don't jump into the water or you will end up back on Suthorn Beach!

In the northern part of these ruins, there are quite a few Caromadillos around. So go ahead and take them out. Afterwards, you will find a **Piece of Heart** atop a pillar on the eastern side of this area (use a Platboom or waterblocks) and on the western part of these ruins, a half-buried **Treasure Chest** we can pull out for Rocktatoes x5.

Head east from the ruins and follow the road north. Eventually, if you continue to the north you will come across a couple of NPCs at a carrot patch which has been taken over by a rift. Approach the rift and head inside. We will arrive in the Stilled Carrot Patch.

Stilled Carrot Patch

Note: This area is part of the Impa's Gift side-quest, but we are including it here because we want to unlock the horse!

We are now in the still world and as you would know by now in these mini-rift areas we have a goal – to find and rescue Tri's friends. There are four glowing orbs hidden around this rift and we will need to find and collect them all to complete the area.

Move across to the first grassy field with some wooden boxes scattered about. Several of these hide rift Zols, but the box in the upper, right is hiding the entrance to a small cave. Head on in there.

In the side-scrolling area here, head past the first Platboom use a Platboom or some Strandtulas to climb the next vertical shaft. At the top, you can find a ledge on the left with a pressure plate. Step on this to open a gate above the first Platboom's location. Head through this gate and destroy the wooden boxes (Caromadillo or Ignizol) to find the first glowing orb.

Back outside, head to the near, left-hand side of the platform and jump across the gap. Again, you will find grass and wooden boxes.

One of these boxes hides another set of stairs leading down to a small basement area. In this area, you will find two rift Spear Moblins waiting for you. Use **Echo**es of your choice to take them all out. One of the two will be holding the second glowing orb.

When you are back outside, continue to the left and up the ramps until you reach some ruins with a collection of large boulders.

Move the boulder in the lower right all the way to the right and then down. Grab the second boulder and drag it all the way to the right. Grab the third boulder and drag it as far as you can south. We can now move to the northernmost boulder. Bind this and jump it out of its location to find a glowing orb where it had been.

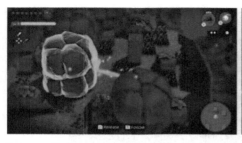 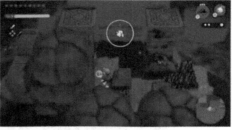

Return all the way to the platform opposite the initial entrance. We can climb the wall behind the stairs leading to the side-scroll area we explored earlier. At the top, head to the left and climb to the next section of floating ruins above (I used waterblocks) to find the fourth and final glowing orb.

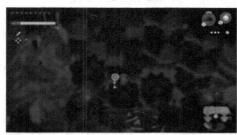 

Finding all five will trigger a few scenes in which Tri and her friends will cleanse the rift. Tri will also gain a bit of XP, but not enough for a new level and will hand over **Might Crystal** x2. We will also find ourselves back outside in the 'real' world.

Hyrule Field

The NPCs outside will tell you that the horse has run off. However, the key to luring it back is right here. Use bind on one of the carrots to pull it out of the ground. This will cause the horse to come running back. This will also complete the Impa's Gift side quest and allow us to use Zelda's horse.

Note: that after completing the quest, pull out another carrot and use it to learn an **Echo – Carrot**. This is particularly handy as if you spawn a carrot, the horse will come running, no matter where you left it on the map previously. With Zelda's horse, we can now also enter the Flag Races mini-game at Hyrule Ranch.

If you continue northeast from this location, you will reach the area we need to go to start the main quest Lands of the Goddesses - Holy Mount Lanayru. Ignore this for now, but keep it in mind, we will be back for it later.

Return to the ruins just southwest of the carrot patch. Make your way to the southwest from the ruins. In the grassy field, you should spot a Peahat by a suspicious collection of stones. Defeat the critter and then pick up the rocks, the middle one is hiding a **Might Crystal**. Just west of this location, you will also find a **Waypoint Stone**.

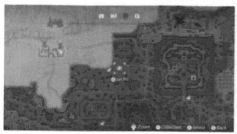 

From this **Waypoint Stone**, there are goodies both to the north and the south. Remember this one as we will be using it as a landmark for the next little bit.

Head northwest from the **Waypoint Stone** to reach a winding, maze-like canyon occupied by Spear Moblins, Ropes and Guays. At the centre of this area, there is a **Treasure Chest** holding a Red Rupee.

Continue to the north to find a cave that we can explore. Whilst you can head in here, you will not be able to find its ultimate prize from this entry point. Instead, climb to the ledge above the cave entrance and use a Holmill on the patch of dirt here. This will create a tunnel, and we can drop down inside for a **Piece of Heart**.

Use a Holmill to dig through the dirt here. Once down, craft some stairs to jump over to the ledge above and on the right. There are sone rolling spike traps here. Jump over one and then follow it – if you can get close enough, you can learn **Echo** – Spiked Roller from it.

Continue to the right and down the ladder. Dispatch the Zols at the bottom. To the left, you should see a glowing blue switch. Change to swordfighter mode and shoot an arrow at it to open the door below. Climb up the nearby rock wall and loot the **Treasure Chest** here for a Golden Egg.

Continue down the next ladder to exit the cave.

Further to the northwest from here you will find the fellow who starts the Acorn Gathering mini-game. There is a different variation on offer here. Have a go at it if you like. If you can do it in less than 20 seconds, you will be rewarded with a **Piece of Heart**.

The entrance to Kakariko Village is just west from here, but ignore this for now and instead, return to the last **Waypoint Stone**.

If you head south from the **Waypoint Stone**, you will come across a collection of tall rocky structures with small pathways winding between them. The entire area is also overrun by copious numbers of Tektites and a Guay or two... so that's fun. Although there are a lot of pillars and Tektites here there are comparatively few points of interest.

On one of the stone pillars on the eastern side of this area, there is a **Treasure Chest** with a Monster Stone. On a pillar to the northwest (the one closest to Kakariko Village) there is a collection of stones, one of which we can pick up for a **Might Crystal**.

From this area, drop down to the left and head west to reach a Moblin Camp. This is guarded by a couple of Sword Moblins and a pair of Spear Moblins. After defeating them all, open the **Treasure Chest** here for Electro Apple x10.

South from the Moblin Camp, you will come across a pool of water, which we explored earlier (there was a **Piece of Heart** here). To the west of this, you can find a small slope leading up to a **Waypoint Stone**.

Further to the west from here is a small desert area. Here you will find the Dude who will give you the Acorn Gathering mini-game. There is a different variation on offer here. Have a go at it if you like, whilst you are here you should also kill one of the small, yellow beasties to learn the **Echo** – Mini-Moldorm.

Head north from the **Waypoint Stone** and follow the path provided until you reach the turn and it starts heading east. Continue to follow this until you find a pair of sloped paths leading north. Climb up these until you can go no further.

At this point, Kakariko Village will be just to the east. Ignore this for now however and instead head west. You will reach a small desert area with more Mini-Moldorms. Climb the stone pillar at the centre of this area for a **Treasure Chest** containing a Red Rupee.

Just southwest from here, at the edge of the platform, you will see a large boulder below. Bind this and then summon a Platboom (or create some stairs or use waterblocks). To lift the boulder up and out of its position. Place it somewhere nearby. Drop down to where the boulder had been to find a **Piece of Heart**.

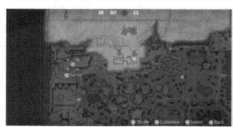 

A short distance to the west from the large boulder we just moved, you will find a cave entrance. If you head inside, you will find that there are some boulders in place preventing us from exploring. To do so, outside the cave, look for a patch of dirt above it. Use a Holmill to create an opening and drop down inside. There is a **Piece of Heart** here. Use your bind to pull the boulders out of the way so that you can escape.

After exiting the cave use a Platboom (or another method of going up) to climb up to the high ledge on the left. There is a Stamp platform here we can use to progress our latest Stamp Rally. Nice!

Head south from the stamp platform to find a rock on its own... pick this up to find a **Might Crystal**... and that is all there is in Hyrule Field for now. However, there is still more to be found before we press onwards!

For now, we want to teleport to the **Waypoint Stone** outside Hyrule Castle. Let us explore Eastern Hyrule Field.

Eastern Hyrule Field

Retrace your steps following the path leading to the east and south until you reach the bridge leading north. After crossing the bridge, head to the east in the direction of Jabul Waters until you reach a 4-way intersection. Head north here.

After a short walk, you should reach the Eastern Temple. There is a **Waypoint Stone** to activate here.

Continue to the north to find a set of stairs leading upwards. Along the wall to the right of this, there is a Stamp platform. Go ahead and use this to keep that Stamp Rally going.

129

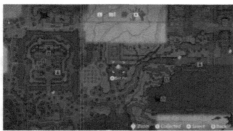 

Make your way up the stairs here. At the top, hop over the wall ahead. There is a Moblin Camp here with two Spear Moblins and two Lv.2 Spear Moblins. Eliminate the lot to unlock the **Treasure Chest** here. It contains Radiant Butter x7.

Return to the top of the stairs and continue to the right. Ascend the next set of stairs to find an entrance to the temple with a fellow named Sago beside it. Speak with him for a new side quest:

● Let's Play a Game

Head back down the stairs and south to the intersection. Make your way back to the west and then north until you reach a large field occupied by a collection of large boulders. The area is occupied by several Octoroks and Sword Moblins. You will find a Red Rupee atop one of the stones here.

Further to the north you will find a bridge leading across the river on the left. Ignore this and continue to the north, defeating some Crows as you go.

Eventually, you will come across another Moblin Camp. This one is guarded by several Spear Moblins and Spear Moblins, one of which is a Lv.2 variant. If you have not already slay this to learn **Echo** – Sword Moblin Lv.2. Be careful of getting too close to the left-hand wall as there are several Tektites in the river who will hop over the wall to attack you if they spot you. Loot the **Treasure Chest** here for a Monster Stone.

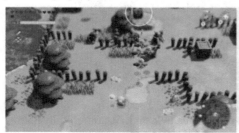 

After clearing the camp, enter the river to the north, fight off the Tektites and Spear Moblin on and around the small islands here. At the northern end of this water, there is a taller platform we can waterblock our way up to with a Stamp platform. Use this to continue our latest Stamp Rally.

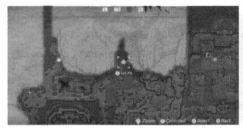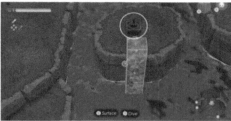

Return to the Moblin camp and follow the path to the east. You will reach a small, lower area inhabited by a Guay and some Caromadillos. The path on the right side of the area leading to the north will lead you straight to a **Waypoint Stone**. In this clearing, you will also find Dampe's house. Here we can proceed inside.

Have a chat with Dampe here and he will hand over Twisted Pumpkin x5 before telling you about his automatons, little critters he can make that we will be able to use out in the field.

Following the initial chat, we need to give him some inspiration using **Echo**es that we have acquired throughout our journey so far. Fortunately, if you have been following the walkthrough to this point, you should have both! We need to summon the **Echo**es on the metal plate here so that he can have a looksie.

- The first creature he is after is "creature with the big eye, the sort that's always jumping around". The **Echo** he is after is a Tektite. If you have yet to find one, you can find these in the river just west of Dampe's hut, or all the way up and down the Zora River in Jabul Waters.

- The second is "something that shoots hot smoke out of its backside to blast forward" The **Echo** that he wants to see for this one is a Mothula. We will have grabbed this **Echo** whilst exploring Dungeon - Gerudo Sanctum.

Once you have summoned both, he will get to work and create an automaton for us. He will reward us with Automaton – Techtite, and a Clockwork Key.

Note: We will now be able to summon Automatons. Hold Left to open the Automaton menu and select the Automaton of choice. Summon this with Y and then wind it up to let it go!

Following this side-quest, you can read Dampe's journal to unlock additional side-quests for him which will unlock further Automatons. The first one available is:

- Explosions Galore!.

Outside of Dampe's house, climb the ledge on the right to find a cave. Inside, there is a fence with a **Treasure Chest** on the left and a pressure plate on the right. Summon an **Echo** through the bars on the right (I used a Caromadillo) and have it move onto the pressure plate to lower the fence. Loot the chest for **Might Crystal** x3.

Just west of Dampe's hut, we can climb up to a ledge above with a collection of suspicious looking rocks. We can pick up the rock at the centre to find a **Might Crystal**.

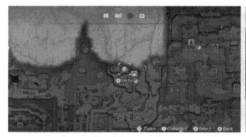

LANDS OF THE GODDESSES

After receiving this quest from the King, you'll notice that three objective markers have appeared on the map. Each of these three objective markers represent the start of a questline exploring the odd phenomenon happening in that region and we will need to complete all three of these quest chains to prod the main questline along.

There are three different locations available, each leading to a different quest chain:

- Lands of the Goddesses - Eldin Volcano (northwest)
- Lands of the Goddesses - Faron Wetlands (east)
- Lands of the Goddesses - Holy Mt Lanayru (north)

Note: Although you can do these things in any order, we suggest hitting Eldin Volcano first. It is the easiest of the three and has arguably the most useful **Echo**es to unlock out of the available options. We would recommend visiting Faron Wetlands second and finally Holy Mount Lanayru as your final stop.

LANDS OF THE GODDESSES - ELDIN VOLCANO

In order to reach Eldin Volcano, we need to first head for Kakariko Village. This is located in the northwestern part of Hyrule Field... and if you have been following along, we will have explored all around it by now, so let us go and explore it properly.

Kakariko Village

As you approach the main entrance to Kakariko Village from the south, you will find a Stamp platform just outside. Go ahead and use this to add the Stamp to your collection. Just inside the gate, there is a **Waypoint Stone** on the left.

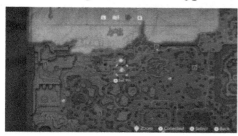

Proceed into the village and you will find a few NPCs around to talk to. There is a general store here that sells the Accessory - Climbing Band for 500 **Rupees**, this is particularly helpful as it increases climbing speed... and we will have plenty of climbing ahead of us.

While we are here, you can open up the lid of the well at the centre of town and jump down inside to find a **Treasure Chest** with Refreshing Grapes x3. You can also check out the graveyard in the northwest part of town for a small patch of dirt that a Holmill can dig up for a **Might Crystal**.

We will be able to check out the Slumber Dojo in the southwestern part of town. This is a mini-game of sorts where you can undertake a number of challenges where you start with nothing and need to overcome challenges by finding and utilizing **Echo**es.

There is also a pair of side-quests available in this area, which we can undertake whilst we are here. They include:

- Cuccos on the Loose
- Questioning the Local Cats

If you approach the guard speaking with the villagers on the eastern side of the town, he will give you a little information about your main quest, triggering the main quest of the region.

As we now have the main quest, let us go forth to complete it - The Rift on Eldin Volcano.

THE RIFT ON ELDIN VOLCANO

The Volcano Trail

After starting this quest in Kakariko Village, proceed up the path leading to the north out of the village. As the path turns to the left, we want to climb up to the ledge on the right for some goodies first. Follow the path to the end to find a weak section of wall to blow up. Inside is a **Treasure Chest** with Monster Fang x6.

Return to the main path and follow it to the left and past a pair of Mini-Moldorms. Continue into the next cave that you come across.

As you proceed through this cave, a swarm of Beetles will attack you. You can eliminate the Beetle Mounds to stop them appearing and fight them off, or simply run past them. The same thing will happen in the cave's second room. Towards the end of this area, however, there is a **Treasure Chest** we can loot for Rocktatoes x5.

After exiting the cave, climb the nearby wall and work your way across the walls to the left. Summon some flying **Echo**es to take out the flaming critter here and learn **Echo - Torch Slug.**

One you reach the ledge on the far left of the climbable walls you will find yourself in a Lizalfos camp. Clear these out and be sure to learn **Echo - Lizalfos** here. Defeating them will also unlock a nearby **Treasure Chest** we can loot for **Might Crystal** x3.

At the top of the sloped path at the rear of this area, you will find a **Waypoint Stone** to activate. Nice!

Before continuing, return to the start of the Lizalfos camp below and look for a small climbable wall leading downwards. At the bottom, follow the path to the left and then north to find a weak section of wall we can blow up. Enter the opening to find a **Treasure Chest** with Accessory - Fairy Flower.

Return to the **Waypoint Stone** and head north.

At the top of the first climbing wall, you will see a second dead ahead. Climb this too. At the top, there is a longer horizontal climbing wall with a Torch Slug, so use some flying critters to deal with it. Hop up to the wall above and climb all the way to the right to find a ledge with a **Piece of Heart**.

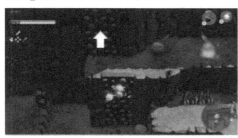

Drop down and climb the first wall once again. This time we will follow the path to the right. As you go, you will come across small steam vents shooting out super-hot steam from cracks in the cliff walls. You can place a rock, or spawn a boulder in front of them to block the steam.

After crossing the first gap, you will come across a pair of steam vents together. You want to place a boulder in front of these – a single rock will not work. Avoid the falling rocks ahead and enter the cave that you come across.

In this cave, you will encounter a Ghirro. These small flying mushroom creatures can blow a concentrated burst of wind at you. This will knock you off an edge if you are too close. Summon some flying **Echo**es and defeat it to learn **Echo** - Ghirro.

The Ghirro **Echo**es are handy. If you spawn one and pick it up, it can shoot a gust of wind, propelling Zelda forwards across gaps. Spawn a Ghirro, grab it and step into the geyser here, you will lift up into the air and we can use the Ghirro to shoot across the gap to a platform on the right.

Once across, use the vent to the north to reach a ledge above. From here, you should be able to see a ledge in the distance with a **Treasure Chest**. Use a Ghirrro and its wind gusts to get you there. It contains a Monster Stone.

Head back to the previous platform and continue to the right. At the top of the first climbing wall, there is a horizontal wall to climb. There are, however, three braziers beside it. Summon a Ghirro to have it blow out all the braziers and then scramble across to the far side.

Exit the cave.

Eldin Volcano

Once outside, climb the nearby climbing walls to the top, avoiding the Torch Slugs (or dealing with them) as you go. At the top, proceed to the right to find the entrance to Goron City. There is a **Waypoint Stone** here to activate.

If you look over the ledge to the south of the **Waypoint Stone**, you can find a small platform below you can drop to. Do so and work your way across the wall to the right past the Torch Slugs. There is a **Treasure Chest** on the far side with a Monster Stone.

Climb back up the previous wall (or head to the right and climb the next they both go to the same location) and head past the **Waypoint Stone** and continue to the right. You will soon come across a Stamp platform for another stamp.

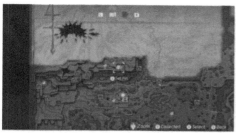 

Continue up the nearby stairs to find the entrance to Goron City. Speak with the Goron here. Note that there is also a Business Scrub off to the left should you want to make some Smoothies.

Goron City

Inside Goron City, you will find most of the area inaccessible due to the large rift here. As such, there is not a whole lot of interest about. As such, lets jump into the rift to continue.

Stilled Goron City

After you enter the rift to reach the Still World, we will need to find and rescue Tri's friends. There are four glowing orbs hidden around this area and we will need to find and collect them all to complete the rift.

From the starting platform, locate some floating boulders in the lower, left. Hop across these to find a small island housing the first glowing orb. It is guarded by a Rift Mini-Moldorm, so be sure to dispatch that before hopping over.

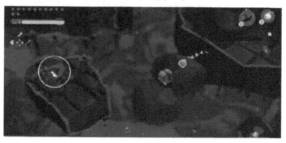

Continue north and up the first two climbing walls ahead. At the top, you will see another wall to climb on the right and more on floating blocks above. Use a Platboom/waterblocks to climb up to the floating walls and continue to the left. Deal with the Zhirro here (a Ghirro, but throws bombs instead of blowing wind) to learn **Echo** - Zhirro. At the top of this area, you will find the second glowing orb.

 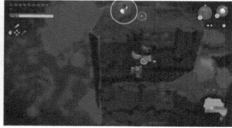

Jump back to the previous floating block and then drop down. Head north from this ledge to find the third glowing orb. Continue to the right and down the sloped path below with a Torch Slug.

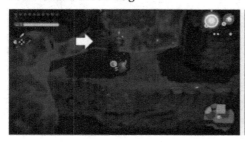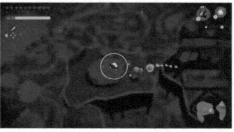

From the sloped path, drop down to the platform in the right. Here you will find a large Goron statue with an opening in its head. Climb down inside to reach a side-scrolling area. Inside there are a bunch of weak blocks, use a Bombfish or a Zhirro to spawn bombs to blow them up. Note that there are some Rift Zols, a Rift Mini-Moldorm and a couple of Blue **Rupees** along the way (if you are interested). At the very bottom of this area, you will find the final glowing orb.

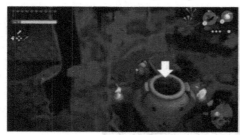

Finding all four orbs will have Tri and her friends cleanse the rift. Tri will also gain a bit of XP, and will hand over **Might Crystal** x2. We will also find ourselves back outside in the 'real' world and the rift will vanish.

Goron City

Once you are back in Goron City, you will be introduced to Darston, the newly minted chief of the Gorons. After a brief bit of thanks, he will run off, leaving you alone to explore. Following the chat, you will be free to wander around the now rift-less Goron City... although there is not a whole lot of interest here for the moment.

To continue, head outside and speak with Darston once again. He will mention that in order to reach the giant rift on Eldin Mountain, we will need to find a pair of missing Gorons – Elder Gol and Elder Silv, because of course we do.

He will add a pair of objective markers to your map, one for each of two little quests that we need to complete in this area. Note that they will become active when we reach the markers, but for the sake of the walkthrough we will start from this location to reach both, grabbing collectibles as we go. The two quests here include:

- Lizalfos Burrow
- Rock-Roast Quarry

LIZALFOS BURROW

Eldin Volcano

Note that throughout this area, you will come across hot springs – these will restore Zelda's health if you have her stand in them. Additionally, you will find pools of lava, which are bad (obviously) and cracked sections of earth with glowing cracks, stepping on these areas will damage you, so don't do it!

From the entrance to Goron City, we want to head to the right (east). Look for a stone ramp leading upwards. Before climbing this, head to the edge of the nearby cliff and look below. You should be able to make out a **Treasure Chest** and a Stamp platform.

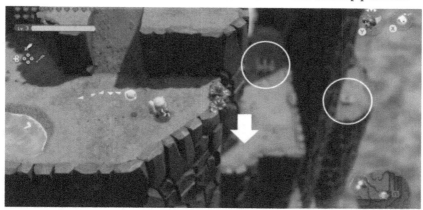

We can simply drop down to the ledge with the **Treasure Chest** and loot it for **Might Crystal** x2. The Stamp platform below can be reached using a Ghirro and its wind gust to propel you over. Activate this to continue with your latest Stamp rally.

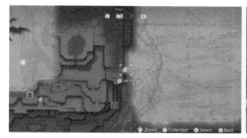

From the Stamp platform, you will see a third, lower platform off to the right. Again, use a Ghirro to fly over to this. Pick up the rock here to find a **Might Crystal**.

Fast travel back to the previous **Waypoint Stone** and head to the right again. This time lets continue up the stone ramp.

After climbing a second ramp, you will encounter a pair of new creatures – Tweelus (there isa third off to the left). These rock-like creatures will hit you if you get close to them and can take a bit of damage, because of the whole rock composition thing. Using a Zhirro with its bombs, or a heavy attacker such as a Dark Nut, you can take them down fairly quickly. After doing so, you can learn **Echo** - Tweelus.

Once the area is clear, continue to the left. At the top of the next sloping path, you will reach a large pool of lava. At this point we can explore to the right or the left. The left path leads to the objective marker, so let us explore to the right first.

As you explore this area, keep your eyes peeled for Zhirros (those bombs will become tiresome if you do not eliminate them) and some Fire Octos. These are dark versions of Octoroks that can live in lava. When they are there, they can be pesky as your **Echoes** will often burn up, you can always bind them and pull them out of the lava to make things easier on yourself. Be sure to grab **Echo** - Fire Octo while you are here.

After climbing the first ramp on the right side, head immediately to the right to find a Fire Octo and s lava stream. Make your way across this for a **Treasure Chest** with a Golden Egg.

Climb up to the platform above the chest. Here you will find a powerful new enemy called a Fire Wizzrobe. These things can shoot fireballs as well as disappear and re-appear, making targeting them difficult. They also have quite a bit of health. Defeating this will allow you to learn the **Echo** - Fire Wizzrobe.

Drop back down to the main path and continue to the north. Spawn boulders to block the steam vents and eliminate the Zhirros as you go. At the end of this path, you will come across a sparkly platform. Use this to learn **Echo** - Lava Rock.

If you backtrack along the path around the corner, you can spawn a lava rock in the lava below and then jump down to it. From here we can hop across to a small island with a **Piece of Heart**.

Make your way across to the lava rock on the geyser to the north. Hop across to the next and the spawn another lava rock into the lava geyser on the left. Hop onto the rock when it is safe to do so and ride the geyser up to the ledge above.

Follow the path here south, past a Rift creature or two and a pair of Torch Slugs. Continue along the narrow ledge here to find a **Piece of Heart**.

From this location, you can drop down to the right to reach a **Waypoint Stone**. Note that if you went left from the entry to the lava pool area, this is where you will have ended up.

To continue, head north from here to reach the entrance to the Lizalfos Burrow.

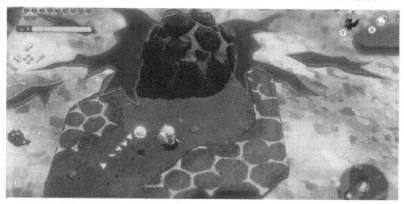

Lizalfos Burrow

As you enter the Lizalfos Burrow, you will come across a pair of Gorons nearby. Darston will show up as well for a chat. After a short chat, the quest will begin properly.

Head through the first doorway. There will be a pair of Lizalfos waiting for you in the next room. Dispatch the pair and then loot the **Treasure Chest** here for Rocktatoes x5. Continue into the next room.

This room is a bit trickier because you will have hot sections of floor and some higher level Lizalfos to deal with. Have your **Echo**es defeat the pair of enemies here to unlock the doors. Darton will also show up for a brief chat here before running off again. Once you regain control, be sure to learn **Echo** - Lizalfos Lv. 2.

The next area is a long hallway with more of those lava-cracked floor tiles in it. There is a Fire Keese and another Lizalfos to dispatch here. If you are having trouble with the Fire Keese, you can use a wind cannon or a Ghirro to blow the fire off of it, making it significantly easier to kill. After dispatching the flying baddie, be sure to check it out for **Echo** - Fire Keese.

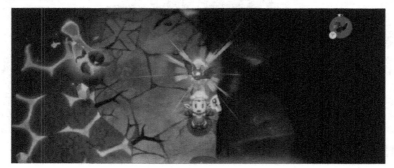

After passing through the next door, you will catch up with Darston. He will kill a few of the Rift Lizalfos in the room ahead for you, leaving a group of three of them for you to deal with.

Once the room is clear, we will be ported back to the entrance where we will have a brief chat to end the quest.

Note: If this was the first of the two quests that we needed to run down for Darston, we can continue by proceeding with the second - Rock-Roast Quarry. If you did that first and this is your second quest for Darston, you can head onwards to The Rift on Eldin Volcano - Part 2.

ROCK-ROAST QUARRY

Eldin Volcano

Note that throughout this area, you will come across hot springs – these will restore Zelda's health if you have her stand in them. Additionally, you will find pools of lava, which are bad (obviously) and cracked sections of earth with glowing cracks, stepping on these areas will damage you, so don't do it!

From the entrance to Goron City, we want to head to the left (west), past the Business Scrub and onwards. Dispatch the Zhirros you come across either side of the bridge here. Before continuing up the ramp, dop down to the south. You can find the entrance to an optional rift here:

- Stilled Western Eldin Volcano Rift

When you are ready to continue, head to the right, climb the wall and then make your way over the bridge once more. Take the ramp leading upwards. At the top you can go left or right. Both paths lead to the same location, but the left path has goodies, whereas the right path does not... so take the left path!

At the top of the first ramp, defeat the Lizalfos and Fire Octos inhabiting the area. On the right side of this area, you will find a small island surrounded by lava with a Stamp platform. Build a bridge over to collect it for your Stamp Rally!

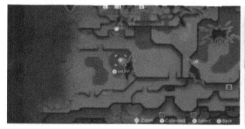

Continue up the next ramp to find a **Waypoint Stone** and the entrance to the Rock-Roast Quarry. Use a Platboom/Water Block to climb up to the left of the entrance to find a Lizalfos guarding a **Treasure Chest** with a **Might Crystal**.

To continue, head into the Rock-Roast Quarry.

Rock-Roast Quarry

As you enter the Rock-Roast Quarry, you will come across a group of three Gorons nearby. Darston will show up as well for a chat. After a short chat, the quest will begin properly.

Follow the obvious path leading off to the left, dealing with the Tweelus and Fire Octo enemies that you encounter along the way. At the end of the path, you will bump into Darston once again. Once the chat ends, go head and examine the pile of food nearby to learn **Echo** - Rock Roast. On the southern side of this platform, you can also find a **Treasure Chest** with Rocktatoes x5.

Backtrack to the start of the area, either by retracing your steps, or defeating the nearby Tweelus enemies and creating a makeshift path of boulders/Tweelus to cross the lava cracked floor.

Once you are back at the entrance approach the three Gorons and create a Rock Roast **Echo**. Each time you do, one of the Gorons will wake up and eat it... except for the third time. Yep, Elder Gol knows the difference between an **Echo** and the real deal. For this fellow you will need to return to the back of the cave and bind one of the Rock Roasts and carry it all the way back.

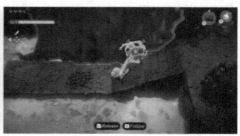

After feeding all three Gorons, a scene will play and the quest will be completed.

Note: If this was the first of the two quests that we needed to run down for Darston, we can continue by proceeding with the second - Lizalfos Burrow. If you did that first and this is your second quest for Darston, you can head onwards to The Rift on Eldin Volcano - Part 2.

THE RIFT ON ELDIN VOLCANO - PART 2

Goron City

After completing Darston's two quests - Lizalfos Burrow and Rock-Roast Quarry we will be able to proceed with this quest. To do so, we will need to head back to Goron City.

Once you arrive, Darston and the two elders will be having a chat. Following the chat, Darston will run upstairs and enter the room behind the large Goron statue.

Once inside, approach the stone carving at the rear of the room. You will see a bolt on the right side of this. We want to bind this and pull it out. This will trigger a short scene and reveal a new doorway we can explore.

Head on inside to continue.

Crater Shortcut

The first room has a large pool of lava and a doorway on the far side. Have some **Echo**es clear out the Keese in here and then use a Ghirro to fly across to the far side.

The next room has a fairly obvious path winding around a pool of lava with numerous wind gusts we can use in conjunction with a Ghirro to fly around the area. After reaching the upper section of the room, look for a lava geyser on the right side of the room.

Spawn a Lava Rock atop the geyser and then ride it upwards. At the top, there is a **Treasure Chest** with a Monster Stone.

From this location we can use a Ghirro wind blast to reach the exit door nearby. This will lead you into a side scrolling area.

Make your way across this area, using the Lava Rocks to cross the pools of lava. When you reach the third pool, you will find that there is a lava geyser that goes much higher than the others. This one leads to the exit.

Before using this, head all the way to the left. On the far side of this room there is a **Treasure Chest** that contains a Purple Rupee. Return to the tall lava geyser and use it to reach the exit.

After exiting, follow the bridge to the north and approach the large boulder. Darston will show up here and remove it from the path. Head through the new opening.

Hop across the platforms in the next room until you reach a **Waypoint Stone** and the entrance to the large rift. Head on inside when you are ready to continue.

Stilled Eldin Volcano

This section of the Still World is filled with lava, and as usual a collection of floating islands and rift-imbued baddies. After entering we want to head north and continue across the pools of lava using Lava Blocks (or other bridging options) until you reach the next large pool of lava – there will be some Fire Octos here.

Proceed to the northern end of this large lava pool. Here, you should see a series of islands leading to the right. Hop across here to reach some solid ground. Follow this area to the south to find a **Treasure Chest** with Rocktatoes x5. Watch out though as there is a rift creature about here that may spot you and attack.

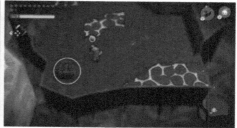

Return to the previous lava pit and head to the far northern end. When you reach the tiered lavafall area, head to the left side to spot a **Treasure Chest** across a gap. Create a path out to this to loot it for a Purple Rupee.

Hop back across the gap and head to the north until you can go no further. Spawn a Platboom here and ride it upwards to reach a climbable wall above. Once up, scramble off to the right to find a ledge with a **Waypoint Stone**.

From the **Waypoint Stone** we want to head to the left, either over the top of the platform (and through some Fire Octos) here, or along the climbable wall at its front (and through some Mini-Moldorms).

Continue to the left and defeat some Rift Zhirros when you come across them. Climb up the ledges here and head back to the right climbing up the walls here until you reach the end of the path.

At the top, you will find a wind gust and sticking out from the wall ahead a number of frozen lava geysers. Our goal here is to use a flying **Echo**, such as a Ghirro (the wind gust is a bonus) to maneuver around the lava here. There is a platform at the centre of this lava wall we can land on. From here we can glide/fly down to another ledge below and to the right.

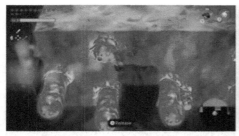

In this location you can find a doorway into which we can walk. This is the next dungeon Dungeon - Eldin Temple.

DUNGEON - ELDIN TEMPLE

Eldin Temple

Upon entering the Eldin Temple dungeon, head on over and activate the nearby **Waypoint Stone**. We can use the nearby hot spring to restore health if required. Proceed through the door to the north when you are ready to continue.

In this room you will have several sections of lava cracked floor to avoid along with a pair of Fire Keese (remember, us a Ghirro or Wind Cannon to extinguish their flames). After clearing the area, you will notice there are three exits to this room. The left side is locked, leaving the top door and that to the right.

Check the top door first. Clear the pair of Rift Zhirros in here. Once the area is clear, we want to destroy the weak blocks here. The one in the back, right corner from the entry point is hiding a half-buried **Treasure Chest**. Yank this out with bind and loot it for Twisted Pumpkin x8.

Return to the previous room and head to the right. Use a Lava Block to work your way to the right side of the room and pop one onto the taller of the two lava geysers here. Ride this up and hop onto the ledge above. Continue through the door here.

This next room has a bunch of vertical wind vents. Our goal is to use them with a flying **Echo** to navigate the area. Make your way to the back, left corner of the room, and use the vents along the rear wall to reach the platform in the back, right. There is a **Treasure Chest** here with a Small Key.

148

Head back to the previous room with the locked door and use the key to proceed through it.

The next room has a pool of lava that will rise up to the top of the room and then recede, draining into three pits on the floor. This will happen on repeat. We will need to navigate the lower level when the lava is at its lowest, and pop down a Lava Block to jump on when the lava starts rising again. You will find that there are a couple of Tweelus enemies here as well, who are not perturbed by the lava.

In this room, there is a half-buried **Treasure Chest** on the lower left with a Golden Egg Along the left-hand wall, there is also a Lava Block. This one is sitting on a pressure plate and pulling it off will reveal it. Step on this pressure plate once it is visible to open the door in the upper right.

Head on through here to continue into a fairly large side-scroll area.

The first section of this side-scroll area consists of a large lava Proceed to the right, using a Lava Block to navigate the lava geysers and continue across the climbing walls. The final geyser may require you to use a bed or trampoline for a little extra height/distance to reach the upper ledge.

The next room has a couple of Fire Keese waiting for you when you arrive. Defeat them. Now this room has a couple of different paths leading out of the area, one leading upwards and another heading down. Let us go down first.

Climb down the ladder, spawn a boulder, and bind it in front of you as you walk into the steam vent. Head down the ladder behind this.

We will reach another side-scroll room. This time around, the lava here will rise and fall, revealing platforms and climbing walls as it does so. We want to head to the left first and pop a Lava Block into the lava here. Climb on this and kill the Torch Slug on the wall above. When it is safe to do so, hit the glowing switch on the left. Return to the ladder we came in from (you can use a Strandtula to climb back up).

This time head to the right, again using Lava Blocks and the climbing walls to proceed. This leads to a small room on the right where you will find a **Treasure Chest** with a Small Key.

Backtrack to the previous side-scroll room (the one with two exits). This time let us proceed upwards. As you climb the first climby wall, time your ascent to avoid the alternating steam vents.

At the top, ignore the first ladder and instead head left. Spawn three boulders atop one another and then bind push them into the far wall to block the steam vents here. Climb the second ladder to find a **Treasure Chest** with the Dungeon Map.

Return down the previous ladder and climb the other ladder we ignored earlier. Continue to the right. Here we will find an exit... and a **Waypoint Stone**.

Proceed through the nearby locked door to start a mini-boss fight.

❖ Boss: Shadow Link

This time around, Shadow Link is armed with bombs which he will lob at you from range. He has a standard bomb, or bombchus, the latter being a wind-up mechanical bomb that will keep moving around the area until it blows up. Again, the goal here is to stay out of the explosions as much as possible and get our **Echo**es to tackle him. Note that he will frequently teleport away and reposition himself elsewhere after taking a bit of damage.

I used a swarm of Crows (although any flying **Echo** will probably work here) to constantly send a collection of swooping **Echo**es I his direction. The flying critters can get at him no matter where he teleports in the room and as they are not on the ground, can avoid the majority of explosions and bombs. You can work your way up to him so that you can hack him a few times in Swordfighter mode, or just keep it safe and bombard him with flying **Echo**es.

After he takes enough damage, a scene will play, and Shadow Link will start glowing purple. At this stage he will move and teleport away from you a little faster, and throw bombs out quicker, but other than that he remains pretty much the same. The good news is that we can use the same tactics here to fight and defeat him.

Following the fight, claim the Bombs of Might from the ground nearby.

Note: The Bombs of Might can be used in Swordfighter mode by pressing A. This will allow you to target objects in the distance. Nice!

To continue, head through the door at the rear of the room to enter another side-scrolly area.

This side-scroll area is even bigger than the last one was. This first room is a bit of a hub with another three exits to explore – upper right, upper left and lower left. The exit in the upper, left leads to the end of the dungeon, and the lower left is locked for the moment, so let us go upper right first!

Climb the first two ladders, dealing with Tweelus as you go, and at the top, head right to find the path blocked by some cracked blocks. Climb to the ledge facing the cracked blocks and switch to swordfighter mode. Toss a bomb into the opening to blow them all up at once. Defeat the Fire Keese and Tweelus behind it before heading up the ladder.

We will reach the first exit to the side-scroll area. Defeat the Tweelus here. Once it is gone, we want to spend some time clearing the broken blocks here. In the back, left corner there is a **Treasure Chest** with a Silver Rupee. In the back, right there is a door leading onwards. Head on through there.

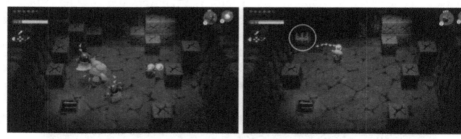

The next room has a Fire Wizzrobe in it. We simply need to defeat this to have a **Treasure Chest** appear with a Small Key.

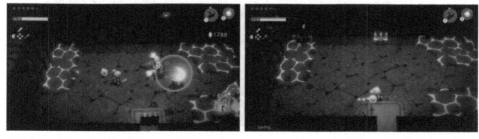

Return to the side scroll room. Make your way along the upper floor of this to the left and break the rift web here. Dispatch the Fire Keese and then destroy the weak blocks to find a **Treasure Chest** that contains a Small Key.

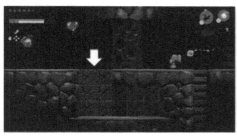

Head to the right and you will see two locked doors, one leading to the upper left, and the other to the lower left. Take the lower left path first.

After exiting the side-scroll area here, you will immediately find a ladder leading to another one. Hop on inside.

This side scroll area is quite a vertical one. Our goal is at the bottom of the room, but it is a good idea to take out all of the enemies (Fire Keese, Ghirros and Mini-Moldorms) as you go.... Because we will need to make a quick ascent shortly and the less distractions about, the better.

When you reach the bottom of the room, loot the fancy **Treasure Chest** here for the Big Key for the boss door. As soon as you loot this, however, the lava at the bottom of the room will begin to rise. We need to quickly climb back up to the top of the room and out of the area. Note that the final ladder will break, so you will need to create a quick bridge to the left, but other than that it is not too tough!

After exiting the area, we want to return to the previous side-scroll area and this time, proceed through the door in the upper, left.

We will exit into a lengthy, lava filled room. We need to make our way all the way to the northern end. Use the air vents dotted around the room and a flying **Echo** to maneuver across the lava pits, avoiding the lava geysers as you go.

When you reach the first lavafall, pop a Lava Block onto a lava geyser to reach the ledge above. From here we can continue using the air vents to cross this second segment. This one has a few Fire Keese, Fire Octos and alternating geyser placements so it is a bit trickier. Upon reaching the far end, however, you will find a **Waypoint Stone** and the door leading to the boss area.

Now that we have gotten all that sorted, all that is left to do is head through the boss door to take on the dungeon's boss.

❖ Boss: Volvagia

Volvagia is a large, snake-like flying dragon. It will pop out from one of the circular openings located around the room. It will remain stationary here and from this location it will launch a series of attacks. After it takes some damage it will exit, fly around a bit and then vanish before re-emerging from another opening to resume its attack.

Note that this arena is made up of a collection of small islands in a lava pool, and due to the boss's attacks, you will need to move between them pretty quickly, so we recommend that you equip the Frog Ring accessory to make jumping (and your maneuverability) a bit easier.

Initially the boss will have two main attacks, a large, green orb which will home in on your location and a series of three fireballs fired off in quick succession. These will not home in on you, so you can simply side-step them.

Our goal is to approach the boss at his location and attack! Note that we can make this a lot easier by grabbing the green orb hanging around its neck with bind and ripping it off. This will stun the boss temporarily. Once you have stunned the boss, you can jump to his location (if the ground is safe) and attack him with swordfighter mode. We can also summon Fire Keese and Tweelus enemies to attack him (they will not be bothered by the fire attacks and can attack even on lava-cracked surfaces). If the boss chooses to appear in the lava-cracked areas, be sure to create a Lava Block beside him so that you can safely attack.

Note that if you or your **Echo**es stand too close for too long , the boss can sweep its head and neck across the ground in front of it, damaging you if you get caught.

After inflicting enough damage on the boss, a second phase of the fight will begin. Fortunately, the fight will not change too drastically as the boss will still use the same behavior as the first phase, he will however pick up a new attack or two. Volvagia will move quicker and also transition between locations a lot more frequently during this phase.

The major new attack has the boss shoot a jet of concentrated fire onto a platform, which will cause it to take on a new 'hot' appearance and limit our ability to use it (although our Fire-proof **Echo**es will have no such issues). The other thing that is different is that his rapid-fire fireballs change up a little and he will now use five, rather than three.

Other than that, the fight plays out in the same way – chase him around, pull his necklace to stun him and then wail on him with your swordfighter mode and fire-proof **Echo**es.

For defeating the boss, you will receive a full Heart Container. Once the scene here runs its course, you will be able to claim it. Additionally, Tri will level up again, unlocking a new ability. Tri will also hand over **Might Crystal** x5. Additionally, you will also be spoken to by the Goddess, Din who will give you a new key item – Din's Sanction.

Speak with Tri by the glowing section of ground on the left side of the room to teleport out of the dungeon.

We will end up back outside in the 'real' world just outside Goron City. Here we can enjoy a few story scenes with Darston and the Gorons. Following this scene/chat, our objectives will update, and we will all be done with this main quest.

Note: With this part of the main quest completed, we should have a few options as to what to do next. These include:

- Eldin Volcano Exploration (Optional)
- Lands of the Goddesses - Faron Wetlands
- Lands of the Goddesses - Mount Lanayru

ELDIN VOLCANO EXPLORATION (OPTIONAL)

After completing the Eldin Temple dungeon and removing the rift from the Eldin Volcano region, you will find that there are a few new areas around the volcano that we can now explore for some new goodies.

Before doing that, however, you can make a brief visit in and around Goron City to find a few newly available side quests that we can pick up:

- Glide Path
  - Glide Path Trailblazer (available after completing Side Quest: Glide Path)
- Ready? Set? Goron!
- The Fireworks Artist
- A Mountain Mystery (requires you to travel to another region and return... I think, unsure of exact unlock requirements.)

We can also make a quick trip around Eldin Volcano to pick up a couple of additional collectibles.

155

From the entrance to Goron City, make your way to the right until you find the hot spring. From this location, look over the edge of the cliff here to spot a small ledge below Drop down to this and loot the **Treasure Chest** here for a Red Rupee.

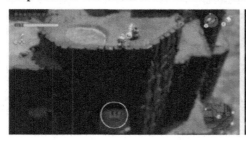

Fast travel to the **Waypoint Stone** outside the Rock-Roast Quarry. Without the rift here, you can climb up to the ledges above the entrance. Continuing climbing upwards and head all the way to the right to find a Stamp platform. Go ahead and use this to continue your current Stamp Rally.

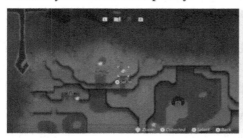

Head for the hot springs above the **Waypoint Stone** for the Lizalfos Quarry. Here you will find a Goron named Ondes we can speak with for another side quest:

- The Flames of Fortune

...and with that we are done with Eldin Volcano for the moment. We still however have a few other bits and pieces that have popped up in other areas at this point, so let us go deal with those!

Hyrule Field

Pay a visit to Dampe in the northeastern part of Hyrule Field. After completing the side quest The Fireworks Artist on Eldin Mountain, you will now be able to complete Dampe's second Automaton side quest:

- Explosions Galore!

Completing this side quest will have his journal updated with three more side quests to attempt. We can complete all three of these now if you like. They include:

- Performance Artist!
- Endless Stomach!
- Chop 'Em In Two!

After completing these three side quests, you will be able to pick up one more from Dampe's journal:

- Get Rich Quick!

Once you are done with Dampe, head on over to Hyrule Castle Town to continue.

Hyrule Castle Town

Finally, we can pay a visit to Hyrule Castle Town. In this location you will find another two side quests to pick up and complete. These include:

- An Out-There Zol (available after completing Performance Artist!)
- From the Heart

After finishing up here, we can travel to Seesyde Village for one last side quest.

Jabul Waters

If you have completed the Side Quest: Questioning the Local Cats in Kakariko Village, you can find a new side quest from a cat on the beach by Seesyde Village:

- A Treat for My Person

...and that is it for the moment.

Note: We should now proceed with the main quest, and we have a few options as to what to do next. These include:

- Lands of the Goddesses - Faron Wetlands
- Lands of the Goddesses - Mount Lanayru

LANDS OF THE GODDESSES - FARON WETLANDS

Lake Hylia

The Faron Wetlands area is located in the southeastern corner of the map. There is no obvious way to reach this however, but there is, in fact, a way and we can get there via Lake Hylia. Go ahead and travel there.

At Lake Hylia, we recommend visiting the Great Fairy once again to upgrade your accessory slots. If you have four slots unlocked already, you can find a **Treasure Chest** with a Might Stone in her area. Looting this will unlock a side quest:

- The Great Fairy's Request

If you do not have the required number of accessory upgrades, you can choose to have the Great Fairy unlock additional accessory slots, then travel to another region and back again to get the **Treasure Chest** to appear.

In Lake Hylia proper, if you did not go and complete the optional rift to the southwest of the Great Fairy's island, now is a good time to do so:

- Stilled Lake Hylia Rift

Before continuing onwards to Faron Wetlands, lets grab some additional loot. There are a few goodies to grab around Lake Hylia that we can grab at this point.

First up, we want to explore along the western shore of the lake. If you follow this south you can find a weak section of wall that we can blow up. This will reveal a cave. Inside is a **Treasure Chest** with Fresh Milk x10.

From this cave, continue to the south and follow the raised path around to the right. There is a small hilltop path here straddling the border between the Lake Hylia and Suthorn Forest regions. At the far eastern end of this path there is a cave. Inside you will find a half-buried **Treasure Chest** with a Golden Egg.

With all that sorted we can press onwards to Faron Wetlands. Make your way to the southeastern part of Lake Hylia and locate the waterfall here. Use a Platboom or waterblocks to climb up to the top of the waterfall.

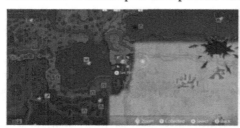

Once up, you will find three paths leading away from this area – a path to the northeast, another leading south and just to the east of the waterfall, a climbing wall leading down into the Faron Wetlands area.

Follow the path here to the northwest to find a Moblin Camp. There are a pair of Spear Moblins and a Sword Moblin Lv.2 here. Defeat them all to unlock the **Treasure Chest** they were guarding for Riverhorse x7. Return to the top of the waterfall and follow the path leading to the south. You will soon come across another Moblin Camp. Clear out the Sword/Spear Moblins here and loot the **Treasure Chest** for Refreshing Grape x10.

Continue south and you will reach a rocky area with a number of Mini-Moldorms. Clear all of these out. Once it is safe to do so, look for a raised ledge in the northern part of this area. Climb up here and slash the lone plant here for a **Might Crystal**.

From the Mini-Moldorm area, head to the west and drop down to the area below. This is a fairly large, open area occupied by Zols and Ropes. Despite its size, all there is here is a single **Treasure Chest** with a Purple Rupee.

Return to the top of the waterfall and descend the climbing wall to the east to reach the Faron Wetlands.

Faron Wetlands

At the bottom of the climbing wall, go ahead and activate the **Waypoint Stone** here.

Speak with the guard here if you like before pressing onwards. Follow the path to the right and then to the south, dispatching the Hydrozol as you go. After a short walk, a brief scene will play introducing the area. After the scene, our next story quest will begin - A Rift in the Faron Wetlands.

A RIFT IN THE FARON WETLANDS

Faron Wetlands

Work your way to the east. As you go you will encounter some Hydrozols your first

Drippitune. These frog-like enemies will sing, causing rain to fall. This will enhance nearby water and electric-based enemies.

A little further on you will find some Hoarders, these crab-like creatures have glowing blue mushrooms on their shells and can hide in amongst other mushrooms to ambush you as you run by. After dispatching these enemies, make sure you learn **Echo** - Drippitune and **Echo** - Hoarder.

After your initial fights, you will come across a pair of Deku Scrubs that we can talk with (you can pull the buried one out of the ground with bind) for a bit of information about the area.

Further to the east we will come across a series of ruins. There is not too much interesting here, but there is a Drippitune and several Hoarders lurking about. Head up the nearby stairs and proceed to the right.

We will find a door guarded by a pair of Deku Scrubs. This is the entrance to The Sweet Spot. Tri advises that this area is where the main rift in the area is located, and we need to get in... unfortunately the guards will not let us in without a Membership Card... so we will need to find one.

You can head south from here to reach Scrubton, the main village in this region. Before doing so however, head to the right/east first.

As you go, you will come across a couple of Hoarders and two new enemy types – a Baby Gohma and some Buzz Blobs. The small pond here has a waterfall to the north. The bottom pool is occupied by Buzz Blobs and at the top of the waterfall there is a Ribbitune who will make it rain.

Baby Gohmas are small spiders that can shoot webs. These will drop on the floor and will slow down your movement speed if you walk through them. The Buzz Blobs live in water and look like tall Zols. These will have a constant aura of electricity around them, which can be expanded when it is raining. You will want to send a rock-based critter such as a Tweelus to deal with them. After dispatching them, be sure to learn **Echo** - Baby Gohma and **Echo** - Buzz Blob.

With the area clear, climb up above the waterfall to deal with the Drippitune here. In the pool above the waterfall there is a small island with a Stamp platform. Go ahead and activate this to keep plugging away at that Stamp rally.

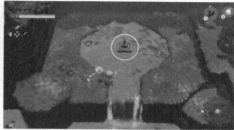

On the left side of this upper area, you should be able to see a webbed opening on the cliff wall. Create a bridge up to this and use a fire-based **Echo** to burn away the web. Behind it you will find a **Might Crystal**.

With all that sorted, return to the entrance to the Sweet Spot. This time, head south to reach Scrubton.

Scrubton

As you arrive in Scrubton, go ahead and activate the **Waypoint Stone** here. As with most towns in the game when you first arrive in this game, there is not a whole lot to do.

There is a Smoothie shop on the eastern side of the village, a prison area on the western side of town and in the centre, a **Treasure Chest** with Radiant Butter x5.

Opposite the **Treasure Chest** is a Deku Scrub who will give you a quick and easy side quest:

● The Rain-Making Monster

If you head directly south from the prison area, you can find a Stamp platform. Go ahead and activate this to add another to your Stamp Rally.

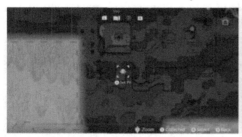 

You can go around and speak with some of the Deku Scrubs here to get a bit of information about where we can go to find a Membership Card. If you chat with all of them, you will have two points of interest we want to investigate - the ruins to the east of Scrubton, or the heart-shaped lake in the southwestern corner of the Faron Wetlands.

To continue, we will need to go explore those two area. The east ruins are closer, so let us check them out first.

Faron Wetlands

Take the path leading out of Scrubton to the east (just east from the Smoothie shop). Follow the path south. At the bottom of the first slope, you will encounter a pair of levelled up Deku Babas. Fight them off to learn **Echo** - Deku Baba Lv.2.

Just past this patch of grass, you will see a 4-way intersection. We want to explore the right path first.

In this area, we will come across a series of stone pillars. In amongst these, you will encounter another new enemy type, a Goo Specter. These things look like green puddles on the ground which will jump up and attack when you get close to them. Be sure to kill one so we can learn **Echo** - Goo Specter.

Climb the stairs to the north, fighting off more Goo Specters as you go. At the top, you will find a Deku Scrub on the left. Have a chat with him here about the Membership Card. He will tell you about his friend Blossu, but sadly will not have any more information about a Membership Card. Whilst we are here, you can enter the cave to the north.

As you enter, you will reach a room with five narrow walkways and statues at the end of each. These are not actually statues, but Armos enemies. These will activate when you get close and hop the length of the lane facing forward. They have a weak spot on their backs, so you will want to spawn **Echo**es behind them to take them out.

After clearing the room, be sure to learn **Echo** - Armos here. The Armos on the second path from the left will have been blocking a ladder leading further into the area, so continue through there.

We will reach a side-scroll area.

In this first room there will be a climbing wall with a pair of Beamos enemies looking over it. These will look back and forth and shoot lasers at you if they spot you. There is a Red Rupee by the Beamos on the upper left. We can break these things with an **Echo** attack to disable them, however, to destroy them completely, you will need to hit them with a bomb. After doing so you can learn an **Echo** - Beamos.

From this climbing wall there are two paths – upper right and lower right. The upper path is locked up for the moment, so let us explore the lower path.

The lower path is fairly linear, but is guarded by numerous Beamos and Keese. Be sure to grab the **Treasure Chest** from the lowest platform as you go for Electro Apple x5. At the top of this area, there is a ladder, but head down the path to the left of this first to find a glowing switch we can hit to open the locked door, allowing you a quick route back to the entrance.

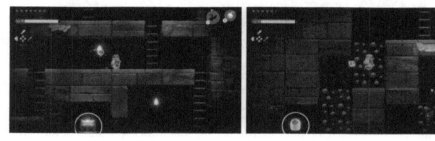

Climb the ladder and at the top, proceed into the room ahead. Here you will bump into a high level Darknut enemy. Use your Darknuts, Darknut Lv. 2 or Ball and Chain Trooper **Echo**es to fight it. Be sure to steer clear as its attacks can wipe out Zelda's health bar really quickly. Defeating it will allow you to learn the **Echo** - Darknut Lv. 3. A **Treasure Chest** will also appear nearby, which you can loot for Accessory - Spin Brace.

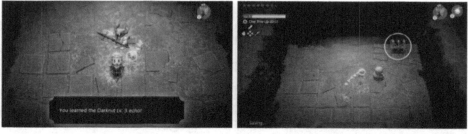

We are all done here for now so make your way outside and to the intersection we came from earlier. This time, we want to take the path leading to the south. As you go, you will encounter a higher level Mothula enemy. Dispatch it and learn **Echo** - Mothula Lv.2.

Ignore the path leading to the left for now and instead return to the previous intersection This time, we are going to explore to the west/left.

After a short jog you will come across a new flying enemy – a Beakon. These critters will screech, alerting nearby enemies to your location. They will subsequently converge on your position. Unfortunately, the clearing where you encounter this is also home to a collection of Hoarders. Defeat them all and the bird. Be sure to examine it once it has been dealt with for **Echo** - Beakon.

Further to the west, you will come across a body of water. Again, you will find a number of Hoarders around. In the water itself, you will encounter Piranhas and a Giant Goponga Flower. On the western side of this water, you will find some Buzz Blobs as well.

Piranhas are particularly vicious fish that can jump out of the water to bite at you – note that you can bind them and pull them out of the water to make them easy pickings for your **Echo**es, whilst the Giant Goponga Flower will constantly shoot pollen-based projectiles towards you. After dispatching all the enemies, take a moment to learn **Echo** - Piranha and **Echo** - Giant Goponga Flower.

On the far, western side of this area, you will find a path leading to the north through some tall grass. As you explore this, be careful as a Lizalfos often wanders around here and can be tricky to spot. After passing through the grass, you will see a Ribbitune on the ledge to the right. Deal with it and the two Ignizols nearby.

Continue to the left and when you reach the next patch of tall grass, watch out for a Baby Gohma hiding here. There is also a **Treasure Chest** behind the grass holding Electro Apple x5.

Keep heading to the west and defeat the Lizalfos you spot ahead. At this point, the path should turn and begin heading south. Again, there will be tall grass here. Watch out for critters hiding once again. Now that the nearby Ribbitune is dead; to make things easier, you can use a fiery enemy to set the grass ablaze and deal with them that way.

As you follow the path south, look for a smaller path on the left side of the main path. This leads to a small clearing with a suspicious arrangement of plants. Spin attack the central plant for a **Might Crystal**.

Return to the main path and continue south. After a short jog, you will see a cave entrance. Whilst you can explore this, you will find it is blocked. Fortunately, there is an alternate entrance nearby. Climb up onto the ledge above the cave entrance and locate the pool of water here. We can dive down inside this to reach the very same cave.

Enter the cave to reach an underwater side-scroll area.

As soon as you arrive, you will find yourself under attack by a high level Lizalfos. Keep summoning aquatic critters to attack it, and use a Bombfish to break the weak rocks below the entrance to reach the bubbles inside. Defeating the monster will net you **Echo** - Lizalfos Lv. 3 and a **Treasure Chest** that contains a Purple Rupee.

 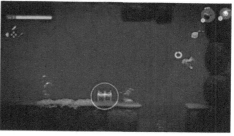

Continue to the left and you will find the path forwards is blocked by a pair of boulders.

Pull the first one back and out of the opening, then swim down and push the second forwards. Swim up the vertical passage here, using a Bombfish to access the bubbles on the left if needed. We will come across another passage blocked by a boulder. Bind this from below and push it all the way to the right. After it sinks, grab it again and pull it out of the opening. We can now swim up to the top.

A short swim to the east, we can surface into a room with a pair of Needleflies. Summon some aerial critters to eliminate them. In this room, use waterblocks to create a vertical path. At the top, jump to a ledge on the left.

At the top there is a platform with an Armos guarding a **Piece of Heart**. Run over to activate the enemy. It will hop along the length of this passage back and forth. In the middle of this passage, you will see a section of roof that is slightly higher. We need to use this location to jump over the Armos I used a Trampoline (but waterblocks will probably work too). Once you are behind it, defeat the Armos and claim your prize.

Drop back down into the water and continue to the left, following the set path and defeating the Bio Dekus as you go. At the bottom, activate the nearby Armos and then defeat it. Defeat another a little further along. Afterwards, stick to the left and swim upwards, through some more Bio Dekus to reach the exit.

Heading up the ladder will put you back outside the cave at the lower entrance.

Head south from the cave and you will find we can head down a slope to the right, or down a climbing wall straight ahead. Both lead to the same area, you will just have some different enemies to deal with - Buzz Blobs to the right, and Hoarders straight.

Between the two paths, you will find a raised ledge with another Stamp platform for your Stamp Rally. Go ahead and activate that.

167

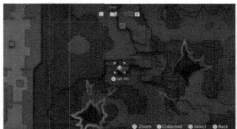 

Drop down and continue to follow the set path here through some more Baby Gohmas and Needleflies. Make your way left/west when you are able to do so and eventually you will arrive at Heart Lake. There is a **Waypoint Stone** here.

Just west from the Waypoint, you will find a Deku Scrub and a rift. Speak with the Deku Scrub and you will learn that he has a Membership Card. He, of course, will not talk with you until you deal with the rift.

As you activate the rift, the Deku Scrub will run by and jump inside. Follow after him.

Stilled Heart Lake

After you enter the rift to reach the Still World, we will need to find and rescue Tri's friends. There are five (!) glowing orbs hidden around this area, and we will need to find and collect them all to complete the rift.

From the start of the rift, we want to head north. After crossing the first web bridge, the Baby Ghoma hiding in the tall grass and the Deku Baba. On the vertical wall here, you should be able to see a small alcove covered in webs. Use a fire **Echo** to burn away the web to reveal the first glowing orb. A second glowing orb can be found behind some webs on the climbing wall to the right.

Climb to the top of the wall here (left side) and send out some flying **Echo**es to knock off the Baby Ghoma at the top. On the top of this platform, you will find another glowing orb beneath a web at the centre of the area.

Make your way across the gap to the west to find a platform with a pond at its centre. In the middle of this body of water there is a tunnel entrance. Dive down to reach an underwater side-scrolling area.

Once inside, proceed to the left and you should see a glowing orb here. It is behind a weak block, the problem? There is a current pushing downwards right beside the block.

We want to spawn a Bombfish, use bind on it from above and then swim against the current to slow your descent whilst holding the explosive fish against the wall. The final glowing orb can be found by following the current down and then swimming right. Defeat the Bio Deku you come across and the glowing orb will be above it's location.

Finding all five orbs will have Tri and her friends cleanse the rift. Tri will also gain a bit of XP, and will hand over **Might Crystal** x2. We will also find ourselves back outside in the 'real' world and the rift will vanish.

169

Following a brief scene, where the two Deku Scrubs are reunited, we will be given a hard "No" when it comes to the Membership Card, they will however mention that Blossu fellow once again... so we are going to have to keep looking.

Faron Wetlands

From Heart Lake, we want to make our way east. When you reach the next lake there will be a few Piranhas about, There is a grassy area by a rift on the west side of the lake with a few baby Gohmas as well. Enter the cave on the right side of the lake.

Upon entering the cave, head north to enter a darkened room. There will be a Beakon here and a bunch of Hoarders. The Beakon will, of course, alert them all to your location. Hop up onto the tree stump in the middle of the room for safety and spawn **Echo**es to clear out the baddies.

The next room is a bit gone, made up of a series of narrow ledges occupied by Hoarders. It is also quite dark, so if you have trouble seeing, consider spawning an Ignizol and carrying it around with you. After the initial area, jump to the back wall and head to the right.

Along this back wall there is another doorway we can explore for some goodies, so proceed inside.

Again, we will find ourselves in a darkened room. Be careful as there are some Baby Gohma's lurking about. In this area, you will find four braziers hidden around the area. Lighting all of these on fire will light up the room and spawn a **Treasure Chest** with a Purple Rupee. There is one beside the entrance, another beside a ramp opposite the entrance, one behind a fence in the back, left corner and another behind a spider web in the back, right corner.

Return to the previous room and find the path on the right that leads south to the exit. Just before reaching the exit, look across the gap to the left and you should be able to spot a **Piece of Heart**.

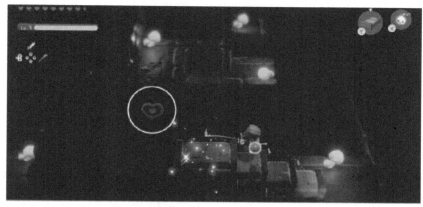

Head back to the exit and continue outside.

As you exit the cave, you should be able to make out a platform above the cave entrance. Use waterblocks or a Platboom, to get up there. Here you will find another suspicious collection of shrubs. Cut down the middle one for a **Might Crystal**.

Drop down and follow the area to the right. As you go you will be attacked by an Electric Wizzrobe. These things can shoot electrical projectiles as well as disappear and reappear, making targeting them difficult. They also have quite a bit of health. Defeating this will allow you to learn the **Echo** - Electric Wizzrobe.

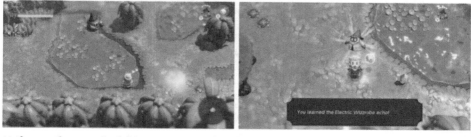

At the northern end of this area, you will find a pair of lit braziers. Head past these and it will start raining. Defeat the pair of Ribbitunes here to stop the rain. You can then light the two tall braziers in the water here to have the statue ahead move, revealing a secret staircase. Inside you will find a **Treasure Chest** with a Monster Stone.

Back outside, look behind the statue for a raised ledge we can climb up to. Do so and head left to find a Stamp platform. Activate this to continue your Stamp Rally.

Return to where we fought the Electric Wizzrobe and continue to the right to find Blossu's house. Activate the **Waypoint Stone** here. As we arrive, we will be treated to a brief scene with some Deku Scrubs chatting it up. Once they finish, approach the rift here and jump inside.

Stilled Blossu's House

After you enter the rift to reach the Still World, we will need to find and rescue Tri's friends. There are five glowing orbs hidden around this area, and we will need to find and collect them all to complete the rift.

From the start, march forward and dispatch the Baby Gohmas and Giant Goponga Flower ahead. After doing so, look behind the flower for a web hiding the first glowing orb.

Climb the wall here and head to the left. As you go, you should find a small alcove with a Giant Goponga Flower in it. This particular enemy is holding a glowing orb. So, eliminate this and claim your prize. Just to the left of this area, is another floating island with three Deku Baba Lv. 2, defeat them and loot the third glowing orb they were guarding.

 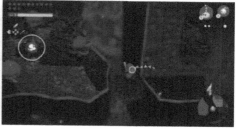

Head back to the climbing wall and climb to the top. Here we want to clear out the baby Gohmas and Giant Goponga Flower. On the right side of this platform, there is a collection of lit braziers floating nearby. Summon a Ghirro to blow them out or a Ribbitune to get the rain to do the same. Hop across these to find a glowing orb on the island on the right below some spiderwebs.

Return across the braziers and climb to the high up platform on the left to find a ladder leading into a side-scroll area.

Once inside, descend the ladder and head to the left. Dispatch the Strandtula here (and the Hydrozol if it drops down to attack). There are three openings in the roof here.

Pop a Strandtula down below the one on the far left and climb up. Destroy the weak blocks here and the Deku Baba Lv. 2 above. The collection of weak blocks that it is guarding contains the final glowing orb.

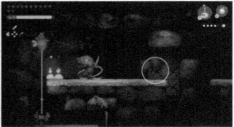

Finding all five orbs will have Tri and her friends cleanse the rift. Tri will also gain a bit of XP, and will hand over **Might Crystal** x2. We will also find ourselves back outside in the 'real' world and the rift will vanish.

Following a brief scene outside, we will learn that the Deku Scrubs are most displeased with us fixing the rift and curtailing their cotton-candy supply. So much so that they are going to throw us in jail.

Deku Scrub Lockup

After arriving in the lockup, a guard will confiscate your Tri Staff, which also means you lose all of your **Echo**es. You will however get a stick in exchange... so better than nothing, I guess. Oh, we also still have Tri with us, so bind can still be used.

When we regain control of Zelda, you will see that the guard dropped his key. Use Bind to grab it. Open the door to escape the cell.

Once outside, you can open another nearby cell for a Red Rupee. You can also look around to find that there are four doors. The door to the south leads outside and you will be captured the second you step outside, leaving the three doors to the north. The middle door is locked, and the right-hand door leads to some guards that we cannot get around just yet, so take the left-hand door first.

This leads to a lengthy room filled with patrolling guards that we will sneak past. We can do this by hopping into a pot and sneaking by all the guards, but it is easier to use a jump out of a pot (it gives you a little extra height) to hop onto the wooden boxes and then from the boxes onto the walls.

In the first area, jump onto the boxes at the bottom of the screen and drop down the far side. When you reach the second guard, use the box at the top of the screen to reach the walk to the left and then jump across to the next box/wall on the left and keep running left and around the corner.

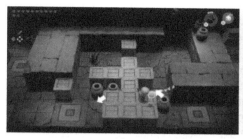 

From the southern end of this wall, we can drop down and sneak by the two Deku Scrubs near the top of the room, using the crates as cover and only moving when they are not looking in your direction. After this group, continue through the door to reach the next area.

As you arrive, you will find some cells in the foreground. There is also a higher ledge on the far right with the door leading to the next area – this is where we need to go to continue.

Before sorting that out, check out the three decorative shrubs on the back wall. Pull away the middle one to find they are hiding a door. Inside you will find a **Piece of Heart** atop a collection of pillars.

 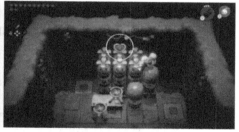

We need to create a set of successively higher platforms to reach the top of the pillars. This setup worked for me – bed > torch > torch on bed > tree > tree on table. From here you can jump to the top.

Enter the right-hand cell. In the lower left of this area, you will find a bed in a ditch. Bind the bed and take it out of the cell by passing it over the door. Take it over to the nearby wall on the right. Grab one of the torches nearby and place it next to the bed. We can then jump from the bed to the torch to the ledge above.

Enter the door here. After a quick chat with the guard, he will hand over the Tri Rod. Once you have it back, switch to swordfighter mode and hit the glowing switch here. Continue through the door that opens.

We will be back in the starting area. This time around however, we want to head down the stairs on the right.

At the bottom, you will see some guards and a short conversation between them indicating that they have a fear of monsters. Rather than following the set route through this area, however, use waterblocks to climb to the wall above their position and work your way across the top of the walls to the far end of the room. There will be one guard on the stairs that we cannot avoid, so summon a monster in front of it and it will freak out. We can then simply run past it and into the door here.

In the next room over, jump into the well to escape the lockup into a side-scroll area.

In the first room, pop a boulder onto one of the wooden boxes to have it sink. We can then bind one on the boxes on the left and drag it beneath the other to create an opening Climb out and proceed to the right, defeating a pair of Hydrozols as you go.

In the next, larger pool of water, you will see a waterfall on the far side creating a downwards current. In the lower, left of this pool of water there is also a collection of crates. If we break through these you can seize yourself a Purple Rupee.

To continue we need to get past the waterfall and to the ledge above it. To do so, create a bridge from the box on the surface of the water, or using water blocks.

The next screen over has a pair of Bio Dekus to eliminate (a Chompfin works well). There are two downwards currents here that we can navigate upwards. The first leads to the exit, whereas the right current leads up to a **Might Crystal**.

There are two solutions to getting up each. The first involves using a box in the vertical path between the two currents – bind this and drag it to the bottom of the wall. Swim off to the sides that you are in the current and then hold ZR to follow the box's movement upwards through the current. The other, simpler method is to just use a Platboom!

After grabbing the **Might Crystal** head for the exit. As you leave you will find yourself back outside in Scrubton. Here Blossu will be standing nearby and will come chat with you. At this point he will hand over his Membership Card... we did it!

The Sweet Spot

Not that we have the Membership Card we can finally go about dealing with the main rift in the region. Head to the entrance to the Sweet Spot and show your card to be permitted inside.

As you enter, we will be treated to a brief scene, after which we will be attacked by a small group of rift spiders. Once this is done, and another short chat, we can jump into the rift here.

Stilled Faron Wetlands

After entering this area, continue forwards until you reach the first larger collection of platforms. You will find a number of Deku Baba and Deku Baba Lv.2 enemies here. At the northern end of this group, there are another two along with a Giant Goponga Flower. Look for a **Treasure Chest** here with a Red Rupee.

The next chain of islands to the north are occupied by Rift Buzz Blobs, Baby Gohmas and Electric Keese. To make things worse, there is also a Drippitune nearby, causing it to rain and amplifying all of the electrical enemy attacks. Clear out the enemies here, being sure to learn the **Echo** - Electric Keese.

In the upper left (northwest) of this group of islands there is an island with a ruin on it. Here you will find the Drippitune, defeat this and the Buzz Blob, Hoarder and Goo Specter nearby. There is also a **Treasure Chest** here with Fresh Milk x4. On the eastern side of this collection of islands, there is another **Treasure Chest**, hidden in a ditch below a web. Burn this away and loot the chest for a Golden Egg.

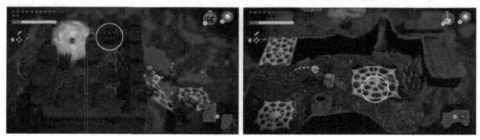

To proceed, head to the northeast to find a **Waypoint Stone** and the entrance to a cave At this point, however, there will be a wall of fire preventing you from entering and six flaming braziers in front. Simply call out a Drippitune here to bring the rain to extinguish the lot, we can now head inside.

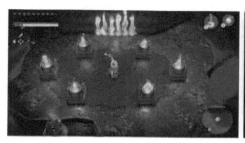 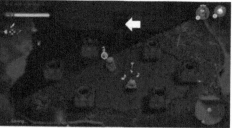

We will end up in a side-scroll area. Use the climbing walls and send out **Echo**es to clear the rift spiders and Beamos as you do . Climb the ladder at the top to escape.

We will arrive in a small puzzle room alongside a pair of Buzz Blobs. Take them out. Once it is safe, have a look around and you should see that there are three green crystals in here.

We need to place an electric enemy by each of the three crystals to activate it – Buzz Blobs work best here as they are innately electric and they are slow, so they will stay in position longer. Drop one by the central crystal and use the higher platforms mid-room to target the two higher crystals by spawning Buzz Blobs from range.

With all three active, the door will open. Head through here for a short scene. At this point, you will have reached the next dungeon. Jump over to the next page to begin Dungeon - Faron Temple

DUNGEON - FARON TEMPLE

Faron Temple

Note: Faron Temple is a bit different from the other dungeons we have encountered so far. It can be confusing and there are multiple entry points inside. We will do our best to explain it, but bear with us!

The main entrance to Faron Temple lies ahead. You can head on inside, but will find that whilst there is a **Waypoint Stone** here, further progress is hindered by the presence of a gate. As such we will need to find another way into the temple from outside.

There are two main entrances at ground level which we can explore:

- Navigate across the floating islands to the left of the main entrance, defeating a Mothula Lv. 2 as you go. This path leads to a grassy area behind the entrance where you can find an opening to explore.

- To the right of the main entrance, you will find Deku Babas and Giant Goponga Flowers guarding an entrance hidden in the tall grass.

Whilst you can explore these in any order, we are going to head to the left first and proceed into the entrance to reach a side-scrolling area. Drop down the first few ledges until you are facing the pit. Summon some flying **Echo**es to deal with the Strandtula and Deku Babas ahead.

After clearing the baddies, summon a Strandtula and keep summoning them to move across the webs to the right until you can get up through the opening in the roof here. Climb up and deal with the Deku Baba Lv.2 at the top to claim the **Treasure Chest** it is guarding. This holds Warm Pepper x10.

Return to the pit below and continue along Strandtulas until you can jump to the platform on the right. Continue up the openings in the roof ahead using Strandtulas to reach the door to the next room.

As you enter, you will find a pair of linked platforms. If you weigh down one, the other will rise. Spawn a pair of boulders on the platform by the entrance. This should raise the second platform on the right up further, allowing you to reach the ladder it had been blocking.

Continue up the ladder here and we will exit into the main chamber of Faron Temple, just behind the gate we had spotted earlier. Step on the pressure plate to the left of the stairs here to lower the gate.

From the entry lobby, enter the door on the left. Dispatch the Electric Keese that you encounter inside. The grass on the left-hand side of this room hides a doorway leading further into the western part of the dungeon.

We will arrive in a dark room. As per usual, this dark area is occupied by several Baby Gohmas, Keese, Hoarders and the occasional Deku Baba lurking about. It is a good idea to spawn and carry about an Ignizol, so you can get the lay of the land. Make your way around this room and light all the braziers on fire – doing so will restore light to the room and you will be able to get around much easier!

On the western side of this room there is a **Waypoint Stone**. There are also five (!) exits. The exit we came from is on the eastern side of the room. There is a locked door just southeast of the entry point, an open door in the very southeastern part of the room and another door to explore in the upper left. There is also a hidden passage doorway in the northwestern part of the area which we will explore later on.

Let us name this room the 2F West Wing. Just because we will be making a few trips back here!

Take the door to the southeast. As you enter, the door will close behind you. There are two pressure plates on the floor here. Now unlike others you may have experienced previously, these pressure plates need to be activated at exactly the same time to open the doors.

To do this, you can activate one of the Armos here (the one on the left is a real one) – this will run over the right-hand pressure plate during its patrol route. We can then spawn another Armos by the left-hand pressure plate so that both touch their respective plates at the same time. Doing so will open both doors.

Head through the door on the right to reach a small room with a **Waypoint Stone** and a pool of water. Dive through here to find yourself outside. After exiting, head to the right from the water and through a couple of Baby Gohma eggs (break them before they hatch!) to find a small opening hidden by webs. Burn these down and continue inside.

The next room has a similar puzzle to the last. There will be two time-sensitive pressure plates. Move the two inactive Armos statues out of the way and spawn two of your own.

Spawn the first on the right, so it patrols up and down the lane with the pressure plate. When spawning the second, we need to make sure our timing is right. Stand on the second tile from the bottom and spawn it just as the first Armos reaches the very top tile on the right side.

Continue through the northern door to encounter an Electric Wizzrobe along with a Baby Gohma. In addition to the baddies, you will also need to avoid stepping on the webs on the floor, which will slow you down. I found the Fire Wizzrobe to be particularly handy here for both clearing the webs and dishing out the damage. After defeating the Electric Wizzrobe, continue through the door to the north.

Activate the **Waypoint Stone** here. We will arrive in a dark room. This area is occupied by several Baby Gohmas and Keese. As with the previous dark area, it is nifty to spawn and carry about an Ignizol, so you can get the layout of the land. Make your way around this room and light all the braziers on fire to have the lights come back on.

This room has four exits. The door on the western side of the room leads out to the lobby area. The ladder on the floor hidden below the webbing to the south leads to a side-scroll area and back outside. The door to the north leads to another side-scroll area, but we will need a Small Key to proceed, so ignore that one for now.

Take the southern ladder first to reach the side-scroll room. Dive into the water and defeat the Tangler below. Continue along the floor of the area to the left and move the boulders out of the way and defeat the Tangler to continue to the left.

Here you will see several passages to the left, however only one of these has a current flowing in the correct direction to take you there. Swim through here and defeat the pair of Biri nearby. Ascend up the far, left hand wall to find a **Treasure Chest** with a Purple Rupee.

Dive back underwater and look for an inactive Armos. We need to bind this and pull it upwards and place it on the ledge in the current above. Head back to the right and then swim into the opening where the Armos had been. With it blocking the current, we can now swim up to the ladder above where we can exit the room.

You guessed it, another dark room! Do your normal thing with the Ignizol carry and dispatch the Baby Gohmas hiding in the darkness. As with the previous dark area, light all the braziers on fire to have the lights come on.

This room has three exits. The door on the eastern wall will lead back to the previous non-side scrolly room and the ladder will take you back to the area we just explored, so we want to open the door on the western side of the room. To do so, we will need to find and activate three green crystals located around the room using an electric **Echo**.

One green crystal is hidden behind some boulders in the southeastern corner of the room, the second is atop the stairs to the north and the third is by the exit door on the western side of the room. Light 'em up and head through the west door.

The next room has a set of stairs at its centre and several baby Gohma eggs around. After clearing them, climb the stairs. You will notice that there are weighted platforms on either side of the room and two time-sensitive pressure plates, one either side of a locked door to the north.

The solution here is a similar puzzle to the Armos puzzles we encountered previously. We want to move the rocks off of both weighted platforms so that they are both at the same height. We then want to spawn one Armos so that it patrols back and forth on the weighted platform in line with the pressure plate. Next, spawn a second on the other weighted platform so it is in line with the first.

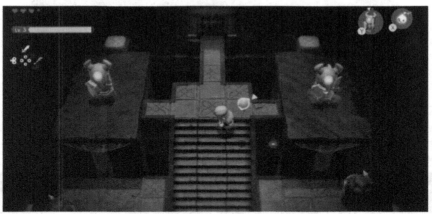

Activating both switches simultaneously will open the door at the northern end of the room and the door along the western wall. Note that the northern door leads to the boss door, but we do not have the key yet (still it is a good idea to run through and activate a **Waypoint Stone** by the boss door). To continue however, you will want to head through the door to the west.

In this small room, you will find a **Treasure Chest** with a Small Key. Use bind on the southern wall of the room to find that it rotates. Pull it backwards to open a secret passage back to the 2F West Wing room (we told you that we would be back!).

On this visit to the 2F West Wing, with our Small Key in hand, we want to head for the locked door along the eastern wall. Inside you will find a **Treasure Chest** housing a Golden Egg.

Return to 2F West Wing and let us check the last door we have not explored yet - the ladder in the northwest corner of the room. We will arrive in another side-scroll area.

As you enter, you will have a pair of weighted platforms, one on the left, and another on the right behind some bars. Head right first and spawn two boulders through the bars onto the platform. This will lower it and raise the other. We can now get beneath the left platform and smack the switch to unlock some doors. As you climb up towards the exit, jump to the platform on the left for a **Treasure Chest** with a Small Key.

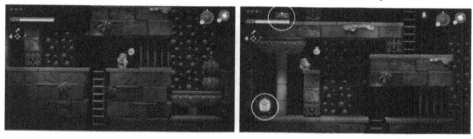

Exit the room.

We will arrive on the 4F of the temple in a room with several Beamos enemies about and a Baby Gohma. Use some ranged **Echo**es to take out the enemies because the webbing on the floor can be troublesome. After clearing the area, we have two doors we can check out. The eastern door leads back to the lobby and **Waypoint Stone** at the very start of the dungeon, whilst the door along the southern wall leads outside.

Head on outside. Once out, dispatch the Crawltulas here and follow the path to the right until you come across a collection of Armos enemies here. Two of these are authentic and a third inactive one blocks the entrance to a room. Bind and pull this out of the way before continuing inside.

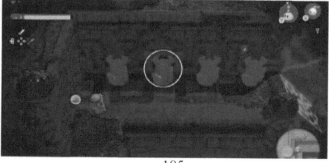

In this room there are three green crystals that we need to activate using an electrical **Echo**. One is located off in the side room to the right (you will need to move the wooden box out of the way to see it). Send a Spark around the wall to it. The other two are atop pillars in a pool of water opposite the entrance. For these, you can create a water block stack between the pillars and the summon a Buzz Blob into it to activate both at once.

With all three crystals active at the same time, a **Treasure Chest** will appear. We can loot this for a Small Key.

Return outside and continue to follow the path to the east (right) and then down to the ground below. Look in the grass near the collection of Deku Babas and Giant Goponga Flowers to find a hidden ladder entrance. Head in here.

We will arrive in a side-scroll area. Upon entering swim to the left and then to the lower area. To the right, there is a **Treasure Chest** guarded by an Armos. Swim close to this to activate it and then bind and pull it backwards, this should reverse its direction. Kill the baddie and loot the chest for a Purple Rupee.

Continue to the far left and exit this area.

We will arrive in a room with a large pit running down its centre and a number of small moving blocks moving back and forth along rails. Excluding our entry point, there are two additional exits to this room, the one in the lower left goes through a room occupied by Beamos and Armos before arriving back in the entry lobby, whilst the platform on the upper left balcony leads to some goodies. Let us do the latter.

In amongst the moving blocks, you will see three green crystals. As is customary, we will need to activate all three with an electric **Echo**. The easiest way to do this is to climb onto the block running the length of the room between the crystals. As you pass each, spawn a Buzz Blob to activate it. Simple!

We can then either use one of the stationary platforms, or the lift platform to make our way up to the balcony above and through the now open door. In here you will find a **Treasure Chest** containing the Dungeon Map. Use the pressure plate to open the door and exit to the entry lobby.

Enter the locked door at the top of the stairs here. A scene will be played as you enter, followed by a mini-boss fight.

❖ *Boss: Duo Deku Baba*

Remember the enemy that stole the Boss Key Chest at the very start of this area? We will get to fight it here. The bud containing the chest will remain closed for us here, but two Deku heads have now sprouted from it, and they will attempt to snap at you and can swallow you (and your **Echo**es) if they can land a bite. The bud itself can also emit a purple poisonous gas if you remain too close to it for too long.

Our goal here is to damage the weak point of each Deku head, represented by a red orb along their stem and attack it to deal some serious damage. Unfortunately, we can't just approach and attack it at any point, instead we will need to stun the heads first. To do so we will need to inflict enough damage to stun them. At this point we can approach the weak point and attack away.

A good way to damage the heads is to summon a bunch of Ignizols. These can damage the boss both by attacking the head, and also if eaten, they will set the head ablaze, inflicting additional damage. You can also use higher level critters or swordfighter mode. Note that you can reclaim your **Echo**es if the boss eats them by binding and pulling the head that has swallowed the **Echo**.

We will need to attack the weak spot for each of the two heads until both have been defeated. At this point, a scene will play, and the boss will run away.

We will now need to track down the mini-boss a second time. To do so, we want to fast travel to the **Waypoint Stone** on the far right on the 2F of the dungeon map. In this room, we want to use the ladder at the top of the stairs that we ignored earlier. Proceed through here to reach a side-scroll area.

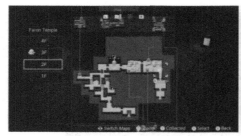

This area has a pair of weight platforms from the get-go. We want to jump onto the first that we come across and spawn two boulders on the left-hand side. This will lower the platform so that we can drop down to the right. Then use waterblocks to ascend to the ledge below the now raised right-hand weight platform. Open the locked door here and continue down the ladder.

Upon exiting, you will find yourself in a room with a **Waypoint Stone**. Activate this and head through the nearby door to find the mini-boss once again.

❖ *Boss: Quadra Deku Baba*

You have just fought this fellow, so the fight should be fresh, and you should have an idea as to what to do this time around. The problem is that the boss has evolved a little since the last encounter, so this one ais a bit trickier. The bud containing the chest will remain closed for us here, but four Deku heads have now sprouted from it.

Much like the last encounter, the boss will use its heads to perform the majority of its attacks. They will attempt to snap at you and can swallow you (and your **Echoes**) if they can land a bite. These heads can now also throw projectiles at you – either rocks, or electrical orbs. The bud itself can also emit a purple poisonous gas if you remain too close to it for too long. Note that as the fight progresses, the boss can also summon a Drippitune, which can enhance the electrical projectiles, making them bigger.

As with the previous fight, our goal is to damage the weak point of each Deku head, (the red orb along their stems). To access this, we will first need to damage the heads sufficiently in order to stun them. Once stunned, we can approach the weak point and attack away. Note that there are two types of heads, the same ones we saw previously (green) and the new ones (blue).

A good way to damage the green heads is to summon a bunch of Ignizols. These can damage the boss both by attacking the head, and also if eaten, they will set the head ablaze, inflicting additional damage. You can also use higher level critters or swordfighter mode. Note that you can reclaim your **Echo**es if the boss eats them by binding and pulling the head that has swallowed the **Echo**.

For the blue heads, you will find they are pretty much impervious to damage in any of our usual methods. However, if you summon a bomb or a Bombfish and get the blue head to eat it, it will explode inside, stunning the head and allowing you to work your magic on the weak spot.

We will need to attack the weak spot for each of the four heads until all of them have been defeated. At this point, a scene will play to end the fight.

Following the fight, the central bud will fall open, revealing the **Treasure Chest** inside. Go ahead and loot this for the Big Key to open the boss door.

With the Big Key in hand, fast travel to **Waypoint Stone** outside the boss door we activated earlier. Rest up, prepare yourself and when you are ready to continue, proceed inside to fight the dungeon boss.

❖ Boss: Gohma

Gohma is a large spider that has a number of different attacks which it can use both with the large eye at the centre of its back, and using its sharp front claws. It can also transition from the wall to the floor and summon little minions to assist it.

190

Initially the boss will take up residence on the back wall of the room and shoot web projectiles from its tail down onto the floor whilst summoning some Baby Gohma eggs which will hatch after a short time. A good idea here is to quickly spawn an Ignizol onto each of the webs it shoots and then once they are all ablaze, spawning more Ignizols by the eggs, either destroying them outright, or quickly killing the Baby Gohmas when they hatch.

The boss will then open the eye at the centre of its back and shoot a laser across the floor This can deal a lot of damage if you let it hit you.

The laser attack also presents an opportunity to hit its weak spot – the open eye. If you can switch to swordfighter mode and shoot the eye with an arrow (or have a flying **Echo** target and hit it), the boss will be stunned. Note that rather than waiting for the laser, you can also expose the boss's eye by targeting the green crystals on its legs – hit them with an electric **Echo** (Electric Keese are good for this).

Once the eye is exposed and has been hit, the boss will fall to the floor, stunned with his eye open. Jump onto its back and wail on the eye in swordfighter mode (with a few choice **Echo**es as backup) to deal some serious damage.

As it recovers, quickly run away from the boss as it will usually perform a quick spin attack using its front legs to knock you off (and damage you in the process). At this point it will either return to the wall, or if you deal enough damage, transition into a second phase.

During the second phase, the boss can do all the things that it did in the first phase, but can also come down to ground level to attack. It has a couple of attacks here that you will want to be aware of. The first has it rear up before performing a sweeping slash attack in front with both forearms. Another has the boss charge at you before slamming its forearms into the ground.

Note that this charge attack is handy if you can avoid it because the slam at the end of it causes Gohma's forearms to get stuck in the ground, taking it out of action temporarily and giving you an opportunity to target the crystals on its legs.

Again, the key is to expose the eye and attack it to stun the boss and then go all in on the damage when the boss is on the floor and its eye is showing. Dealing enough damage to this in the second phase will end the fight.

For defeating the boss, you will receive a full Heart Container. Once the scene here runs its course, you will be able to claim it. Additionally, Tri will level up again and will also hand over **Might Crystal** x5. Additionally, you will also be spoken to by the Goddess, Farore who will give you a new key item – Farore's Sanction.

Speak with Tri by the glowing section of ground on the left side of the room to teleport out of the dungeon.

We will end up back outside in the 'real' world just outside the Sweet Spot. Here we can enjoy a few story scenes involving the Deku Scrubs and Sthe town of Scrubton. Following this scene/chat, our objectives will update, and we will all be done with this main quest.

Note: With this part of the main quest completed, we should have a few options as to what to do next. These include:

● Faron Wetlands Exploration (Optional)

- Lands of the Goddesses - Eldin Volcano (if you have not been there yet)
- Lands of the Goddesses - Mount Lanayru

FARON WETLANDS EXPLORATION

Faron Wetlands

After completing the Faron Temple dungeon and removing the rift from the Faron Wetlands region, you will find that there are a few new areas around the wetlands that we can now explore for some new goodies.

Before doing that, however, you can make a brief visit in and around Scrubton to find a few newly available side quests that we can pick up:

- Cotton-Candy Hunt
- Looking for Bempu
- Mobbing Mothulas!
- The Mythical Deku Snake

We can also make a quick trip around Faron Wetlands to pick up a couple of additional collectibles.

From the Heart Lake, head east until you climb the ledges. At the top, just before reaching the lake, you should see a grassy area above. This had previously been occupied by a rift. With the rifts gone, you can find a **Treasure Chest** here with a Red Rupee.

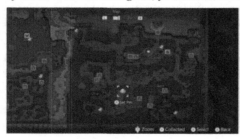

...and that is it for the moment.

Note: We should now proceed with the main quest, and we have a few options as to what to do next. These include:

- Lands of the Goddesses - Eldin Volcano (if you haven't been there yet)
- Lands of the Goddesses - Mount Lanayru

LANDS OF THE GODDESSES - HOLY MOUNT LANAYRU

Northern Sanctuary

To reach Holy Mount Lanayru, we want to head north and across the moat from Hyrule Castle to reach the Northern Sanctuary area. This is a church and an adjacent graveyard that have been impacted by rifts. You will find a Business Scrub outside of the church for your Smoothie-making pleasure and a **Waypoint Stone** just south of the graveyard which we can activate for that sweet, sweet fast-travelly goodness.

From the **Waypoint Stone** area, we want to make a quick detour to the east first. When the main path here starts to head south, we want to explore off to the north. In this area you will encounter some Sword Moblins and a new enemy type – a Ribbitune. Kill them to learn **Echo** - Ribbitune.

In the water just east of this location, there is an island with a cave that we can explore. Inside there is a pool of water with a downwards current. Create a Platboom in here and ride it up, through the current to reach a **Treasure Chest** with Floral Nectar x3.

Return to the rift here at the Northern Sanctuary. Note that this is an optional rift, but completing it will allow you to find a few more goodies in the nearby graveyard, so let us do it!

- Stilled Northern Sanctuary Rift

After clearing the rift, explore the graveyard to the east of the church. One of the graves here can be bound and pulled to reveal a Red Rupee. At the eastern end of the graveyard, there is a larger grave atop some stairs. Light the braziers either side of this to have a hidden passage appear. Continue inside.

Inside the cave, follow the winding passage all the way to the left, defeating the Ghinis as you go. In the larger area at the end of the room, you will be able to see a teddy bear. We can interact with this to learn **Echo** - Stuffed Toy.

Enter the next door and clear out the Ghinis here. There is a glowing switch behind the wall at the northern end of this room. Spawn a Ghini and then lock onto the switch to have it pass through the wall and hit the switch for us. Head through the door on the right that opens.

This next room is occupied by a much larger Ghini. As it spots you it will attack and a bunch of smaller Ghini will flood into the room to assist it. Summon a few **Echoes** to take them all out (a pair of Peahats made short work of them for me). Afterwards, you can learn **Echo** - Ghini Lv. 2.

proceed through the next door on the right for a **Treasure Chest** with a Golden Egg. Step on the pressure plate to exit the room and head back outside.

Locate the road to the west of the church and follow it to the north. As you go, look for a **Waypoint Stone** on the left – this marks the entrance to the Eternal Forest area which we will explore a bitt later.

For now, continue north, dispatching the Rope enemies as you go. During your trek, you will encounter a soldier and a friendly NPC whom we can talk to about Holy Mount Lanayru, the NPC will want you about the temperature.

At the end of this path, you will find a cave that is blocked by rubble. Go ahead and blow this up with a Bombfish (or Bomb of Might) to create an opening. Proceed inside.

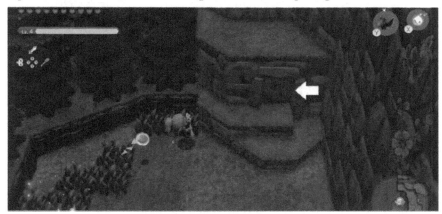

Upon entering the cave, create a Platboom to your left and ride this up to reach the climbing wall high above. Navigate across this to the right, sending out aerial **Echo**es to deal with the Keese along the way.

On the far side of the gap, there is a column of weak blocks. Create a bridge up to this and detonate a bomb beside them to take them out. Behind the wall, pop a bomb onto the lift platform so that it carries it up and explodes the blocks above. We can then ride the lift upwards.

At the top, you will find another lift platform, again blocked by weak blocks. Head left and use waterblocks to reach the area above the lift. Break the blocks here with a bomb... That is not the end of them though! Head left to find a **Treasure Chest** behind more weak blocks that holds Warm Pepper x9.

Make your way up the climbing wall here. Send out some flying **Echo**es to dispatch the Peahat that attacks midway up. At the very top of the wall, break the weak block here and then bind and move the giant boulder all the way to the left.

Return to the lift and ride it all the way up, using one more bomb to destroy the final weak blocks at the top. We can now reach the top of the lift and continue right.

Head up the ladder and then continue outside to reach Hebra Mountain. At this point we will receive a new main quest - Rift on Holy Mount Lanayru.

RIFT ON HOLY MOUNT LANAYRU

Hebra Mountain, Lower

As soon as we begin this quest after leaving the previous cave, you should see a **Waypoint Stone** off to the left. Go ahead and activate this.

Follow the path to the south to encounter a Snomaul. These evil snowman enemies will roll their body segments at you at high speed. Simply attacking their heads will make short work of them. Defeat it to learn **Echo – Snomaul**.

Keep moving south, fighting off a few more Snomauls the wind will pick up and ice will crystalize around the edges of the screen.

Note: Just like in Breath of the Wild and Tears of the Kingdom, if you stay in the cold too long, Zelda will begin losing health. This is indicated by the crystals around the edges of the screen. We will need some kind of warmth or protection to survive.

If you went and crafted some cold-resistant smoothies as we suggested earlier, now is the time to break them out. If you don't have any, you can also summon and carry about

196

an Ignizol, which will keep you warm, or run between the braziers dotted along the main path up the mountain.

From the start of the cold area, you can climb the ledges on the left to find a Stamp Platform. Go ahead and activate this to keep your Stamp Rally kicking along.

 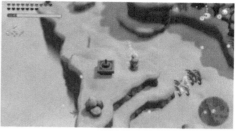

Just south from the main path there is a half-buried **Treasure Chest** containing Twisted Pumpkin x3. To the right of this you will encounter some Leever enemies, small, buried enemies with blades on top that will spin towards your location. Defeat them to learn **Echo** - Leever.

Return to the main path and follow it to the northeast. There will be some braziers here if required. Note that in addition to more Snomauls, you will encounter some Ice Keese here too.

Ice Keese are annoying as they will freeze most regular enemies solid, rendering them useless if they touch them, as such you want to use an elemental variant such as a Fire Keese or Fire Wizzrobe to make short work of them. Be sure to learn the **Echo** - Ice Keese from one of them.

At the end of this initial path, you will see a large, sleeping creature off to your right - this is a Yeti, and we need to chat with it to continue. If you somehow miss it, Tri will point it out to you as well. Before approaching this, however, there are a few more goodies to collect first.

From the yeti's location continue to the north. There is an open area here dotted with tall columns of ice (you can melt these using fire) and enemies including Leevers and Snomauls. On the right-hand side of this area, you will find a half-buried **Treasure Chest** with Twisted Pumpkin x6. On the northern end of the area, you can melt some ice pillars to find a cave we can explore.

Inside the cave, defeat the Snomaul ahead and then use some fire to melt the ice pillar below. You will find a collection of ice blocks here that are shimmering. Approach and interact with these to learn **Echo** - Ice Block.

Either melt the ice blocks here into a stairway, or get rid of the lot and make your way up to the ledge above using an alternate means. At the top, defeat another Snomaul and continue right.

You will see some ice blocks on the floor. Ignore these for the moment and climb the wall to the right to find a **Treasure Chest** above with Floral Nectar x8.

Drop back down and melt away the ice blocks here. At the bottom you will come across a body of water stretching away to the right with ice blocks floating on it. Note that the water is ice cold and will damage you if you fall in it, so spawn ice blocks to work your way to the far side of the area.

Make your way up the vertical shaft here. I found it difficult manipulating the ice blocks, so I melted them all and created little bed staircases between each of the side platforms until I reached the climbing wall at the top. At the top, you will find a Snomaul on the left to kill. Follow this upper ledge all the way to the left to find a **Treasure Chest** housing a Golden Egg.

Whack the switch here to open the gate and make your way back outside.

Once outside, spawn a Platboom and use it to reach a ledge above the cave we just explored. There is an ice column here surrounded by grass that we can melt for a **Might Crystal**.

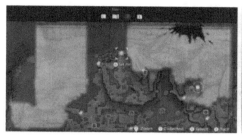 

With all that sorted, head on back to the sleeping yeti we spotted earlier. Approach and interact with it for a short scene and a chat. He will introduce himself as Conde, pull out a lamp (a heat generating lamp) and bid us to follow him.

Once the chat ends, run after the yeti, avoiding the enemies as you go. After a short jog he will lead you to a broken bridge. Speak with him here and respond to his question with "yes" and he will jump you across the gap. What a guy!

After crossing the gap, head south and activate the **Waypoint Stone** here. Continue up the slope to find Conde's house. Speak with him at the entrance to head inside.

Once you are free to roam around Conde's house, you will need to examine a few objects to prompt time to speed along. The first is the picture of Conde and his family on the back wall. A second is a diary on the table, and the third the crate of shovels and pickaxes just inside the door.

With all three of these points of interest examined, Conde will notice that the storm outside has settled down a little and we can now proceed. He'll run outside and begin cleaning up.

To continue, we need to enter the cave that Conde just cleared for us. Before doing that, however, now that the storm has passed, and visibility is a little better we can backtrack to the area we just came through to grab a side quest and some collectibles.

From the entrance to Conde's house, head south to find a small clifftop path leading way to the right. Follow this to the end to reach a fairly large Moblin camp.

In this area you will encounter several Spear Moblin Lv. 2 and Sword Moblin Lv. 2 enemies. There are four of these baddies out in the open (two of each type) and two more Sword Moblins hiding inside blocks of ice around the area. After defeating the lot of them, loot the **Treasure Chest** they had been guarding for Radiant Butter x10. Look for a path through the trees in the northeast corner of this Moblin camp.

Follow this to the end to find a cave entrance. Inside you will find a high-level Sword Moblin defeat this using your big damage **Echo**es. Defeating it will enable you to learn **Echo** - Sword Moblin Lv.3 and have a **Treasure Chest** appear. We can loot this for Accessory - Energy Belt.

Return to the Moblin Camp and head for the guard tower on the western side of the camp. Climb on top of this and you should be able to spot a Stamp platform in a small clearing in the trees nearby. Jump up onto the tress and down into the clearing to grab the Stamp for your Stamp Rally.

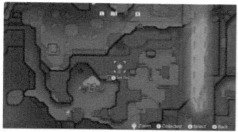 

From the **Waypoint Stone** by Conde's house, follow the path leading away to the north There are Ice Keese, Snomauls and Leevers to deal with or run by here. Follow the path after it turns to the left and across the face of a waterfall.

Just past this waterfall you should see a ledge above that we can climb up to. There is a **Treasure Chest** here that contains Monster Guts x11.

Drop down and continue following the path south, past some more Snomauls and Ice Keese. We will soon reach the broken bridge that Conde jumped us over earlier.

Proceed to the west from the bridge and when the path turns a corner, hop up on the ledge to the left. Defeat the Wolfos and Ice Keese here. In the southwestern corner of this ledge, you will find a patch of grass with a rock at its centre. Pick up the rock to find **Might Crystal**.

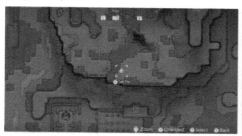 

Return to the main road and follow it north. As you go, look for a small snowy slope on the right side of the path. Climb this and follow the raised ledge at the top to find a small sheltered area with a Business Scrub. Behind him, you will find a **Waypoint Stone**. We can make Smoothies here if needed and he will also offer up a simple side quest:

- Getting it Twisted

With all that sorted, we are good to continue. Return to Conde's house and head to the cave behind his house that he cleared earlier. Before entering, spawn a Platboom and use it to reach a ledge above the cave. There is a block of ice here we can melt for a **Might Crystal**.

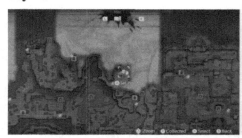

Proceed into the cave. The first room is filled with boxes and ice columns. They are of course hiding the exit door which can be found in the back, right hand corner. Clear the obstructions and head on through. Defeat or run past the Ice Keese in the next room and continue into a third.

This next room has a bunch of Ice Blocks and an exit on the right. There is a Spear Moblin hiding in the upper right corner, and a second exit (the one that goes further into the cave) behind some Ice Blocks in the upper right corner. Before continuing, check the door on the right first for some loot.

As you enter, drop to the ledge below and you will find a sloped path leading upwards. There will be a large snowball constantly spawning and rolling down the slope here before breaking on the wall. There is a small side platform midway up the ramp. Stand by the ends of this, and you should be able to interact with and scan the snowball for **Echo** - Snowball as it rolls by.

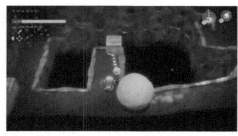

Spawn a boulder, or some other object, bind it, and hold it in front as you walk up the slope. The snowballs are weak and will fall apart as they touch it, so keep them in front until you reach the top. There is a **Treasure Chest** here with a Purple Rupee.

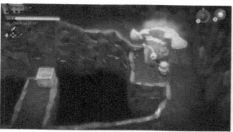 

Return to the previous room and this time, take the doorway in the upper left corner of the room. You will come across Conde who is shoveling snow into a rift, trying to clean it We will have a bit of a chat here.

After the chat, melt the ice column on the left and continue through the door. Here you will find the entry point to the rift. Hop on inside.

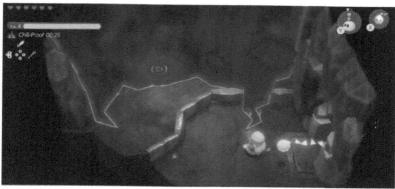

Stilled Hebra Mountain Cave

After you enter the rift to reach the Still World, we will need to find and rescue Tri's friends. There are five glowing orbs hidden around this area, and we will need to find and collect them all to complete the rift.

Upon starting the rift, hop across to the smaller island to the south. We then want to work our way across a series of small islands leading to the west. Note that these are occupied by ice columns, so be sure to melt those to proceed. On the larger island at the end, there is an ice block with the first glowing orb.

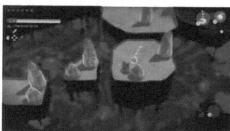 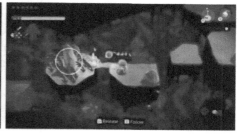

Return to the starting platform and then head to the west. There is a large ice-covered platform here with a pair of Snomauls about. Defeat them all before melting the central ice column to find the second glowing orb.

From the starting platform head north and then take the first right onto an icy walkway. Follow this icy path to the end, fighting off or avoiding the ice Keese as you go. When you reach the solid ground at the end of this path, there will be a glowing orb on a raised ledge above.

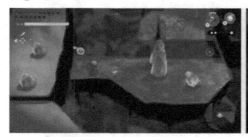 

Return to the main path and continue to the north. At the top, head west and jump across the gap. There will be trees sticking out of this platform that we can use as platforms. As you ascend this platform, look out for an icicle we can melt for another glowing orb. At the very top of this platform, you will spot another smaller island on the right. Defeat the Rift Spear Moblin here and hoover up the final glowing orb.

Finding all five orbs will have Tri and her friends cleanse the rift. Tri will also gain a bit of XP, and will hand over **Might Crystal** x2. We will also find ourselves back outside in the 'real' world and the rift will vanish.

Hebra Mountain, Lower

Once you arrive back in the cave, make your way to the previous room to find Conde. Before we get a chance to talk with him he will jump away, leaving us behind. Enter the door at the rear of the room that had previously been covered by the rift.

We will find ourselves in another side-scroll area.

Proceed to the right and you will spot a Spear Moblin Lv. 2 between to collections of Ice Blocks. We can either melt these all away and fight it, or strategically melt them so that you can climb over its position and on to the right without disturbing it.

In the next room, you will need to climb upwards whilst avoiding a snowball that will constantly roll down through this area. When you reach the top of the room, defeat the Snomaul and then jump across to where the snowball is coming from when it is safe to do so. There is a **Treasure Chest** here with Monster Stone.

Climb up the ladder in the upper right of the room. Once you exit the side-scroll area, proceed outside to find yourself back on Hebra Mountain, just a bit higher up.

Hebra Mountain, Middle

As soon as you exit the cave, activate the **Waypoint Stone** on the left. This immediate area is occupied by a large, frozen pond. Remember, that ice cold water will damage you if you step in it, so do your best to stay out of the drink!

Before exploring the main body of water, head to the right first. This leads to another small pond where you will encounter an Ice Wizzrobe. Much like the Fire and Electric variants, these things can shoot icy projectiles which will freeze you solid as well as disappear and re-appear, making targeting them difficult. They also have quite a bit of health. Defeating this will allow you to learn the **Echo** - Ice Wizzrobe.

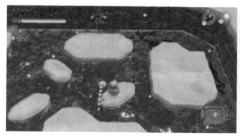

Look on the southeast corner of this small lake to find a half-buried **Treasure Chest** under the water. Pull this out and loot it for a Red Rupee.

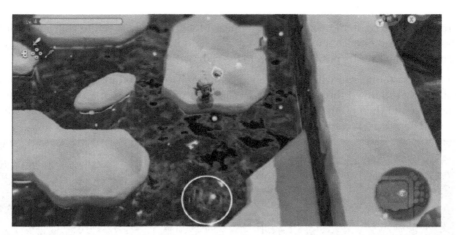

Return to the larger lake. It's time to make our way across this. Note that this lake is inhabited by Ice Keese and Ice Octos, a new type of Octorok that can live in the icy cold water. So, work your way across the small islands cautiously, dispatching enemies as you go. Make sure you defeat at least one Ice Octo to learn **Echo** - Ice Octo.

In the southwest corner of this lake, you will find a **Piece of Heart** on an island. Melt away the ice on the island and work your way up to the prize at the top.

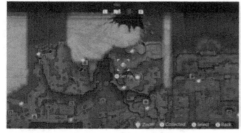

Continue across the large lake and to the northwestern side. Finally, you should see a cave leading into the mountain (we need to go there to progress). Just before reaching this, you should see a waterfall on the left. Go check that out first.

Use the small section of land on the left side of the waterfall to create a stairway of beds jutting out from the waterfall. From this, summon a Ghirro (or another flying beasty) and glide down to the sneaky out of sight ledge on the left.

206

In this area, melt the ice column in the grass here for a **Might Crystal**.

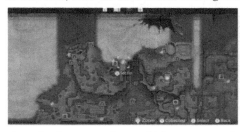 

There is also a cave here which we can explore. Inside, you will immediately encounter a high-level Tektite enemy, so eliminate it and then learn the **Echo** - Tektite Lv. 2 from its corpse.

Head through the next doorway to reach a larger room filled with water and numerous small icy islands. Again, you will encounter Lv. 2 Tektites here along with a small collection of Ice Octos further into the room. Clearing all the enemies will have a **Treasure Chest** spawn. This contains Accessory - Ice Spikes.

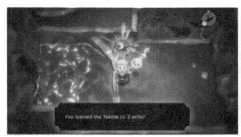 

This accessory is particularly useful in this area as it will reduce the amount of slipping and sliding Zelda will do when navigating ice. Nice!

Head back outside and proceed back across the gap (or fast travel back to the **Waypoint Stone**) and head for the cave in the northwestern part of the large frozen lake.

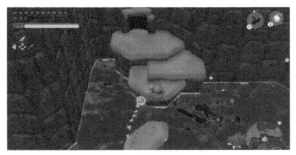

The first room of this cave has numerous weak, cracked tiles on the floor and a Zhirro that will fly about lobbing bombs at you. Defeat the enemy and climb to the ledge at the rear of the room.

The next room is made up of a series of icy paths with wind cannons aimed at them. Unfortunately, most of our stuff will simply slide off along the ice if you try to block the wind. That is except the Waterblocks! Proceed through the area placing a waterblock in front of each air vent. Defeat the Gustmaster at the end of the area and then use a Ghirro to glide across the next gap and through the door on the left.

In this room you will need to defeat all of the enemies to continue. There are two ice Keese about, but also a sneaky Zol hiding behind the ice blocks in the upper right. With the enemies clear, the two doors will unlock.

Head left first. This room has a whole lot of ice blocks. Melt the ones on the left side of the room to find a **Treasure Chest** with Monster Guts x6. Return and head right. Defeat the pair of Freezards here (use fire **Echo**es to deal with them quickly, a Fire Wizzrobe can one-shot them) to learn **Echo** - Freezard.

In the next room there isn't much interest outside of a Sword Moblin in some ice. The room after this features a pair of Spear Moblins. We can also take the ladder to reach a side-scroll area.

As you progress through this area, keep your eyes peeled for the icicles hanging from the roof. These will fall periodically, damaging you if they hit. Time your movements past them to avoid them (obviously).

The first room is fairly straightforward. The second room is too, although in addition to the icicles you will also need to watch out for some Ice Octos positioned along the main route. Have a fire **Echo** or two handy to deal with them.

When you reach the elevator, you will see a pair of jets of icy water either side of the shaft above. Bind one of the pots to the left as you step on the lift and use it to block the left-hand jet. You can then move to the very edge of the lift to avoid the right-hand jet. On the second lift, climb the nearby ladder and shoot an Ice Block in front of the upper ice jet – you can then jump down onto the lift as it passes and ride it upwards.

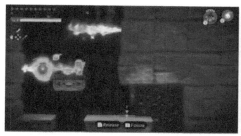

Climb up the ladder in the upper left of the room. Once you exit the side-scroll area, proceed outside to find yourself back on Hebra Mountain, once again a bit higher up.

Hebra Mountain, Upper

Upon exiting the cave, follow the narrow path provided, dealing with an Ice Keese or two as you go. You will soon encounter a new enemy called a Moa. These things are dangerous, but only in a group setting where they can attack alongside other enemies. Killing other enemies will usually have them run off – so be sure to target this one first so you can kill it to learn an **Echo** - Moa.

Follow the path to the left, being careful to avoid the falling snowballs which will drop down from above and roll down the slope. After the second snowball platform, climb the wall ahead. From the top of this wall, you will see the obvious path to the right, but also a lower path on the left.

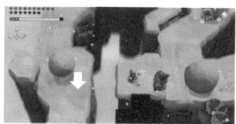

Jump down to this lower area and work your way up the hill, dodging snowballs (or using a boulder as a blocker). As you go, you will spot a rock pillar on the right side of the path with a **Piece of Heart**. Climb up to grab this.

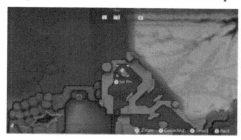

Continue along the set path here back to the south (again maneuvering around snowballs) to find yourself back at the top of the rock wall we climbed earlier. Proceed to the right from here and look for a ledge to the side of the path with an ice crystal. Melt this to find a **Might Crystal**.

 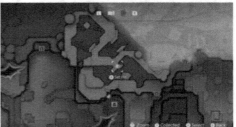

Keep following the path upwards until you find a **Waypoint Stone** and Conde. Approach this area for a scene.

We now have a relatively large slope heading upwards towards the summit.... And of course, there are snowballs rolling down it. Before heading north however, there are paths leading way to the left and the right that we can explore first.

On the left path, continue up the slope here to find a small ledge off to the side with a half-buried **Treasure Chest**. This contains a Purple Rupee. Further up the slope is the location of a side quest (which we can't do yet). As such, return to the main slope and head to the right. At the end of this path, you will find the Stamp Guy. Speak with him here for a side quest

- Stamp Stand Swallowed!

If you complete this side quest, you will be able to plonk another Stamp from the now present Stamp platform to prod that Stamp Rally along.

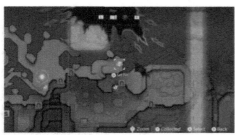 

Note: If you have been following this walkthrough, this should be your 25th and final Stamp. As a reward, the Stamp Guy will give you **Outfit** - Stamp Suit. Nice!

Return to the main slope and follow it upwards to the top. Here you want to locate the cave on the eastern side of the slope. Head on inside.

Once inside, work your way to the left, using the climbing wall and avoiding the snowball Climb the ladder. Defeat the Ice Octo on the platforms ahead, or drop to the ledge below (and avoid the snowball) to continue back to the right and up the next ladder.

Use the next series of climbing walls to avoid the snowballs and continue your ascent. As you reach the next ladder, note the ledge on the left. Head over to this and climb to the top (again avoiding snowballs) to find a **Treasure Chest** with Monster Fang x4.

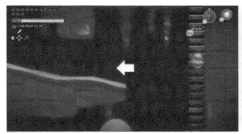 

Return to the ladder and climb up and out of the side-scroll area.

In the cave atop the ladder, you will encounter a new enemy – Temper Tweelus. These are similar to the Tweelus enemies you will have encountered on Eldin Volcano, but these ones can light themselves on fire. Dispatch one of them for **Echo** - Temper Tweelus.

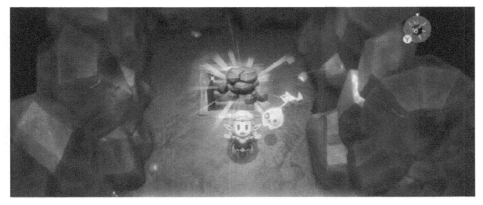

Note that you can use the hot spring here (green water) to restore Zelda's hearts if needed. Continue outside when you are ready to continue. As you exit the cave, activate the **Waypoint Stone** here.

After a brief scene and chat with Conde here, approach the rift atop the mountain and head on inside.

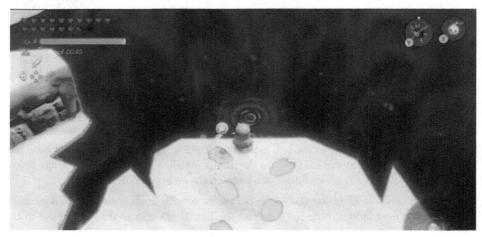

Stilled Hebra Mountain

This rift is a little different from others we have encountered previously. Whilst the others have a single location, this rift joins two different Stilled locations together so it's a little bit bigger. The second of these is home to the Lanaryu Temple, which is our next dungeon.

After arriving in this area, you'll notice that in addition to floating islands, there are also clouds that are thick enough to stand on and function as platforms as well, so that is a thing and it's handy. From the start, begin your journey north, defeating the Tornado enemies here.

At the northern end of this initial area, you want to create a bridge to the area to the left. Clear out the Rift Spear Moblin and the Rift monsters that the nearby orb will spawn.

Just past this area, you will see some sparking clouds nearby, approach and interact with one of these to learn an **Echo** - Cloud. To the left of this is a floating island with a **Treasure Chest** containing a Monster Stone.

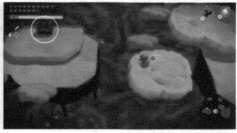

Return to the main path and head north, taking care of the pair of Ghirros as you go. We need to make our way to the larger island to the northwest. Here there is a cave that we can explore.

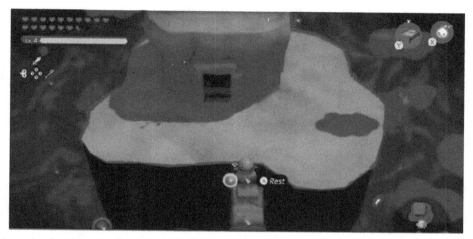

Once in the side-scroll area, make your way to the right across the floating islands and deal with the pair of Ghirros here.

If you continue along this section of the level, there will be a **Treasure Chest** with a Red Rupee. After nabbing this, return across the gap and use Platbooms to climb to the upper section of the level. Once up, head all the way to the left and break open the weak wall here to find a **Treasure Chest** behind it holding Warm Pepper x3.

Continue to make your way to the right, across to the tall vertical platform and then down the drop afterwards, until you reach some climbing walls. Freeze Slugs will inhabit these. These monsters will patrol up and down the walls, freezing you (and **Echo**es) if you touch them, or the trail they leave behind. Use some flying critters to deal with them and then examine one for **Echo** - Freeze Slug.

At the top of this room, use the ladder to escape the side-scroll area.

Stilled Holy Mount Lanayru

Upon exiting the previous cave, you will now be in the new Stilled area, Stilled Holy Mount Lanayru. Go ahead and activate the **Waypoint Stone** here.

Head across the cloud platforms to the south (watch out for the Ice Keese) and from the second, proceed across the gap to the east to reach solid ground. Use a Platboom to reach the raised ledge above.

There will be a frozen pond here occupied by Ice Octos. At the northern end of this point, you can find a cave we can explore. Inside there is a **Treasure Chest** containing a Purple Rupee. Create a stairway using beds to reach it.

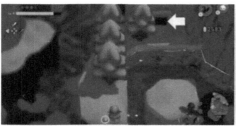

Return outside and this time, head to the east from the pond. Defeat the Wolfos here. Use a Platboom from its location to reach the ledge above. Clear out another Wolfos and some Rift enemies here. Continue north to find a larger cave entrance.

After a short scene here, continue to the right and enter the next doorway to reach the next dungeon, Dungeon - Lanayru Temple.

LANAYRU TEMPLE WALKTHROUGH

Lanayru Temple

Upon reaching the Lanayru Temple, you will want to go ahead and activate the nearby **Waypoint Stone**.

The next room of the temple has a fan on the wall and a grey series of tiles along the ground linking the fan with a pedestal in another room. These objects are a big feature of this dungeon, so you will be seeing them plenty. Before getting started and following the grey tiles, you can defeat the two Ice Octos in the room to the right first for a **Treasure Chest** with Rock Salt x5.

Head through the door on the right. As you enter you will see the pedestal linked to the fan in the previous room. There is a pool of water to the right and on an island on the far side, a red orb. Create a path across the water, bind the orb and take it back to the pedestal. Doing so will melt a chunk of ice in the previous room, revealing a ladder we can climb down.

214

We will be in a side-scroll area. Dispatch the first two Snomauls here. Above the second, you will see a pair of icy geysers shooting out of the ceiling above.

Between these ice geysers is an opening in the roof. If you create a stairway from the upper ledge on the right, you can use a Strandtula to get up through it. You will need to create your final platform below the left-hand geyser and quickly spawn the Strandtula as the geyser will break your platform when it activates. There is a **Treasure Chest** up here with Monster Fang x3.

Drop down and continue down the ladder on the far right.

The next room features more ice vents and an Ice Keese. Use the boulder here to block the ice geysers as you go and continue into the next room.

This room is a bit trickier. You will see a locked door on a ledge to the right with a pair of steam vents below it. On the left side is an open door with ice vents in front. Between the pair is a fan mounted on the wall, leading away to the left-hand room. Make your way through the left-hand door first.

We will find ourselves in a room with a pedestal and a red orb. This time around, however, they are behind a fence with an ice geyser between them. We want to spawn a boulder/ice block through the bars and in front of the ice geyser and then bind the orb and pop it onto the pedestal. Return to the previous room to find the icy floor has melted Dive down on the left-hand side of the room to find a Small Key.

After grabbing the key, re-enter the room with the pedestal. This time around, grab the orb and drag it through the ice geyser. This will transform it from red to blue. Pop the blue orb into the pedestal and it will re-freeze the previous room. Make your way up to the ledge behind the steam vents and continue through the locked door.

Another side-scroll area! The initial part of this area consists of a climbing wall with ice jets shooting out across it and large icicles forming on the roof above and dropping downwards. We want to bind the icicles when they appear and then climb down the wall using the ice as a blocker for the vents. Repeat the process ascending the next part of the wall.

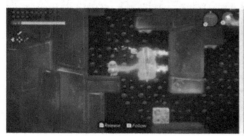 

Repeat this icicle blocking scenario until you reach the ladder in the lower right which will take you to the next floor of the dungeon.

The next area has a pair of gaps, each of which is occupied by ice vents, requiring us to maneuver around them. Above the first gap, there is a sneaky hidden opening. Use a Platboom to reach this and continue inside to find a **Treasure Chest** with a Golden Egg

 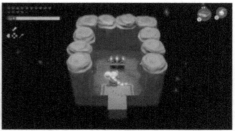

The second gap in this room is harder to cross than the first, it is bigger, there are more ice vents and the ledge we want to reach is higher up. The easiest way to get up is to summon a Platboom, ride it up and then use a flying **Echo** to glide across to the upper platform whilst the upper set of ice vents are briefly inactive.

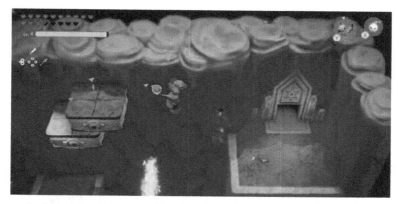

As you reach the next room, you will find a giant ice wall separating the area into two sides and an assortment of symmetrical ice blocks lined up with both sides mirrored. The door on the right is open (but out of reach) and the door on the left is locked. You should note that on the right side of the room, there is a brazier here. If you move the block in the same location on the left, you will find a ladder leading downwards. Head on down!

We will be in another side-scroll area. As you enter, you will find a climbing wall below and on the wall opposite the entrance, a pedestal for an orb. Make your way down the wall here, being careful to avoid the ice vents and take out the Freeze Slugs.

At the bottom of this room, you will find a fire orb on the right. We want to bind this and take it to the pedestal at the top. We can carry this past the first set of vents when they turn off, but the second set will remain on. As such carry it to the ledge on the right. Here, create a stack of water blocks to swim up to the upper section of climbing wall above.

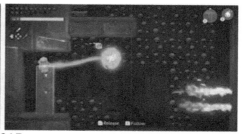

217

We can then head straight for the pedestal and pop the orb in there. This will melt the large ice wall in the room above. This will enable us to head through the open door on the right side of the room.

In this room there are two pressure plates on the floor here. If you went to Faron Temple you will have encountered these already, if not, these pressure plates need to be activated at exactly the same time to open the doors. To do this we want to push the ice block here – it will slide to the right and onto the pressure plate. As it hits the pressure plate, have Zelda step on the other pressure plate just inside the door. Loot the **Treasure Chest** that appears for a Small Key.

Return to the main room and then head through the locked door on the left.

The room we arrive in is occupied by several Temper Tweelus enemies, along with hot springs dotted about and ice vents located around the room. Try and fight the Temper Tweeluses (or is it Tweeli?!?) one at a time before moving on to the next. Defeating them all will have both doors unlock, and a **Treasure Chest** appears with the Dungeon Map.

Through the door on the left, you will find a **Waypoint Stone**. Use the hot spring here to heal up if needed before continuing to the north for a mini-boss fight.

❖ *Boss: Hot Spring Zol*

This boss is essentially a giant Zol that is made up of hot water. This thing is pretty much invulnerable... that is until you figure out its weakness, which is ice. Using ice **Echoes** and having them land attacks on the boss will cause the monster to freeze solid. At this point, you can inflict damage – so bring out your heavy hitting **Echoes** here and swordfighter form to slash away.

I found Freezards to be by far the best option here, their constant spray of icy air in front can freeze the boss pretty quickly, especially when you have a couple of them going at once. You can also use Freeze Slugs, Ice Wizzrobes or Ice Keese, all are capable of freezing the boss.

The boss itself only has a couple of attacks - first it can jump high in the air and attempt to land on you. Fortunately, you should be able to see its shadow on the floor, simply move away from this to avoid getting turned into a Zelda-flavored pancake. After this attack a collection of stones will also fall down form the ceiling at random around the room – again use the shadows as a guide as to where not to be.

The most important ability the boss has, however, is that after damaging the boss enough, it will split in two, and you will need to defeat these smaller Zols which will once again divide into two. Continue to defeat them until they are too small to keep splitting, and end up dying instead. This will end the fight.

After finishing the fight, head through the next door to reach another side-scroll area.

In this area, you will need to find and light four braziers located around the room. Doing so will open the locked gate in the lower left of the area.

After descending the first ladder, you will find the first brazier behind a chunk of ice on the left. Melt this and then toss an Ignizol into the brazier to ignite it. Proceed down the next ladder and melt the ice on the right. Continue straight to the right to find the next brazier.

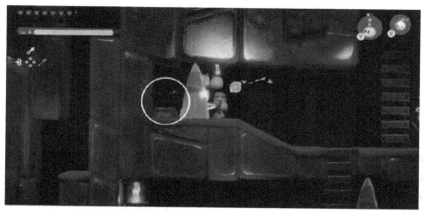

This brazier is a little tricky as it is in a small, contained area above a pool of frozen water. To reach this, I created a stack of ice blocks so that I could stand beneath the opening in the roof and then summoned a Fire Keese up into the opening... it eventually lit the brazier (but took a while).

Head back to the left and you will find two more ladders leading down. Take the first one you come across. In this lower area a collection of icicles will constantly spawn on the rooftop and drop down. The brazier is on the far side of these. Wait until they drop and then throw an Ignizol across the gap and into the brazier.

Head back up the previous ladder and down the next on the left. We will reach a lower area with the final brazier. Defeat the Fire Keese here. There is a pair of bars overhead. We want to spawn an Ignizol just past them. We can then target the brazier and have it hop across to and light it.

With all four braziers now alight, head for the now open exit. Before leaving the room, destroy the brazier to the left of the exit ladder. Use water blocks to climb up the vertical shaft here to the very top to find a **Treasure Chest** with a Silver Rupee.

After grabbing the loot, drop back down the shaft and descend the ladder to the next floor of the dungeon below.

Upon entering, continue to the south and you will find the chest with the Big Key behind a fence here. Stepping on the yellow pressure plate in front of it will trigger a snowball to roll down a hill nearby towards a larger yellow switch, but this will break on the chunks of ice around the room. We will need to come back for this.

You will notice that there are two rooms out of his area, one at the bottom of the screen and another over on the right. The right-hand door leads down to the lowest level of the dungeon and the boss door. You can activate a **Waypoint Stone** here, but there is nothing else we can do, so head through the door opposite the Big Key chest.

This next room has a fan on the wall along with a blue orb and a pedestal, however the two are separated by a large, ice wall. For now, continue into the room to the south.

Here you will encounter several enemies including a Moa, Deku Baba, and some Freeze Slugs. A lot of the room is made up by a pool of frozen water with a few little platforms scattered about. After clearing them all, loot the **Treasure Chest** by the southern exit for Twisted Pumpkin x3. Head through the door to the south once again.

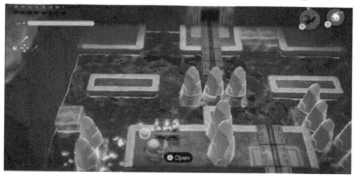

We will arrive in a large room with a big ice block on the floor, a fan on the wall and two exits. The left door is out of action for the moment, so to begin we want to head to the right and then immediately into the door to the north.

As you enter, there will be a red orb. Past this is a fairly lengthy icy walkway that leads to the pedestal we want to insert the orb into. Of course, the game won't make this easy for us as we will heave several ice vents, Ice Octos, Freeze Slugs, Ice Keese and a Temper Tweelus to avoid along the way. It's a good idea to clear the walkway of enemies, and block the ice vents first before grabbing the orb and walking it through to the pedestal as a victory lap (you can also just make a run for it... worked for me!). Placing the orb on the pedestal will melt the ice in the previous two rooms.

In the previous room, jump into the water on the right and dive under the half wall here. Use some **Echo**es to eliminate the Tektites here and then swim to the far, right to find a **Treasure Chest** with a Monster Stone.

Swim back to the left and continue through the door to the west.

Jump into the new pool of water here. There is a pressure plate under the water here. Use bind to seize the nearby boulder and place it atop the pressure plate. This should open the door on the left. Let's check that area out next.

As you enter this next room you will see another pair of those pressure plates that we need to activate simultaneously. Unfortunately, with the room in its current state we will be unable to use them. As such, for now we want to venture through the door on the left.

This side room will look familiar. We have another red orb and pedestal combo out of reach behind a fence. This time around however, you will have two steam vents and an ice vent between the orb and its destination. Summon some boulders to block both steam vents and then drag the orb through the ice vent and onto the pedestal. This will freeze the water in the previous room.

With the floor now frozen, we can activate both pressure plates at once, either by using the sliding ice block or an Armos **Echo** to activate one, whilst we run Zelda over to step on the second at the same time. Successfully doing so will open the door to the north.

The next room is occupied by a White Wolfos. These are similar to the regular Wolfos enemies, but do a lot more damage and can take many more hits before dying themselves. Additionally, they can summon a couple of regular Wolfos enemies to attack you as well. Use your high-level **Echoes** here (Darknut Lv.3 made short work of them). After defeating it, make sure you learn **Echo** - White Wolfos.

Further to the north is a large, water-filled room. Here you will need to make your way around the perimeter of the room with a red orb. However, there are several Freezards and ice vents along the route we need to take. As such, do a dry run first, clearing out the enemies and blocking the ice vents before grabbing the orb and carrying it around to the pedestal.

Return to the room south of the Big Key chest (you can use the door on the eastern side of this room for a shortcut).

When you arrive, use an Ignizol to light the brazier just inside the door. Next, grab the blue orb and drag it through the lit brazier to change it to a red orb. Place it on the pedestal to the left. This will melt the ice in the room we saw the giant snowball earlier. Once this has occurred, the orb should return to its initial position. Grab this blue orb and pop it onto the same pedestal to freeze the room once again.

223

We can now return to the north and step on the yellow pressure plate. The snowball can now roll down the slope, across the ow flat icy surface and onto the large pressure plate here. This will open the gate, allowing us to loot the **Treasure Chest** for the Big Key.

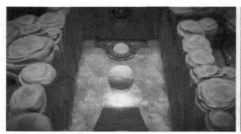 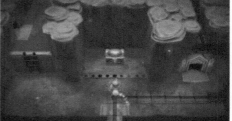

Head down the stairs on the right, rest up in the hot spring here and proceed through the boss's door when you are ready for a fight.

❖ *Boss: Skorchill*

This boss is a large Yeti-like creature with a fancy helmet that makes him pretty much invulnerable to damage. To make things worse, you will also fight this boss on an icy floor, so if you don't have the Ice Spikes accessory, its going to be a lot more difficult than it needs to be!

The boss has several attacks that we will want to familiarize ourselves with. Firstly, he can use an overhead slam if you are in front of him. He can also jump about, causing a number of icicles to fall down from the roof at random... so be sure to avoid them. The boss can also spin around with his arms held out at high speed and bounce around the arena. If you can avoid this, eventually he will get dizzy and stop temporarily to recover.

The key to this fight is the horns on the boss's helmet. You can target these with your elemental **Echo**es and landing a blow will destroy them - you will need to hit all three to stun the boss. Initially the boss will have blue horns, and you will need to use fire-based **Echo**es to destroy them (if you haven't been to Eldin Volcano yet, you can use ignizols or Braziers). Once the boss's helmet is damaged, you can use bind to yank it off his head. At this point he is no longer protected, so summon your hardest hitting **Echo**es and charge into attack using swordfighter mode.

After dealing enough damage to the boss, the helmet's horns will turn red, meaning ice **Echo**es are now your go-to. We will need to repeat the same process of removing the helmet and wailing on him here. In addition to the color change, the boss will also pick up a couple of new fire-based attacks.

The first new attack sees the boss charging up with fire. When you see him doing this you want to put some distance between your location and the boss because once he is done, he will unleash a large fiery whirlwind near his location that can eat up and damage anything within a good chunk of the arena's real estate. His other attack is a volley of fireballs which you will need to stay on the move to avoid.

When you have inflicted enough damage to him in this stage, he will change up again and this time the helmet will boast horns of both colors. In addition to this, Skorchill will also be able to use both his fire and ice-based attacks. Keep plugging away at his health, removing his shiny hat, and dishing out damage when he is vulnerable to end the fight.

For defeating the boss, you will receive a full Heart Container. Once the scene here runs its course, you will be able to claim it. Additionally, Tri will level up again and will also hand over **Might Crystal** x5. At this point, you will also be spoken to by the Goddess, Nayru who will give you a new key item – Nayru's Sanction.

Speak with Tri by the glowing section of ground on the left side of the room to teleport out of the dungeon.

We will end up back outside in the 'real' world just outside where we will meet up with and chat to Conde once again. Following this scene/chat, our objectives will update, and we will all be done with this main quest.

Note: With this part of the main quest completed, we should have a few options as to what to do next. These include:

- Mount Lanayru Exploration (Optional)
- Lands of the Goddesses - Eldin Volcano (if you have not been there yet)
- Lands of the Goddesses - Faron Wetlands (if you have not been there yet)

Note: If this is your third dungeon in the Lands of the Goddesses main quest, a scene will play here. Afterwards, the next main quest - The Prime Energy and Null will begin automatically.

MOUNT LANAYRU EXPLORATION

Hebra Mountain and Holy Mount Lanayru

After completing the Lanayru Temple dungeon and removing the rift from the Hebra Mountain and Holy Mount Lanayru region, you will find that there are a couple few new points of interest around these mountainous areas that we can now explore for some new goodies.

Before doing that, however, you will want to make a brief visit to Conde's house. Head on inside and he will have a new side quest for you:

- Snowball Magic

The other thing we want to do is make your way back up to the middle section of Hebra Mountain, to where we crossed the large icy pool. In this location, head to the east to where the Ice Wizzrobe was located. Here we can climb up onto the ledges overlooking his area to find a **Piece of Heart**.

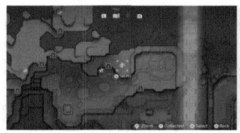 

...and that's pretty much it for the snowy mountains!

Suthorn Prarie

Whilst there is still not a whole lot to do in Suthorn Forest, there are a couple of new things about! Firstly, if you head back into Suthorn Village, now that we have the Snowball **Echo**, we can finally complete the side quest:

- What is Snow... Really?

...and with that we are good to continue.

Note: With this part of the main quest completed, we should have a few options as to what to do next. These include:

- Lands of the Goddesses - Eldin Volcano (if you have not been there yet)
- Lands of the Goddesses - Faron Wetlands (if you have not been there yet)

Note: If Lanayru Temple was your third dungeon in the Lands of the Goddesses main quest we will want to proceed with the next main quest - The Prime Energy and Null.

THE PRIME ENERGY AND NULL

Eternal Forest

This main quest will begin after completing the third of the three dungeons in Lands of the Goddesses (Dungeon - Eldin Temple, Dungeon - Faron Temple and Dungeon -

Lanayru Temple). We will start it in Zelda's bedroom in Hyrule Castle.

Exit the bedroom and you will find general Wright waiting for you. After a brief chat, he will mention that he is heading off to the Eternal Forest to wait for us.

The path to the Eternal Forest can be located midway between the Northern Sanctuary and the cave leading to Hebra Mountain. Look for a **Waypoint Stone** on the left side of the path as you head north – this is where we need to go!

Note: The Eternal Forest here is a bit of a maze, and your map and mini-map will not function properly here... at least until we solve the area's big puzzle. So, bear with us, we'll do our best to make it not as confusing!

From this you will want to head west and into the forest. At the first split in the path head north and at the second split in the path, head to the west. As you go, look for another **Waypoint Stone**.

After activating this, head a little further to the west to find General Wright and some guards. As you approach them, a scene will play.

Following the scene, approach and interact with the glowing tablet on the ground here. This will rise out of the ground and a ball will appear nearby. We can inspect this for **Echo** - Ancient Orb. Bind this and pop it atop the nearby pedestal. This will have one of the lights on the tablet light up. You guessed it, we will need to find another five pedestals to solve this puzzle.

From the nearby **Waypoint Stone**, head directly south and drop down to a slightly lower section of ground. Dispatch the Caromadillo here and create an Ancient Orb **Echo** to place on the pedestal here.

Return to the first pedestal and continue directly east. Look for a small, grassy path leading north in what looks to be a dead end. Follow this to the end and climb up to find a Tresure Chest with a Monster Stone.

Drop back down and continue south. After a short walk you should come across a Sword Moblin Lv.3 guarding a half-buried **Treasure Chest**. Take the hostile out and pull the chest from the ground for a Purple Rupee.

Follow the path south, dispatching a Sword Moblin Lv.2 as you go. When you reach a tree in the middle of the path and there are paths south and to the east, head east first and then north when you can. Defeat the Deku Baba you come across and then do your thing with the pedestal here.

Return to the previous split and continue to the south, looking for a ledge below and on the left. Drop down here and dispatch the Spear Moblin Lv.2 and Rope here. In this location you will also find the third pedestal to activate.

Climb up the ledges to the main part of the forest and continue to the west to find the next pedestal in the middle of the path.

Continue to the right/east until you come across a Sword Moblin Lv.2. There is a half-buried **Treasure Chest** here with a Monster Stone. You will also find the final pedestal on the eastern side of this area.

With all six pedestals socketed, return to the glowing tablet, and interact with it. A scene will play, after which a path will open leading to the north.

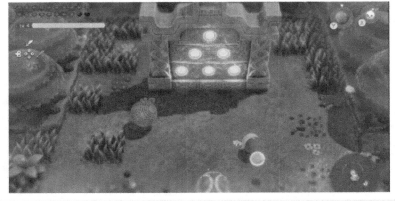

Note: The opening of this path will also dispel the illusion over the forest and your map will now return to normal, showing you the layout of the land.

Before continuing to the north, there are a couple of things we can do in the first here. The main one is picking up the most powerful combat **Echo** in the game. We will want to do this so that we have a bit of a weapon going forward (there is lots of combat in our near future!).

Head southwest from the pedestal and look for a patch of mud with some hoofprints in it This is our clue! Head in the direction of the hoofprints to find another mud puddle with more hoofprints. Continue to follow these until you reach a large muddy clearing (you can't just go there; you need to follow the hoofprints). Here you will encounter a Lynel.

The Lynel is a powerful centaur-like creature wielding a large sword and is able to zip around the area very quickly due to the whole, half-horse thing its got going on. It hits like a truck and can knock out multiple hearts, or kill even your toughest **Echoes** in a couple of hits, so be sure to summon your heavy hitters and be prepared to keep spawning them. After killing it, we can learn **Echo** – Lynel.

In the northwest corner of the area with the Lynel, you can climb up on top of the trees to find a raised ledge nearby with a suspicious looking collection of shrubs. Spin through the middle one to find a **Might Crystal**.

We can now follow the path that the tablet revealed to us to the north. After doing so you will come across the Deku Tree. Speak with it here and it will activate the elevator in front of it, transporting you down to an area below.

After exiting the elevator, continue to the north to watch a scene with Shadow Zelda. Once the scene has ended, there will be a glowing rift in the wall at the rear of the area. Interact with this.

Head on inside to the Stilled Ancient Ruins, which is where we can finally complete the main quest we picked up near the midpoint of the game - Rescuing the Hero Link.

RESCUING THE HERO LINK

"Rescuing the Hero Link" Walkthrough

❖ *How to Complete*

"Rescuing the Hero Link" is a story quest that will remain in the Adventure Log until the final dungeon in **Echo**es of Wisdom. You'll need to complete "Lands of the Goddesses" before this one, so your first goal should be to get rid of the giant rifts in Eldin Volcano, Holy Mount Lanayru, and Faron Wetlands. After you've received all three sanctions from the goddesses, you'll awaken in your room at Hyrule Castle. The one responsible for the rifts, Null, has created an **Echo** of Princess Zelda and plans to use it to claim the prime energy.

Go to Eternal Forest and speak with general Wright. You'll then need to activate the monument and place **Echo**es of the Ancient Orb in the pedestals around the Eternal Forest. Doing so will open a path deeper into the forest, where you'll meet the Great Deku Tree. Confront the fake Zelda, and the Triforce of Courage will open a gap to the Still World in search of Link. You will then have to traverse the Still World to fight the **Echo** Zelda. The easiest way to navigate the Still World is to use the Flying Tile **Echo**, but you'll likely have to fight some enemies along the way. The final Still World has sections of each region you've visited, such as lava columns from Eldin and icy floors from Holy Mount Lanayru.

Tip: You should swap Accessories as you go to make the terrain easier to navigate.

When you confront the **Echo** Zelda, you'll also find Link trapped in a crystal prison. You should use your strongest **Echo**es in this battle, such as the Lynel or Lv. 3 monsters. You can also shoot the **Echo** Zelda while she's in the air by using the Hero's Bow. When she falls stunned, use Swordfigher Mode to get in as many hits as you can.

After the fight, use Swordfighter Mode and shoot an arrow at Link's crystal prison. This will trigger a cutscene and "Rescuing the Hero Link" will be marked complete in your Adventure Log. You can then speak to Link to enter Null's Body, the final dungeon in the game. However, doing so will cause Zelda to lose Swordfigher Mode, as she'll return all of Link's equipment. For the last stretch of the game, you'll team up with Link and need to rely on your **Echo**es to fight.

Things to Do Before "Rescuing the Hero Link"

❖ *How to Prepare for Final Dungeon*

❖ *Might Crystals and Heart Pieces*

If you haven't already done so, you should fully upgrade Swordfighter Mode. This means getting a max energy bar (lv. 4) and upgrading the sword, bow, and bombs to level 3. If you're missing **Might Crystal**s, then leave the Still World and start working on any remaining side quests or minigames. You should also look around Hyrule, since many **Might Crystal**s are hidden in tall grass or buried in the ground. If you have the Might Bell, equipping it will make it easier to track down **Might Crystal**s.

Make sure you've done all 50 side quests and the minigames to get Heart Pieces. You should try to get max hearts before facing off against Null. It also won't hurt to visit the Smoothie Shop and create smoothies using a Golden Egg as one of the ingredients. Golden smoothies heal 15+ hearts and can be combined with a Tough Mango to give Zelda some extra defense.

❖ *Accessories*

- Complete "Let's Play a Game" and "Cotton-Candy Hunt" to get the Curious Charm. "Let's Play a Game" is found at the Eastern Ruins in Eastern Hyrule Field. "Cotton-Candy Hunt" requires the completion of "Let's Play a Game" and "A Rift in Faron Wetlands." If you've done these already, then speak to the Deku Scrub near the totem pole by the well you used to escape the Scrubton prison. You'll then need to track down the same monster you fought in "Let's Play a Game," only now, Smog has moved to the Faron Wetlands Ruins. To reach them, head north from the Deku Scrub's house that was swallowed by the rift. The Curious Charm will reduce the damage that Zelda takes.

- If you didn't grab it before Jabul Waters Rift, you should purchase the Zora's Flippers (350 **Rupees**) from the River Zora Village.

- You can also do the quest "The Zora Child's Fate" for the Zora Scale, which increases Zelda's Dive Time. This side quest can be accepted by speaking to the River Zora child by the waterfall in the River Zora Village.

❖ *Power Up Tri*

Another thing you should do is finish clearing up any remaining rifts. If you look at your map, you should be able to tell if there are small rifts remaining in Hyrule. These aren't required to complete the game, but if you want to raise Tri's level to 11, you're going to need to do them. The optional rifts are:

- * Stilled Carrot Patch
- Stilled Northern Sanctuary
- Stilled Lake Hylia
- Stilled Hebra Mountain Passage
- * Stilled Southern Hyrule Field
- Stilled Eastern Zora River
- Stilled Western Eldin Volcano
- Stilled Lower Suthorn Forest
- Stilled Heart Lake

* These rifts will only appear in side quests. The Carrot Patch spawns in "Impa's Gift" and the Southern Hyrule Field rift appears in "From the Heart."

Aside from Stilled Lake Hylia and Stilled Northern Sanctuary, all optional rifts can be completed after clearing "Still Missing" main quest. You'll gain a small boost of experience and **Might Crystals** by completing the rifts.

FInally, since Zelda won't be able to use Swordfighter Mode against the final boss, you should learn the following **Echo**es before returning Link's equipment:

	Where to Find
Lynel	Eternal Forest - Follow hooftracks in the dirt (south of the **Waypoint Stone** in Eternal Forest) to track down the Lynel.
Darknut Lv. 3	Faron Wetlands - In a cave far east of Scrubton's Smoothie Shop.
Lizalfos Lv. 3	Faron Wetlands - In a cave north of the Heart Lake.
Sword Moblin Lv. 3	Eternal Forest or Mount Lanayru - In the western clearing in Eternal Forest. - In the western cave by the frozen lake with the Waypoint/fast-travel stone.
Chompfin	Zora Cove or Stilled Jabul Waters (Temple) - Chompfins swim around the abandoned ship in western Zora Cove. - You'll find two Chompfins in the Jabul Waters Temple.

Null's Body

Upon arriving in the dungeon, proceed through the first door. You will see Link in the distance. Follow him along the set path here and into the second door.

As you enter, you will be set upon by rift enemies. Here you will get to see just how good Link is with his weapons – he will be able to do quite a bit of damage! Pull out some high levelled summons to help him out and defeat all the enemies as they appear (I encountered 3x Boarboblins, 3x Keese, and a Lynel). Once you have cleared them all out, the next door will open, allowing you to proceed further.

In the next room some vines will pop up separating us from Link. He will continue to the north on the left side of the room, whilst we will need to head through the north door on the right side of the room.

Here you will come across a pair of locked doors. To open these, look on the far, right side of the area to spot a glowing orb. We need to hit this to open the doors. Either spawn some flying enemies and get them to target it, or spawn a Beamos or other projectile enemy on the platform floating opposite the orb and have them do the same. Once the door is open we can proceed.

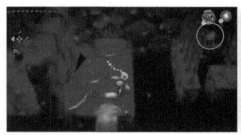 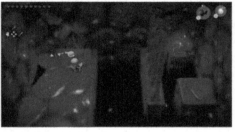

The next room is another fight room. Link will face off against a Freezard, Darknut and Spar Moblin, whilst we need to deal with a Wolfos, Tektite and Giant Gaponga Flower. Summon a high-level **Echo** to have it clear out your side of the room before sending **Echo**es through the bars running up the centre of the room to help Link out (or if he finishes first, he can use his arrows to help you out).

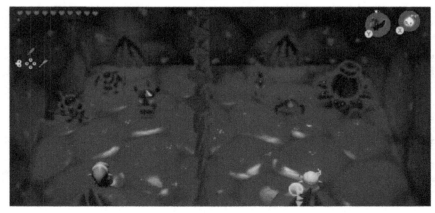

Defeating the enemies will have the northern door open. Head on through and continue down the stairs you come across to reach a side-scroll area.

In this first room, you can either use bond and follow to have the moving platform take you across the first gap, or alternatively build yourself a bridge across.

When you reach the second gap, wait until the upper platform lowers opposite your location and bind it to hold it in place. Next, wait for the lower platform to start heading to the left and drop down to it. When you reach the left wall, use follow to have the upper block carry you up the narrow shaft here to the next ledge. You can also use a Strandtula to create a rope up the narrow gap if the first option is a bit tricky!

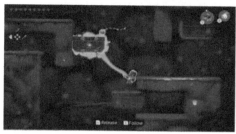 

On the next screen across, have some **Echo**es dispatch the Gustmaster below and then summon a flying **Echo** and grab it so that you can glide across the gap.. or alternatively, make a bridge over to the left-hand ledge. Continue down the ladder and defeat two more Gustmasters on the left and then proceed across the gap.

After a short jog you will come across some vertical wind vents and, you guessed it, another Gustmaster. Clear out the enemy and then summon and grab a flying enemy. Make your way to the upper wind vent and from the top of this glide down to the platform the Gustmaster had occupied. From here we can spawn a Strandtula or two to the left and climb the webbing up and to the left to reach the next ledge.

With this puzzle sorted, climb the nearby ladder to exit the area. You've just completed the final side-scroll area in the game, give yourself a pat on the back... but not for too long as we still have work to do!

After exiting head to the right to reach another puzzle room where you are separated from Link.

In this room your goal is to get link to the upper ledge on the far right, where some rift webs that his weapons can destroy appear, behind which is a pressure plate which will open the doors.

There are a couple of ways to solve this problem. It is possible to bind Link through the bars and maneuver him up to the upper platform. However, I had more luck spawning a

Platboom into Link's room by the back wall and having him ride it up to the ledge above.

After solving the puzzle, head through the now open door to be reunited with Link. Continue through the next door and then follow the lengthy walkway all the way to the north in the next room. Head through the door here.

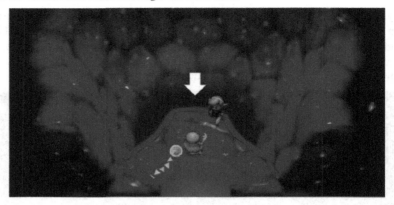

At this point, we will be in a small room with a giant pit. When you are ready to go, jump into the pit. After landing, a scene will play, and you will encounter the final boss.

❖ Boss: Null

This is it, the final boss in the game! Null appears as a large, spherical creature with three taloned arms sprouting from its central core. This fight is quite a bit longer than the others you may have fought thus far and takes place over three distinct phases. The good news is you should have a ton of high-level **Echoes** by now and Link is no slouch when it comes to damage output.

Initially Null will move around the arena, slamming its arms into the ground, creating small hand-like projectiles that will race along the ground towards you. You will need to run to the side to avoid these.

The boss's weak points are the red sections of its 'arms' linking the talons to its core. Link is pretty good at getting in there and knowing exactly what to do, so play support and summon some **Echoes** to back him up. After destroying all three arms, Null will fall to the ground stunned for a short time – make sure you summon your high-level **Echoes** beside it as this is your opportunity to inflict damage.

After doing this for the first time, Null will vanish into the walls of the arena. At this point, the taloned arms will emerge from the walls at random before sinking back into the walls and re-appearing elsewhere. During this part of the fight, the boss can perform those very same slam and claw projectile attacks... and again we will need to target ad destroy its arms. Note that you can target and bind these, so when you see Link or your **Echo**es near one, be sure to grab it and pull it out of the wall to expose its weak spot to make targeting of it easier for your allies.

Destroying all three arms will have the boss jump back out of the wall and revert to its initial state. Again, take out its arms to return it to the walls. We will need to continue damaging it both in the walls and out in the open as it transitions between each time you clear out its arms. Note that from its second adventure into the walls, in addition to the slam attacks it can also place residual pools of purply death fluid on the ground. This will remain for a short time before dissipating, so steer clear!

Once you have dealt enough damage to it, a scene will play. At this point Zelda and Link will be separated, and we will end up in a side-scroll area.

During this stage of the fight, we will be underwater. Null will swim to the right and we need to follow it. As you go you will want to pay attention and swim through the large bubbles that appear occasionally to replenish Zelda's air meter. They blend in a little with the background, so keep your eyes peeled.

In this underwater phase, Null will have several tail-like growths trailing after its main core, each holding one of Tri's friends. We need to attack these to release them and deal damage to the boss. Your best friend here is the Chompfin **Echo** and with Tri at max level you should be able to summon two of them at once.

Of course, its not that simple though as throughout the fight, Null will summon Vocavor, the boss from Jabul Ruins. Whilst we can't actually attack this, it will create water vortexes which we will need to maneuver around. As you progress, you will also encounter additional rift enemies including Biri and falling Sea Urchins, so make sure you avoid them.

After dealing enough damage to the boss, a scene will play, and we will end up back in the original arena with Link where the third and final phase will begin.

The final phase of the fight is similar to the first, although the boss will now have five claws instead of three and can move around a lot quicker. Much like the first phase, our goal is to target and destroy all the limbs so that we can have free rein to attack the core. The boss will then retreat into the walls and pop its arms out in random places to attack. It will then alternate between the two states.

During this phase when out in the open, the boss will pick up a few notable attacks, many of which include summoning rift versions of the many boss monsters you have fought throughout the game. Initially you will get the following two (more will join later):

● Seismic Talus – This will appear at the centre of the room hold its arms out straight and perform a spinning attack.

● Mogryph – A couple of Mogryph clones will appear around the outside of the arena and each of them will summon sand vortexes.

When it disappears into the walls we will have a couple of new things to note. Firstly, rather than the slam attacks from the first phase, the boss will this time summon **Echo**es (Moblins, Boarboblins, Lizalfos and Darknut). A dark shadow will also appear on the floor and will come after Zelda – after a short time a hand will erupt from the floor where the shadow is, attempting to grab you. As long as you keep moving though you should be able to avoid it.

After returning from the walls, Null will pick up a couple of additional boss moves which he will use when he is in the room with you, which he can use in addition to the Seismic Talus and Mogryph abilities he used earlier. These include:

- Ganon – Three clones of Ganon will appear around the room and will perform Ganon's dashing stab attack using his spear one after another. This will increase to six clones before the end of the fight.

- Skorchill – A pair of Skorchill clones will spawn and perform Skorchill's spinning attack that has him zipping around the room at high speed. The number of clones will increase to three towards the end of the fight.

- Gohma & Mogryph – Gohma and Mogryph will appear together. Gohma will spawn on the back wall and shoot webs down onto the arena floor. You will quickly want to run around and summon an Ignizol onto each to burn it away ASAP as a pair of Mogyrph clones will then show up and fire of a pair of sand vortexes.

- Ganon & Seismic Talus – two Ganon clones will spawn to use their stab attacks, then the Seismic Talus will appear at the centre of the arena for a spin attack, followed by two more lunging stabs from Ganon clones.

Essentially though the strategy remains the same – avoid the attacks, wail on the arms and then the core when it is exposed. After dealing enough damage, Null will collapse at the centre of the arena with the Prime Energy it has swallowed exposed.

At this point we need to use Bind to grab this and pull it. Mash the button prompt that appears on the screen to yank it out of Null. This will end the fight.

Following the fight, you'll be treated to a few scenes and the credits will roll. You've gone and saved Hyrule, Huzzahs are in order! Well done!

Note: Once the credits have run their course, you can choose the continue option from the main menu. Here you will find that your save file here is now marked with a star, indicating that you have completed the game. Reloading this save will place you in the area just before the final dungeon, allowing us to return to Hyrule and round up any missing stuff.

There are a few new things to note:

- Firstly, your map and journal will be updated allowing you to see how much you have left to find.

  - press Y on the map to bring up your collectibles and see how many Pieces of Heart, Stamps and **Might Crystal**s you have to go.

  - On the **Echo**es page of the journal, the number of **Echo**es unlocked out of 127 will be shown in the upper right.

  - On the Quest page you will see the number of completed Side-quests out of 50.

- If you have not found all the **Echo**es yet (although you should have them all if you have been following along!), you can speak with the Deku Tree, and he will tell you the regions where you can find any that are missing.

238

SIDE QUESTS

WORLD

Recipes, Please!

Smoothie and Potion making has a side quest connected to it in Zelda: **Echo**es of Wisdom, called 'Recipes, Please'. This quest is divided into two parts - the first challenges you to create 10 recipes and then the second asks you to make an additional 20 recipes. This means you need to make 30 Smoothie, including the Potion, recipes in total.

After making 10 recipes, you'll be awarded with the Survey Scope accessory. Equipping the Survey Scope will make ingredients and Monster Stones appear a little more often when you're either defeating monsters and breaking objects. This will make it easier to build up your ingredient collections for making more recipes.

Once you've made a total of 30 Smoothie recipes, you'll get the Survey Binoculars accessory. The Survey Binoculars have an even higher chance of making ingredients and Monster Stones appear during your adventures.

You don't need to visit a specific Business Scrub to start or complete 'Recipes, Please'. Instead, you can simply continue this quest whenever you run into any Business Scrub.

SUTHORN PRARIE

Finding the Flying Plant

Location: Speak with the man near the lower, left house in Suthorn Village after completing Dungeon - Suthorn Ruins.

This fellow wants us to retrieve a flying plant from somewhere in the Suthorn Forest to the east. Now if you were following our walkthrough, we will have picked this up already and is in fact the Peahat. Simply pull out a Peahat **Echo** in front of him.

If you do not have the Peahat **Echo**, we can make a quick detour to go grab it. From the Warppoint Stone closest to the Suthorn Ruins, head south to find a lower path we can drop down to. Defeat the Spear Moblin here and you will find a cave. Examine the torches either side of the door for **Echo** – Brazier.

Enter the cave here. Continue upwards and you will encounter a Peahat. These plant enemies have thorns around their base and will spin at high speed whilst converging on your position. Wait for their spikes to retract and they stop for a moment before sending out your **Echo**es to attack. Defeat this and then examine it for **Echo** - Peahat.

Once you have the Peahat, simply summon an **Echo** of it in front of the quest giver to complete the side quest.

- Reward/s: Might Stone

The Blocked Road

Location: Approach the ruins in northeastern part of the Suthorn Prairie. A fellow named Verley will ask for help.

After starting this side-quest, look behind the NPC to see the roadblock that he was speaking about. It is made up of both boulders and wooden boxes. We want to move these elements out of the area using Bind so that they are no longer blocking the road.

Note that you can burn the wooden boxes, but you will still need to move the boulders by hand. As long as you grab the lower item in each of the three stacks here, you can move the entire stack at once, so you'll only need to make three trips.

Once you have cleared the road, speak with the fellow once again to complete the side quest.

- Reward/s: Rupee x20

Up a Wall

Location: Approach the ruins in northeastern part of the Suthorn Prairie. A fellow named Verley will ask for help.

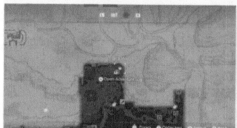 

After approaching this area and receiving the quest, all you need to do is simply defeat the pair of Spear Moblins at the base of the ruins. Use any combination of **Echo**es you have, or use Swordfighter mode.

Once they have been defeated, another scene will play and we will chat with Verley to end the side-quest.

GERUDO DESERT

Beetle Ballyhoo

Location: Speak with Raslett, the Gerudo outside the house left of the General Store in Gerudo Town after completing main quest - Still Missing.

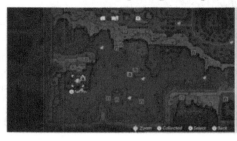 

It turns out this particular Gerudo warrior has been sent on a patrol to deal with some beetles and beetle Mounds but is terrified of Beetles. She asks that we go in her stead, and since we have nothing better to do, let us do just that.

To find the Beetle Mounds, we need to head for a cave to the northeast of Gerudo Town. It is located just east from the **Waypoint Stone** by the entrance to the Ancestor's Cave of Rest, and is just west of a Borblin camp.

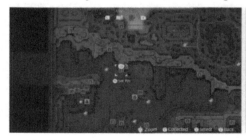 

Inside the cave, head to the right to encounter Beetles. These things will pour out of the Beetle Mounds nearby and will continue to do so until you remove them. Pull out an **Echo** or two to hold them back (Peahat is good). Head up the ramp here and destroy the mounds. Afterwards, if you have yet to do so, you can learn both **Echo** – Beetle and **Echo** – Beetle Mound.

Destroying all of the Beetle Mounds will also update your objectives. Return to Gerudo Town and speak with the quest giver once again to complete the side quest.

- Reward/s: Accessory – Heart Barrette

Dohna's Challenge

Location: Speak with Dohna on the eastern side of Gerudo Town after completing main quest - Still Missing.

After accepting this quest, we will be testing out Dohna's security arrangements. Here we will have the goal of sneaking into Gerudo Town palace's treasury and stealing the goodies inside. We can find the entrance on the western side of the roof of the palace building.

There are two ways to enter the treasury. We can enter via the door here, or alternatively can climb to the ledge above the door and use a Holmill on the patch of sand here. This will create a hole we can drop down into which will put us roughly halfway through the area.

Inside the treasury, we will be presented with a stealth challenge. We need to move past all the patrolling guards to reach the end.

If entering from the door, the first guard will patrol in a square pattern around a central cabinet. Follow her and continue to the right. The second guard patrols up and down the room. Wait until she walks towards the top of the screen before running across the mouth of the path she walks.

The next two guards patrol around a pair of square cabinets in synch. Note that if you used the Holmill, you would drop onto the right-hand cabinet here.

To continue, we need to go to the right and up some stairs. Before doing so however, sneak by the pair of guards cutting laps of the cabinets here. At the very northern end of this area, you will find a **Treasure Chest** containing Chilly Cactus x10.

Head back south and then to the east and continue up the stairs. At the top, there will be another patroller, this time taking an L-shaped route. Follow her and then continue north when able to do so.

The final guard is standing in front of the room with the **Treasure Chest** we want to loot. Create a pot **Echo** and throw it to one side to distract the guard. While she goes to investigate, quickly run in and loot the **Treasure Chest** for **Outfit** – Silk Pajamas.

After looting this chest, we will be ported back outside for one final chat with Dohna. Once the chat ends, the side quest will be completed.

- Reward/s: **Outfit** – Silk Pajamas

Elusive Tumbleweeds

Location: Speak with the Gerudo on the western side of Gerudo Town..

After starting this side-quest, you will need to track down one of the tumbleweeds that you have been seeing blowing around the desert and bring it to her. To do so, you will need to grab one using Bind and then drag it back to the quest giver.

You will find tumbleweeds all over the desert, but the best place to do so is just south of Gerudo Town (less walking back!). The other thing to note is that the tumbleweeds are incredibly fragile. If they touch anything on the way back they will fall to pieces, and you will need to go grab another.

After nabbing one, enter the main gate to Gerudo Town, left at the top of the stairs, immediately up the next set of stairs, left again and then up to the quest giver. This is the quickest and easiest route.

After bringing her a tumbleweed, the side quest will be completed.

- Reward/s: Might Stone x2

Gerudo Tag Training

Location: Speak with the Gerudo in the northwest part of Gerudo Town, outside of the left hand door leading into the palace.

In this side quest, we essentially need to run after and 'tag' the Gerudo. She is however very fast, and you will not be able to keep up with her. If you do chase her however, you will discover that she will do a large lap of the town.

To catch her we want to take some time to create a roadblock somewhere along her route I placed three boulders by the top of the entry stairs. We then want to chase her into the roadblock. She will pause briefly, allowing you to catch and tag her.

After tagging her, a conversation will play out after which you will complete the side quest.

- Reward/s: Chilly Cactus x6

245

The Flying Tile

Location: Speak with the Gerudo on the right at the top of the stairs at the entrance to Gerudo Town.

This Gerudo warrior wants us to investigate what she describes as a flying tile. The thing she is talking about is in fact an enemy type called a Flying Tile. We will not encounter these until you reach the Gerudo Sanctum dungeon at the end of the areas – so be sure to learn an **Echo** when you do!

Once you have the **Echo**, simply pull out an **Echo** of a Flying Tile in front of her. Doing so will complete the side-quest.

- Reward/s: Rupee x50

Tornado Ghost?

Location: Speak with the Gerudo on the right at the top of the stairs at the entrance to Gerudo Town.

This lady wants us to investigate a tornado ghost that she spotted. Fortunately, if you were following our walkthrough, we will have picked this up already before arriving in Gerudo Town and we can complete the quest right away. The thing she is talking about is in fact a Tornado enemy. Simply pull out an **Echo** of a Tornado in front of her.

If you do not have the Tornado **Echo**, we can find one in the Gerudo Sanctum dungeon, or in the eastern part of Gerudo Desert when the sandstorm is active. You can also find them in a room at the end of the cave in the ruins south of the Oasis.

Once you have the Tornado, simply summon an **Echo** of it in front of the quest giver to complete the side quest.

- Reward/s: Fresh Milk x10

Wild Sandstorms

Location: Speak with the Gerudo guards in the barracks of the palace in Gerudo Town after completing main quest - Still Missing.

Note: To get this side quest to appear, you must have also tracked down and defeated both Lamola mini-bosses in the region – one in the western desert and one in the eastern desert. They are found in the following locations:

- *Western Desert – just northwest of the Stamp platform west of the Oasis.*
- *Eastern Desert – just north of the **Waypoint Stone** on the eastern side of the desert.*

After accepting the side quest, we will need to find and eliminate one final Lanmola. This Lanmola is located in the eastern desert, in the same location as the previous Lanmola had been north of the **Waypoint Stone**. Approach the bubbling sand to fight it.

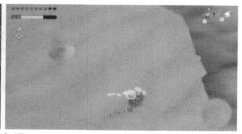

❖ *Boss: Lanmola*

The Lanmola is a large, centipede like enemy that will initially cover the ground in quicksand, yep the entire arena will be quicksand this time, unlike the previous encounters where there were little islands of safety. You will need to constantly jump, or use Accessory – Gerudo Sandals to prevent Zelda from sinking.

*Additionally, this Lanmola will constantly have additional monsters helping it out – both Sand Piranhas and Aruroda will make appearances. This makes it much more difficult than the other Lanmolas. It is important that you keep some **Echo**es of your own, preferably flying ones (so they don't need to contend with the quicksand), out to deal with them whilst you focus on the boss itself.*

Outside of the arena and the additional monsters though, the fight is essentially the same as previous. The boss will bury under the ground, move towards you, and then emerge from the ground, throwing a collection of boulders about the area before diving back underground again.

To defeat it, take note of the hook-like tail that it has, this is the key to victory. As Lanmola moves away from you, you want to grab its tail with bind and then pull backwards. This will pluck it out of the ground and have it collapse on its side. Use this opportunity to run in and wail on it using Swordfighter mode.

We essentially need to repeat this process until it dies.

Defeating the Lanmola will have it drop a bunch of **Rupees** and a **Piece of Heart**. Huzzah!

At this point, we can also head on back to Gerudo Town and speak with the bickering guards in the armory to report your success and complete the side quest.

- Reward/s: Accessory – Gold Sash

HYRULE FIELD

Let's Play a Game

Location: Speak with Sago by the entrance to the Eastern Temple in Hyrule Field, East.

After accepting the quest, head on into the temple. We have a little mini-dungeon ahead of us. Huzzah!

In the first room you will encounter your first Spark enemies. These things will travel around a set path on walls, or blocks (in this case blocks). If you get touched by one, they will electrocute you, dealing quite a bit of damage (mercifully, not forcing you to drop your weapons like in Tears of the Kingdom though!). We want to kill one of these (Sea Urchins are king!) for **Echo – Spark**.

Continue through the next door. In this area, you will see a golden receptacle in the upper left. We need to get all three of the Sparks in this room to enter the receptacle. The one getting around on the outer wall should do it by itself, leaving the two in the middle of the room.

Spawn some boulders to create an extension of the central wall out to the socket to have the Sparks jump inside, or alternatively just grab them with bind and pop them into the receptacle. Once all three have been captured, the door will open.

The next room has two doors. An open door on the right and a locked door on the left.

Enter the door on the right first. There will be a fence running the length of the room midway across and two Octoroks and a receptacle on the far side. Use your ability to summon **Echoes** at range and spawn some monsters to take care of the Octoroks. Note that you want to try and not disturb the wooden boxes here (they will direct Sparks into the receptacle as is).

Once the enemies are dead, send a Spark along the bottom wall (summon it through the fence) and another along the top wall of the room. They both should travel around and enter the receptacle. This will have a **Treasure Chest** spawn holding a Purple Rupee.

Return to the previous room. Let's get that left hand door unlocked.

On the rear wall of this room, you will see a ramp. Move the boulder away from the bottom of the ramp and position it on the other side. The Spark doing laps around the perimeter of the room will head up the ramp and into the receptacle. Place another Spark **Echo** by the base of the ramp to have it do the same, opening the door.

After entering the now unlocked door, there is a **Treasure Chest** with two Sparks patrolling around it. Use bind to pull this out of the danger zone and loot it for Rock Salt x5

Use the nearby ladder to descend into a side-scrolling area.

Head to the right, defeating the Sparks on the platform ahead (note there is also a level 2 Caromadillo on the platform below). On the next screen over, there will be more Sparks. This time around they are patrolling platforms and will be moving in and out of the pool of water below. Swim carefully beneath the first Spark to find a **Treasure Chest** on the floor. It holds a Purple Rupee.

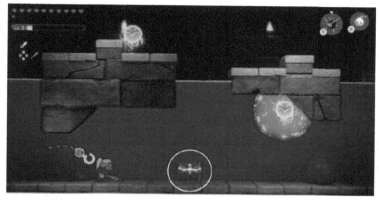

Swim up and out of the water through the opening in the crates provided to the right of the next patrolling Spark platform. Continue down the ladder to reach another room. Head through the next door for a boss fight.

❖ *Boss: Smog*

Smog is a large, sentient electrical cloud (yes, you read that right). This thing behaves in much the same way as the Sparks we have encountered throughout the lead up to the fight have done. It will stick to walls and blocks and patrol around them. If you touch it, you will get zapped. So don't touch it! The boss will also regularly fire out electrical projectiles which we will want to avoid where possible.

Our goal here is to damage the boss. His movement is a bit erratic however, so you can spawn boulders to extend the existing walls here and trap him in a smaller area to make it easier. I had a lot of success spawning a bunch of Pathblades, but Sea Urchins will work as well. Note that it is immune to Sparks, so don't bother with those.

After damaging him a few times, he will split up into three smaller clouds. These will then take off and act independently of one another as they move around the room. Just like Smog, touching them is a no-no and they will occasionally fire off some electrical discharge.

During this stage, we need to get all three clouds back together to re-form Smog. Use boulders to trap them in a smaller area until they merge. This can be a bit tricky as they all have a mind of their own.

Once you have merged all the clouds back into one, Smog will reappear and will attack as he did preciously – zipping around the room and launching electrical projectiles. He moves a bit faster this time around, but otherwise acts the same.

The same pattern will repeat once again. Again, hitting him enough will have him split up again, this time into five clouds. Again, round them all up and get Smog to re-form and then take down Smog once he has returned. Defeating him this time will end the fight.

For defeating this boss, you will be rewarded with a bunch of **Rupees** and a **Piece of Heart**. A portal will appear as well, allowing you to teleport back to the start of the area.

With all that done, exit the temple and chat with Sago outside. Report your success to him to complete the side quest.

- Reward/s: Accessory – Ancient Charm

Runaway Horse

Location: Speak with the farmer at Hyrule Ranch..

This side quest requires us to track down a missing horse and return it to the farmer at the ranch. The good news is it is not all that far from the ranch itself, so it will not take us long to do so. Head to the west until you find a small body of water with an island at its centre. Atop this island is the horse we are looking for.

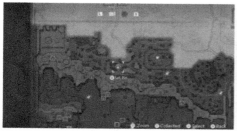 

Jump down to the island and create a path out – a bed should do the trick. Once you have done so, ride the horse back to the ranch. Note that the horse will automatically jump obstacles the same height as what Zelda can jump, so don't bother pressing the jump button, as it won't do anything!

Once you have gotten the horse off the island, ride back to Hyrule Ranch and park it in front of the farmer. This will trigger a brief chat and the side quest will be completed.

- Reward/s: Horse Riding

Automaton Engineer Dampe

- Location: Find Dampe in Hyrule Field just northeast of the Hyrule Ranch.

After spotting Dampe, you will need to defeat the nearby Crow that he was yelling at. Doing so will have him speak with you again and encourage Zelda to visit him in his house in the eastern part of Hyrule Field. He'll even mark its location for us, what a guy!

From the **Waypoint Stone** at Hyrule Castle town, follow the path leading to the east and south until you reach the bridge leading north. After crossing the bridge, continue to the north and through a large field occupied by a collection of large boulders. The area is occupied by several Octoroks and Sword Moblins. You will find a Red Rupee atop one of the stones here.

Further to the north you will find a bridge leading across the river on the left. Ignore this and continue to the north, defeating some Crows as you go.

Eventually, you will come across another Moblin Camp. After clearing the camp, follow the path to the east. You will reach a small, lower area inhabited by a Guay and some Caromadillos. The path on the right side of the area leading to the north will lead you straight to a **Waypoint Stone**.

In this clearing, you will also find Dampe's house. Here we can proceed inside. Have a chat with Dampe here and he will hand over Twisted Pumpkin x5 before telling you about his automatons, little critters he can make that we will be able to use out in the field.

Following the initial chat, we need to give him some inspiration using **Echo**es that we have acquired throughout our journey so far. Fortunately, if you have been following the walkthrough to this point, you should have both! We need to summon the **Echo**es on the metal plate here so that he can have a looksie.

The first creature he is after is "creature with the big eye, the sort that's always jumping around". The **Echo** he is after is a Tektite. If you have yet to find one, you can find these in the river just west of Dampe's hut, or all the way up and down the Zora River in Jabul Waters.

The second is "something that shoots hot smoke out of its backside to blast forward". The **Echo** that he wants to see for this one is a Mothtula. We will have grabbed this **Echo** whilst exploring Dungeon - Gerudo Sanctum.

Once you have summoned both, he will get to work and create an automaton for us. He will reward us with Automaton – Techtite, and a Clockwork Key.

Note: We will now be able to summon Automatons. Hold Left to open the Automaton menu and select the Automaton of choice. Summon this with Y and then wind it up to let it go!

Following this side-quest, you can read Dampe's journal to unlock additional side-quests for him which will unlock further Automatons. The first one available is - Explosions Galore!.

- **Reward/s**: Automatons

Explosions Galore!

- Location: Read Dampe's journal in Dampe's Hut after completing Automaton Engineer Dampe.

 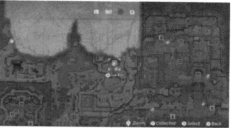

Following the initial chat with Dampe after reading his journal, we need to give him some inspiration using **Echo**es that we have acquired throughout our journey so far. We will not be able to complete this side-quest when we initially pick it up, but once you have completed the story dungeon on Eldin Volcano, we are good to go.

The first creature he is after is "a creature that spits stones out of its mouth". The **Echo** he is after here is an Octorok. If you have yet to find one, you can find these in bodies of water Suthorn Prairie, Hyrule Field and the Zora River in Jabul Waters.

The second clue is a "there's a guy up on Eldin Volcano who crafts fireworks, so you might check there." The **Echo** that he wants to see for this one is a Firework. In order to get this **Echo**, you need to complete the side quest - The Fireworks Artist.

Once you have summoned both, he will get to work and create an automaton for us. He will reward us with Automaton.

After completing this side quest, you will unlock a set of three follow ups from Dampe's journal:

- Performance Artist!
- Endless Stomach!
- Chop 'Em In Two!

Reward/s: Automaton - Tocktorok

Performance Artist!

- Location: Read Dampe's journal in Dampe's Hut after completing Explosions Galore!.

 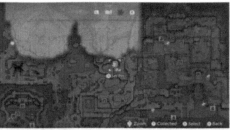

Following the initial chat with Dampe after reading his journal, we need to give him some inspiration using **Echo**es that we have acquired throughout our journey so far.

The first creature he is after is a "jiggly monster with cute little eyes". The **Echo** he is after is a Zol. If you have yet to find one, you can find these all over Hyrule Field, Suthorn Beach and Suthorn Forest.

The second is not an **Echo**, but a key item. The clue he gives is "something melodic around Hyrule Ranch". The item we are after is the Prismatic Music Box and to get this, we will need to compete in and complete the Middle Course of the Flag Races at Hyrule Ranch.

Note that to unlock this, you must have Zelda's horse, which means you will need to complete both of the Runaway Horse and Impa's Gift side quests. Additionally, you will need to complete the Short Course to get the Medium Course to unlock. Once you have done so, beat the Medium Course under the target time to receive the key item.

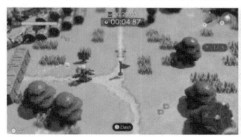 

Once you have summoned the Zol and spoken with Dampe, chosen the "I want an automaton" option and handed over the Prismatic Music Box, he will get to work and create an automaton for us.

Reward/s: Automaton - Gizmol

Endless Stomach!

- Location: Read Dampe's journal in Dampe's Hut after completing Explosions Galore!.

 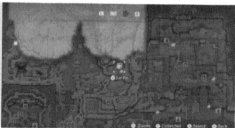

Following the initial chat with Dampe after reading his journal, we need to give him some inspiration using **Echo**es that we have acquired throughout our journey so far.

The first creature he is after is a "creature that swallows things whole with its massive jaws". The **Echo** he is after is either a Bio Deku or a Deku Baba (both will work). If you have yet to find one, you can find these in some caves in Jabul Waters, along with the Dungeon – Suthorn Ruins, Dungeon – Jabul Ruins and Dungeon – Hyrule Castle.

The second is not an **Echo**, but a key item. The clue he gives is "...a special part to strengthen its ability to clamp down on things... and the guy who spreads acorns has just such a tool". The item we are after is the Steel Trap and to get this, we will need to compete in and complete one of the Acorn Guy's Acorn Gathering mini-games.

There are several locations to try out the Acorn Gathering mini-game, but the one that gives us what we need is the variation found on the far, western side of Hyrule Field. Just north of the Gerudo Desert. We will need to complete this challenge with a time under 60 seconds to earn the Steel Trap.

Once you have summoned the Bio Deku/Deku Baba and spoken with Dampe, chosen the "I want an automaton" option and handed over the Steel Trap, he will get to work and create an automaton for us.

Reward/s: Automaton - High-Teku Baba

Chop 'Em In Two!

- Location: Read Dampe's journal in Dampe's Hut after completing Explosions Galore!.

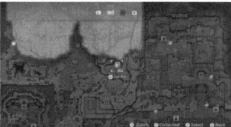

Following the initial chat with Dampe after reading his journal, we need to give him some inspiration using **Echo**es that we have acquired throughout our journey so far.

The first creature he is after is a "monster with a sword who fights alongside others". The **Echo** he is after is a Sword Moblin. These can be found in Moblin Camps across Hyrule Field... so you should have one already!

The second is not an **Echo**, but a key item. The clue he gives is "...a special weapon. I heard the leader of the dojo in Kakariko Village has a rare sword." The item we are after is the Heirloom Katana and to get this, we will need to compete in and complete six challenges in the Slumber Dojo in Kakariko Village.

Once you have summoned the Sword Moblin and spoken with Dampe, chosen the "I want an automaton" option and handed over the Heirloom Katana, he will get to work and create an automaton for us.

Reward/s: Automaton - Roboblin

Get Rich Quick!

- Location: Read Dampe's journal in Dampe's Hut after completing Performance Artist!, Endless Stomach! and Chop 'Em In Two!.

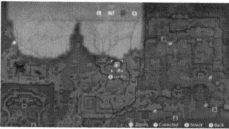

Following the initial chat with Dampe after reading his journal, we need to give him some inspiration using **Echo**es that we have acquired throughout our journey so far.

The first creature he is after is a Crow. These can be found in Hyrule Field or by the entrance to Gerudo Desert from Suthorn Prairie. There will also be one where you found Dampe in Hyrule Field initially... so you should have one already!

The second is not an **Echo**, but a key item. The clue he gives "I'll need a real special flashy somethin'. Speakin' of, I think I met a Gerudo who's got a real shiny thing... If memory serves, she was researching something at the oasis in Gerudo Desert." The item we are after is the Golden Fan.

To attain the Golden Fan, we need to head for the Oasis in Gerudo Desert. Here we will need to partake in the Mango Rush mini-game. You will need to complete the Radiant Seed variant of the mini-game. To unlock this, you must first complete the Standard Seed difficulty level.

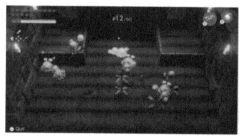

Once you have summoned the Crow and spoken with Dampe, chosen the "I want an automaton" option and handed over the Golden Fan, he will get to work and create an automaton for us.

Reward/s: Automaton - Goldfinch

HYRULE CASTLE

A Curious Child

- Location: Speak with the child by the lower, left house in Hyrule Castle Town.

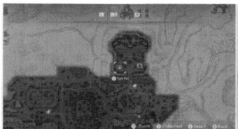

After speaking with the child, we will discover that he has a fondness for Zols which we need to assist him with by bringing him samples to swoon over. There are three Zols in total that the boy wants to see, and we will need to learn and summon **Echo**es of all three different Zols for him to complete the quest.

The first is a regular Zol. You will have come across one of these on Suthorn Beach earlier in the game (and the game would have prompted you to catch one), but if not they can also be found in Suthorn Prairie. The second type of Zol the boy is after is the fiery variant - an Ignizol. Again, if you have been following our walkthrough, you will have one by now. If not, you will find these in a couple of caves in the Suthorn Forest, Suthorn Ruins dungeon and in a cave on the western side of the Zora Cove in the Jabul waters area.

Finally, the boy wants to see a Hydrozol, the water-based Zol type. The closest place to find one of these is in the Jabul Waters area where they can be found in a cave on the western side of the Zora Cove. Note that the boy will not be happy with a regular Hydrozol, instead you will need to place it in the nearby fountain so that it increases in size. Drop the giant Hydrozol in front of him to satisfy his request.

Once you found and summoned all three **Echo**es for the boy, the quest will come to an end.

Reward/s: **Might Crystal**

An Out-There Zol

Location: Speak with the child by the lower, left house in Hyrule Castle Town after completing both A Curious Child and Performance Artist! side quests.

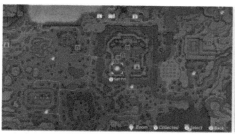 

After speaking with the child, we will discover that he has a fondness for Zols which we still have not satisfied after showing him the first three. Fortunately, upon completing Performance Artist! for Dampe, we will have an Automaton that does just the thing – the Gizmol.

After acquiring this Automaton, summon it in front of the boy and after a short chat, the quest will come to an end.

Reward/s: **Piece of Heart**

From the Heart

- Location: Speak with Romi just north of the fountain in Hyrule Castle Town after completing the first of the three dungeons during Lands of the Goddesses.

After speaking with Romi at the beginning of the quest, she will hand over a Happy Clover. Following our chat, we will then need to enter Hyrule Castle and speak with the king, at which point we will hand the Happy Clover over to him. As you do so, a guard will come in and tell us that Romi has gone missing.

Head for the southern gate to Hyrule Castle Town and speak with General Wright here.

He will tell you to follow the path and look for her along the way. Now, you can 100% do this, and speak with various soldiers along the way for new hints, or alternatively look at your map to spot a new rift just southwest of Hyrule Castle Town.

Either following the path, or looking at the map will lead you to the entrance to the new rift. This is just southeast of Hyrule Ranch. Approach the rift and head on inside.

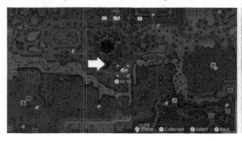 

❖ *Stilled Southern Hyrule Field*

After you enter the rift to reach the Still World, we will need to find and rescue Tri's friends. There are three glowing orbs hidden around this area and we will need to find and collect them all to complete the area.

From the starting location, you should see Romi nearby. Follow the path here to the left and hop across the trees to reach a climbing wall. Clear the Torch Slugs here and climb to the top. Here you will encounter several Mini-Moldorms. Defeat them all, one of these critters is holding the first glowing orb.

 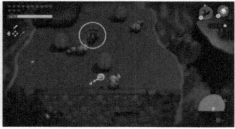

Head across the trees to the right until you reach another, larger platform. There will be a group of three Peahats here along with a Rift Zol. The Rift Zol is our target here as it is carrying the second glowing orb. From this platform continue to the right and then south to reach a large, vertical water-filled platform. This is occupied by a group of Tanglers, one of which is holding the third and final glowing orb.

 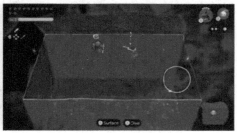

Finding all three orbs will have Tri and her friends cleanse the rift. Tri will also gain a bit of XP, and will hand over **Might Crystal** x2. We will also find ourselves back outside in the 'real' world and the rift will vanish.

Once you are back in the real world, a scene will play showing Roni reunited with her father, we will also end up back in the throne room of Hyrule Castle, where after another chat, the side quest will draw to a close.

Reward/s: **Outfit** - Customary Attire

Impa's Gift

- Location: Speak with Impa in the throne room of Hyrule Castle after completing the Dungeon - Hyrule Castle.

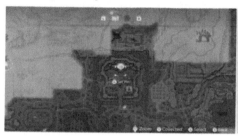 

After receiving this quest, you will learn That Impa has been training a horse for you over at the Hyrule Ranch. It is time to go claim it! When you arrive and speak with the little girl in the upper, left corner you will find that the horse has run off.

Head out of Hyrule Ranch to the north and follow the path to the right. If you haven't explored this area previously, you should come across a fellow named Dampe fighting with a Crow. Kill the Crow for him to start a new side-quest:

- Automaton Engineer Dampe

Continue to follow the dirt path here until it heads south and when you can, follow it to the east once more. At the next intersection, we want to follow the path to the north along the bank of the Hyrule Castle moat.

Eventually, if you continue to the north you will come across a couple of NPCs at a carrot patch which has been taken over by a rift. Approach the rift and head inside. We will arrive in the Stilled Carrot Patch.

We are now in the still world and as you would know by now in these mini-rift areas we have a goal – to find and rescue Tri's friends. There are four glowing orbs hidden around

263

this rift and we will need to find and collect them all to complete the area.

Move across to the first grassy field with some wooden boxes scattered about. Several of these hide rift Zols, but the box in the upper, right is hiding the entrance to a small cave. Head on in there.

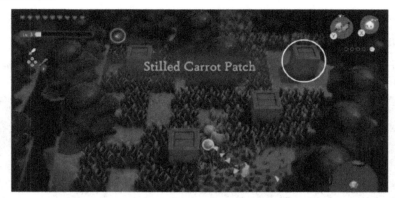

In the side-scrolling area here, head past the first Platboom use a Platboom or some Strandtulas to climb the next vertical shaft. At the top, you can find a ledge on the left with a pressure plate. Step on this to open a gate above the first Platboom's location. Head through this gate and destroy the wooden boxes (Caromadillo or Ignizol) to find the first glowing orb.

Back outside, head to the near, left-hand side of the platform and jump across the gap. Again, you will find grass and wooden boxes.

One of these boxes hides another set of stairs leading down to a small basement area. In this area, you will find two rift Spear Moblins waiting for you. Use **Echoes** of your choice to take them all out. One of the two will be holding the second glowing orb.

When you are back outside, continue to the left and up the ramps until you reach some ruins with a collection of large boulders.

Move the boulder in the lower right all the way to the right and then down. Grab the second boulder and drag it all the way to the right. Grab the third boulder and drag it as far as you can south. We can now move to the northernmost boulder. Bind this and jump it out of its location to find a glowing orb where it had been.

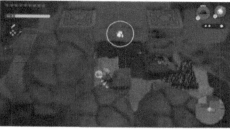

Return all the way to the platform opposite the initial entrance. We can climb the wall behind the stairs leading to the side-scroll area we explored earlier. At the top, head to the left and climb to the next section of floating ruins above (I used waterblocks) to find the fourth and final glowing orb.

Finding all five will trigger a few scenes in which Tri and her friends will cleanse the rift. Tri will also gain a bit of XP, but not enough for a new level and will hand over **Might Crystal** x2. We will also find ourselves back outside in the 'real' world.

The NPCs outside will tell you that the horse has run off. However, the key to luring it back is right here. Use bind on one of the carrots to pull it out of the ground. This will cause the horse to come running back. This will also complete the side quest.

Note: that after completing the quest, pull out another carrot and use it to learn an **Echo** – Carrot. This is particularly handy as if you spawn a carrot, the horse will come running no matter where you left it on the map previously.

Reward/s: Zelda's horse, Flag Races mini-game at Hyrule Ranch

One Soldier Too Many

Location: Speak with Beecher, one of the soldiers by the southern entrance to Hyrule Castle Town after completing Dungeon - Hyrule Castle.

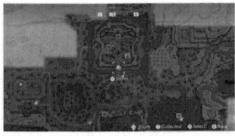 

After starting this quest, we will learn that there are one too many soldiers in Hyrule Castle Town and our goal is to discover which of the soldiers is the imposter. To do this you will need to talk with each of the soldiers around the town. Those you can speak with will conveniently get a speech bubble over their heads.

To make it quick, there are a couple that you will want to speed with to progress. The first is the soldier by the fountain. The second is the soldier atop the western wall. He will suggest we go to the armory and speak with the soldier inside.

Whilst chatting with the soldier in the barracks, Beecher will enter the room. He will ask you a question and you will have three dialogue choices. The correct answer is "The **Echo** took it." After this, we will be given a new objective – to look for a soldier with some damaged equipment.

If you speak with Beecher once again, he will ask you first, which soldier you suspect of being the **Echo**. He will give you three options – near the well, near the fountain or in the barracks, we can then back out of the conversation. Now that we have three options, head outside and inspect the three of them. Once you know the answer, return to the barracks, and speak with him once again.

The answer is "Near the well." And then he will ask you which piece of equipment has been damaged. The correct answer is "The lance." (if you look closely at the suspect soldier, you will find the sharp tip of the lance he is holding is missing!)

Once you have given both answers, General Wright will enter the barracks and get involved. After a brief chat, where we learn the truth about the '**Echo**,' the side quest will be completed.

Reward/s: Golden Egg

Big Shot

- Location: Approach the River Zora on the boat in Zora Cove, just south of Seesyde Village after completing main quest - Still Missing.

As you approach the boat with the stranded River Zora, this quest will immediately start. All you need to do is simply defeat the nearby enemies consisting of a pair of Chompfins (and possibly a Tangler) in the water beneath the boat. Use any combination of **Echo**es you have (Chompfins work well against Chompfins!), or use Swordfighter mode.

Once they have been defeated, another scene will play, and we will chat with the River Zora to end the side-quest.

- Reward/s: Riverhorse x10

Deliver the Grilled Fish!

Location: Speak with the woman on the docks on the eastern side of Seesyde Village.

After startin the quest, exit the village via the dirt ramp to the north. When you reach the river, cross the fallen stone pillar here. Clear out the Moblin camp on the far side and loot the **Treasure Chest** they had been guarding for Riverhorse x10.

At the northern end of this camp, you will find a higher ledge that we can make our way up to. At the top, you will find Anube, the lady's son. We need to deliver the Grilled Fish to him. Unfortunately, he won't accept an **Echo**, we need to provide the fish that the quest giver drops on the dock.

As such once you have cleared the camp, return to the docks, request a new slab of Grilled Fish and use bind to carry it back to the clearing. Create a path up to the boy and drop the Grilled Fish in front of him.

After a brief chat, he will accept the fish, demolish it and then fall back to sleep. At this point we can return to Seesyde Village and speak with the quest giver to complete the side-quest.

- Reward/s: Bubble Kelp x10

Out of Bubble Kelp

- Location: Speak with the Business Scrub on the beach by the Waypoint south of Crossflows Plaza.

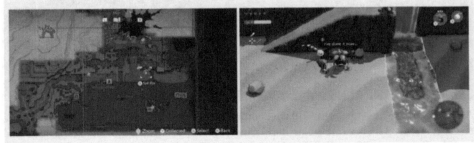

After speaking with the Business Scrub, you will be required to bring him Bubble Kelp x3 If you have these on you already, simply speak with him once again to hand them in. If not, we'll need to go and find some.

The good news is that the General Store in the Sea Zora village, a short swim through Zora Bay to the southeast has Bubble Kelp in stock. You can simply purchase the required amount there. Additionally, you can find it in grass, **Treasure Chests** and by defeating enemies in the nearby area. The nearby side-quest - Deliver the Grilled Fish! also issues you with Bubble Kelp as a reward.

Once you have found Bubble Kelp x3, return it to the Business Scrub in order to complete this short Side-Quest.

- Reward/s: Rupee x20

Precious Treasure

- Location: Speak with the Zora by the entrance inside the Sea Zora Village after completing Dungeon - Jabul Ruins.

After accepting the quest from this Zora, you will learn that he needs something to hold some precious objects in... and you will not have much more to go on. Fortunately, its actually not too difficult once you figure out what needs to be done!

What our friend is after is, believe it or not, a **Treasure Chest**. The good news is, if you have been following along there is a **Treasure Chest** directly south of the entrance to the Sea Zora Village which we would have looted earlier. It is the one that was surrounded by Sea Urchins and contained a Red Rupee.

Use bind to grab the chest and swim back to the Sea Zora island. Rather than re-entering the village, you will find that the quest giver is now standing atop the island itself. Take the **Treasure Chest** to him and deposit it in front of him to complete the side quest.

Reward/s: Monster Stone x3

Secret Chief Talks

- Location: Approach the Sea Zora on the small island west of the large island with Sea Zora Village after completing main quest - Still Missing.

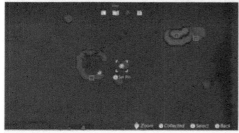

Upon starting this quest, you will learn that the pair of Zora chiefs are acting strangely, and we will be tasked with figuring out what sorts of shenaniganry are afoot. The first thing we need to do is head for Dradd's hut in the River Zora Village. Speak with Inawa inside and we will learn that he is missing.

Exit to the River Zora Village. We will need to speak with some of the inhabitants here to find out where Tellum has gone. Those that have information for us will have a speech bubble over their heads. One is located just outside of Dradd's hut and the other in the middle tier of buildings.

To find Tellum, enter the cave behind the middle section of huts (like we did to clear the rift here earlier). Head up the slope to the right and then swim all the way to the right-hand wall to find a River Zora in some grass. This is the fellow we are looking for. Speak with him here.

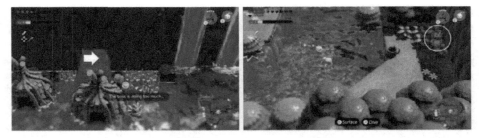

We now know where to go – it is that island on the eastern side of Zora Cove where we rescued Kushara from the cave in in earlier in the main questline. Head inside and speak with the two chiefs to trigger a conversation to end the side quest.

● Reward/s: Accessory - Gold Brooch

The Zappy Shipwreck

Location: Speak with the man on top of the boat in Seesyde Village after completing main quest - Still Missing.

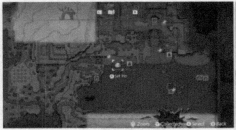

270

After starting this quest, our first port of call is a large ship located in the southwestern part of Zora Cove. Be careful as you approach this because there will be a Chompfin in the water beneath it. Once you have found the ship, climb aboard, and use bind on the hatch on the right side to open it up. Jump down into the opening.

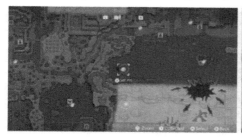

The inside of the ship here acts as a mini-dungeon of sorts. So, it is a bit longer than our typical side quest... but there are puzzles and loot to be had, so that is good!

In the first room you will find some Sea Urchins and Keese. We want to break all of the wooden boxes along the rear wall of the room. Doing so will reveal a hidden doorway we can enter. Proceed through the next hallway and then into a larger, half flooded room.

This larger room is occupied by quite a few enemies. Near the entrance you will encounter Tektites and Keese and as you progress to the left, you will find Sea Urchins underwater and some Octoroks on some platforms by the far wall. Head through the door by the Octorok platform.

In this next room, hop onto the storage shelf to the left first for a **Treasure Chest** with Rocktatoes x5. To continue, you will need to dive into the pool of water in the middle of the room.

We will enter a side-scrolling swimming area. This area is occupied primarily by Tanglers, but you will also encounter a few Sea Urchins and Bio Dekus hiding in the dark Be sure to activate the crystals when you see them to avoid surprises! At the bottom of the first area, you will find a **Treasure Chest** containing a Purple Rupee.

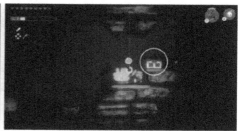

Swim all the way to the left and then take the vertical passage upwards to exit the water.

Upon entering the next room, there will be a **Treasure Chest** on a shelf in the back, left of the room. It contains Electro Apple x5. Look at the section of broken wall near the roof in the lower, left. Create a path up to this and hop over the wall here.

In the next area, there is a statue behind a fence and a pressure plate on the left side. You should know what to do here! Use bind on the statue and build a little set of stairs for yourself so that you can move the statue onto the pressure plate. This will open the door.

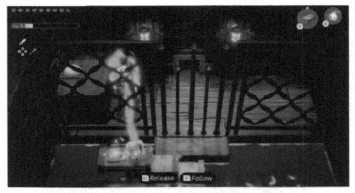

Head on into another large, open area. Here you will encounter another large collection of enemies. By the entrance, there will be Hydrozols and a Poe, and in the water to the right a Chompfin and Biri, there are also several Sea Urchins dotted around the area to watch out for. There is a **Treasure Chest** in the lower, right corner of this room with a Red Rupee.

Once the area is clear, look on the wall opposite the entry door to find a weak area. Hit this with a Bombfish to create an opening and proceed inside. Destroy all of the crates in the room here to find a **Treasure Chest** with a Gold Rupee (300 **Rupees!**).

Head through the door in the back, right of the larger room and then in the next hallway continue through the door on the left. We will reach a room with a boss waiting for us.

❖ *Boss: Zappy Monster*

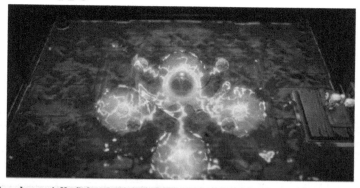

This boss is a large jellyfish who is surrounded by a collection of smaller Biri creatures. The large Biri at the centre is the boss itself, whilst the outer collection of Biri are damaging distractions.

*Initially the Biri will be connected to the main Biri by an electrical tether, and they will spin around the central core in a counterclockwise direction. As they go, some will be electrified, whilst others are not. Our goal here is to use an **Echo** (Chompfins are good) to get in and kill the non-electrified Biri.*

As the spin is happening, the boss will fire out small electrical projectiles at random, which you will want to avoid. After a bit of spinning, the Biri will converge on the central body. They will rest here for a moment, giving you the opportunity to take a few of them out. Be careful however as after a brief pause, they will all start sparking before unleashing a giant electrical explosion.

Once you have defeated all of the smaller Biri, the central jellyfish will be completely stunned. Quickly run in and hack away at the larger creature with swordfighter mode to dish out some big damage.

After damaging it sufficiently, the big jellyfish and its entourage will still do the spinning thing, but will now also be able to move around the room and chase you – be sure to avoid getting cornered. However, the same general strategy remains here – defeat the smaller Biri to stun the main body of the boss and then hack it up.

Once you have dealt enough damage to the boss, the fight will come to an end.

For defeating this boss, you will be rewarded with a bunch of **Rupees** and a **Piece of Heart**. A portal will appear as well, allowing you to teleport back to the start of the area.

With all that done, exit the ship and make your way back to the quest giver in Seesyde Village. Report your success to him to complete the side quest.

- Reward/s: Accessory - Fairy Bottle

The Zora Child's Fate

- Location: Speak with the Zora child by the destroyed houses in River Zora Village after completing the main quest - Chaos at the River Zora Village.

After speaking with the child, we will need to head into the nearby hut where we will get to speak with his mother. The mother asks you to bring her monsters so that she can study them. We will need to learn and summon **Echo**es of three different monsters for her.

The first is a 'sinister looking' fish. The monster she is looking for is a Tangler. If you have not got this **Echo** yet, you can find these around Zora Cove and in some of the caves along Zora River. Summon one into the pool of water in front of her.

The second monster she wants to investigate is a Bombfish. These are located in a cave midway up the Zora River, just past Jabu-Jabu's Den. Again, we will need to spawn one of these in the water at the centre of the room.

Finally, the lady wants us to bring her an electric jellyfish. The monster she is looking for is a Biri, and these can be found on the eastern side of Zora Cove. Once you have the Biri **Echo**, simply summon it in front of her to trigger a cut-scene to end the side quest.

- Reward/s: Accessory - Zora Scale

LAKE HYLIA

The Great Fairy's Request

Location: Loot the **Treasure Chest** in the Great Fairy Fountain after unlocking the fourth Accessory Slot.

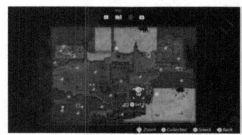

After accepting this side quest, the Great Fairy will ask you for a special piece of jewelry. To do this we will first need to head over to Gerudo Town in Gerudo Desert. We want to speak with the lady in the General Store here. She mentions that she can craft the required item, but will need us to rustle up a few items for her first – a Floral Seashell and a Magma Stone. We need to track both these items down to continue.

To find the Magma Stone, we need to head for Goron City on Eldin Volcano. In this area, head for the General Store and speak with the Goron with the '!' above his head. He will mention that Magma Stones can be found in the Lizalfos Quarry, but it has now been re-overrun by Lizalfos enemies.

Head for the Lizalfos Quarry and fight your way through the initial rooms, defeating the Lizalfos, and Fire Keese as you go. In the room at the back of the quarry, there will be a group of three Lizalfos Lv.2 enemies. Fight and defeat all three of these to trigger a scene after which you will be rewarded with the Magma Stone.

To find the Floral Seashell, we need to head for the Sea Zora Village in the Jabul Waters region. Speak with the Zora behind the General Store on the left side of town. Turns out this Zora has a Floral Seashell, but wants an Unfortunate Smoothie in exchange for it.

If you have an Unfortunate Smoothie, you can do a straight swap for the key item, but if you do not, you will need to head for a Business Scrub and craft one. It is fairly easy - simply combine any monster part with a fruit (e.g., Monster Horn and Electro Apple). Once you have one, return to the Zora and make the exchange.

After acquiring both the Magma Stone and the Floral Seashell we need to mosey on back to the General Store in Gerudo Town and fork them over. In exchange the shopkeeper will give you the Lovely Pendant.

With the Lovely Pendant in our possession, we can now proceed back to the Great Fairy Fountain in Lake Hylia. Speak with the Great Fairy once again and hand it in to complete the side quest.

- Reward/s: Accessory - Might Bell

KAKARIKO VILLAGE

Cuccos on the Loose

- Location: Speak with the woman by the empty cucco enclosure on the western side of Kakariko Village.

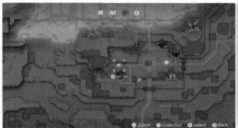

After speaking with the woman, we will be required to find five of he cuccoos that have escaped the enclosure and are now wandering about town. To do this, approach one and pick it up, take it back to the enclosure and throw it inside. Easy!

The five cuccos can be found in the following locations:

- One is found just south of the cucco enclosure.

- Another is by the main (southern) entrance to Kakariko Village.

- One cucco is wandering around in the area with the well.
- A cucco can be found in the graveyard area north of the cucco enclosure.

The hardest cucco to find is on top of the windmill in the northeast corner of the village.

After returning all five to the enclosure, the woman will speak with you once again to complete the side quest.

Reward/s: Fairy Bottle

Questioning the Local Cats

- Location: Speak with the old man behind the well in Kakariko Village.

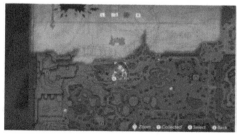 

After starting this quest, we will be tasked with tracking down the man's missing cat. To begin we need to head for the general store and speak with the woman standing outside. She mentions that she has the Cat Clothes that the old man wants us to retrieve, but we need to do a favor for her first.

She will point out a cat by a windmill in the northeast corner of the village. Make your way up here and you will find that the cat is fast asleep. We need to get it to move.

To do so, use the Grilled Fish **Echo** (if you do not have it, you can find it in Seesyde Village in Jabul Waters). And place it in front of the cat. Once it has moved, we can then use a Holmill on the patch of dirt it had been sleeping on to find the Secret Stash.

277

After a short scene and chat here, we will end up with the **Outfit** - Cat Clothes. These clothes have the special ability that allows you to speak with and understand cats. We will be using this to chat with the local cats for clues to figure out where the old man's cat is.

Whilst you can spend some time tracking down and chatting with each of them, the cat that gives you the information that you need is found on the roof of the house in the southwest part of the village (just south of the cucco enclosure). This will direct you to a second cat, found on top of the windmill in the northwest corner of the village who will tell you where to find the target cat.

Apparently the cat we are looking for has fallen asleep in a tree to the east of town. So, let us have a look. If you follow the road leading out of town to the east, you will eventually find the cat atop a tree. It will be close to the entrance to a cave.

Get up onto the tree and speak with the cat. It will run off back to town. At this point, return to Kakariko Village and speak with the quest giver once again to complete the side quest.

Reward/s: Refreshing Grapes x10

278

ELDIN VOLCANO

Glide Path

- Location: Speak with the Goron outside of the entrance to Goron City and to the right by the hot spring after completing Dungeon - Eldin Temple.

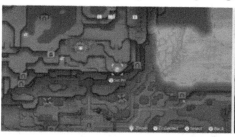 

After speaking with this Goron here, agree to his question to start a glide challenge. Essentially, a bunch of vertical wind gusts will appear, and we will need to use a flying **Echo** to glide between them. These are fairly straightforward and any flying **Echo** (Albatrawl, Crow, Ghirro, etc.) should do the trick.

We need to glide into the wind gusts and hover in them for a short time to gain more altitude before gliding to the next. If you can glide between the gusts all the way to the goal flag without touching the ground, you will complete the side-quest.

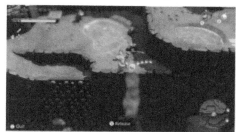 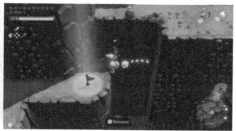

After completing this side quest, you will unlock a follow up - Glide Path Trailblazer.

Reward/s: Rock Salt x10

Glide Path Trailblazer

- Location: Speak with the Goron outside of the entrance to Goron City and to the right by the hot spring after completing Side Quest: Glide Path.

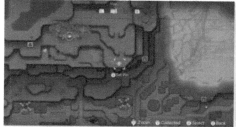 

If you speak with this Goron again after completing the first gliding challenge, his brother Disian will show up and challenge you to try the more advanced path. Agree to do so. We are in for a bit more of the same for this side-quest, but it is a little trickier.

As with the previous side quest, essentially a bunch of vertical wind gusts will appear, and we will need to use a flying **Echo** to glide between them. These are fairly straightforward and any flying **Echo** (Albatrawl, Crow, Ghirro) should do the trick. We need to glide into the wind gusts and hover in them for a short time to gain more altitude before gliding to the next. You will want to fly through these in a zigzag pattern – so up, down, up, down, etc. all the way to the end.

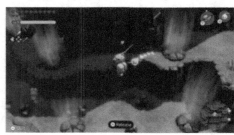 

This time around however you will have more wind gusts available as well as more hazards to avoid, these include falling rocks and steam vents shooting outwards from the cliff face. If you can glide between the gusts all the way to the goal flag without touching the ground, you will complete the side-quest.

Reward/s: **Might Crystal** x2

Ready? Set? Goron!

- Location: Speak with the Goron outside of the entrance to Goron City and to the right after completing Dungeon - Eldin Temple.

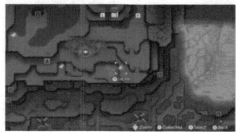 

This side quest is essentially a race between us and a Goron from the entrance to Goron City to the entrance to the Lizalfos Burrow. This fellow can roll fairly quickly and is unperturbed by the lava-cracked blocks along the main path which means if you attempt to race him in the traditional way, you will not have much luck beating him.

Fortunately, there is a much quicker way. From the starting line, run back to the left and just to the left of the entrance to Goron City you will find an alcove in the cliff. If you place a Platboom In here and then a couple of Trampolines atop it (other stuff might work, but Trampolines worked for me) we can jump up to the ledge above.

Once up it is a short run to the left and then north to reach the goal flag, well ahead of the competition. Besting him in the race will complete the side-quest.

Reward/s: **Rupees** x50

The Fireworks Artist

● Location: Speak with Basa in the upper, right room of Goron City after completing Dungeon - Eldin Temple.

Once you have received this side-quest, we will need to track down and grab some Blastpower Soil. All that we have to go on is that it can be found somewhere near the top of Eldin Volcano and that there will be golden flowers like those in Basa's room about to tip us off to its location.

To find them, we want to fast travel to the **Waypoint Stone** outside the Rock-Roast Quarry. From this location, head a short distance to the left to find a collection of golden flowers. At their centre, you will find a sparkling spot. Interact with this to find the Blastpower Soil.

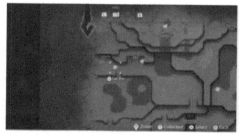

Once you have the Blastpower Soil, make your way back to Goron City and speak with Basa once again for a scene/chat to complete the side quest.

Following the scene, be sure to interact with the launchers in Basa's room here for an **Echo** - Firework. Although not part of this quest, it is a requirement for Dampe's side quest - Explosions Galore!.

Reward/s: **Rupees** x50

The Flames of Fortune'

- Location: Speak with the Goron named Ondes near the hot springs above the **Waypoint Stone** for the Lizalfos Quarry after completing Dungeon - Eldin Temple.

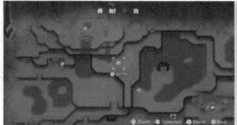 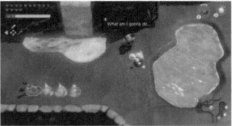

After accepting the side quest, Ondes will pop a piece of flaming coal on the ground nearby. We need to grab this using bind and take it to the entrance to Goron City. Note that the coal is on fire, and we need to keep it alight. Dragging it through lava, lava-cracked platforms or flaming enemies such as Torch Slugs will rekindle it.

The fastest way to take it to Goron City is to head south from the start location and drop down to the area with the **Waypoint Stone** outside the Lizalfos Quarry. Here, hold the coal over some lava to light it up again and then drop down to the south.

 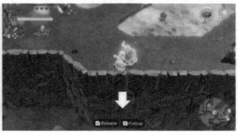

We can then follow the path to the right in order to reach the entrance to Goron City. Place the flaming coal on the ground in front of the Goron to the right of the entrance. Doing so will complete the side quest.

Reward/s: **Might Crystal** x2

A Mountainous Mystery

Location: Speak with the Goron just inside Goron City after completing Dungeon - Eldin Temple. You may need to travel to another region and return to get it to appear.

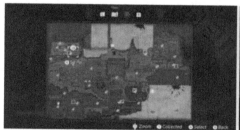

Upon starting this side quest, we will learn that our buddy Darston has gone missing. To find him, we need to head to the Summit Cave, which will now be accessible now that the big rift is gone from the area. It can be found just north of and on the ledges above the Lizalfos Den.

As you enter you will find Darston waiting for us by an open door. After a short chat and ominous statements about a fire giant, we can go forth and explore.

Follow the path and push the Lava Block provided onto the geyser to the right to reach the ledge above. Continue around the corner using the climbing walls here. From the second, spawn a Lava Block onto the geyser on the right. Ride this up to the higher ledge above.

As you round the next corner you will find another lava pit. Hop onto the nearest Lava Block and spawn another on the geyser to the north. Bind the Lava Block off to the right and then jump across to the northern platform, place the bound on the geyser along the northern wall. Summon another Lava Block onto the second geyser here to reach the next ledge.

In the next room there are several platforms linked by wooden bridges and covered in grass. After a short time, this will catch alight, so stay back and wait for it to burn off before making your way north. Dispatch or avoid the Fire Keese as you go.

After reaching the eastern side of the room, use bind to remove the boulders to the north and climb the wall behind them. At the top, bind the Lava Block in the back, right and dragging it over to the geyser on the back, left. Spawn another Lava Block on the nearest geyser and then use the pair to reach the upper platform.

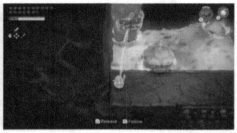

Descend the ladder at the top into a side scrolling area.

Exploring this area is hazardous due to the lava at the bottom of the room repeatedly rising upwards to a fairly high point before lowering again. We need to obviously move to the right when the lava is at its lowest point and quickly find high ground as it rises to avoid it and then press onwards once it recedes once again.

As you hop across the first collection of platforms, you will come across a climbing wall. If you head up, there is a Torch Slug above and a **Treasure Chest** with a Purple Rupee.

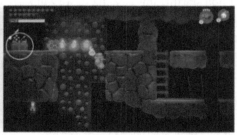

Continue to the right, avoiding the lava as you go. When you reach the far right, you will find a shallow pool of lava with narrow opening above. To get up here, you will want to spawn a Tweelus on the far, right of the lava pool and then stand on top of it. It will float in the lava and carry you up the shaft and to the exit.

Proceed through the door in the next room to reach a boss fight.

❖ *Boss: Fire Talus*

The Fire Talus is the giant we were warned about. It also bears a striking resemblance to the Seismic Talus we fought in the first dungeon.... Except it's on fire. It is a large rock monster with a number of different damaging abilities. Our goal is to target and attack its weak point using our **Echo**es or swordfighter mode.

Note that throughout the fight, the boss will be covered in flames and this will increase the amount of damage he can do and set you on fire if he hits. To debuff him somewhat, you can create a stack of waterblocks and get him to attack them. This will extinguish some of its flames temporarily.

The Talus's weak spot is a glowing, purple orb which will change locations as the fight progresses. Each time you damage the boss enough, the purple rock will fall to the ground. Alternatively, you can also use bind to pull the core out of the boss. Either way, once the core is clear of the boss, you want to transition to Swordfighter mode and attack it until the boss re-forms.

The boss can perform a punch attack, where his fist will fly towards you as a projectile. He can also perform a slamming attack, where he will bring both hands down on the ground in front of his location. After damaging its core for the first time and the weak spot changes position, it gets a new attack where it holds its hands out and spins around.

During the first part of the fight, the weak spot will be at the boss's base, making it relatively easy to target – a high level Darknut or Caromadillo can get the job done here. Wait until the boss performs a slam attack, then move behind it and summon your enemies to get a solid attack window.

The weak spot will then move to the boss's right shoulder (our left). This one is a bit trickier to target by a melee enemy, so wait for it to perform an attack and then send an **Echo** in to attack, or use some aerial monsters to swoop at it. In the final part of the fight, the weak spot moves to the boss's head. We will need to wait until it performs the slam attack and then use bind to pull the orb out.

After smashing the purple core for the third time, the fight will end.

For defeating the boss, you will receive a **Piece of Heart** and a bunch of **Rupees**. A portal will appear as well, allowing you to teleport back to the start of the area. Here we can chat with Darston to complete the side quest.

Reward/s: Accessory - Goron Bracelet

Cotton-Candy Hunt

- Location: Speak with a Deku scrub in the northwest corner of Scrubton after completing Dungeon - Faron Temple AND the Let's Play a Game side quest.

After accepting this quest, we need to make our way to the Hidden Ruins in the southern part of the Faron Wetlands. If you have not been here yet, you will want to travel to Blossu's house and then head west.

In the area with the Electric Wizzrobe, head to the northern end of this area, you will find a pair of lit braziers. Head past these and it will start raining. Defeat the pair of Ribbitunes here to stop the rain. You can then light the two tall braziers in the water here to have the statue ahead move, revealing a secret staircase. If you have been here previously, it will still be open.

Inside you will find a **Treasure Chest** with a Monster Stone. At this point, you will also find an opening at the back of the cave that we can enter (this was caved in previously). A mini-dungeon awaits!

The first room we come across should look familiar, it looks just like the East Ruins we explored in the Let's Play a Game side quest. Again, throughout this dungeon, we will have Sparks everywhere and we need to direct them into the golden receptacles to open doors.

In this first room you can use boulders to redirect the sparks into the receptacle, or alternatively, just spawn a couple of Spark **Echo**es right next to it. This will open the door on the right.

The next room has several recesses in the floor covered by spider webs and a few baby Gohma eggs about. Deal with the enemies and burn away the webs. The receptacle is in the upper right, again we can spawn **Echo**es beside it, but if you want to do it in the intended way, you will want to remove the boulders blocking the paths between the recesses in the floor so that the existing Sparks can reach their destination.

We will come across a room with a receptacle and three Sparks behind a fence. We need to get all three of these into the receptacle. The first Spark is circling a rock – spawn a couple of additional rocks beside this leading to the receptacle.

The second Spark is circling the perimeter of the room. Spawn a boulder by the stone block closest to the fence and bind it. Hold the boulder by the fence so that the Spark moves onto the rock and then quickly walk forward with the bound boulder so that the Spark can then continue around the stone block, back to the boulder and then into the receptacle.

The final spark is cutting laps around the stone block at the rear of the room. To get this one, spawn a monster **Echo** by the Armos to activate it. As the Armos patrols back and forth, the Spark should jump to it and then to the outer wall of the room. We can then get it into the receptacle the same way we did the previous Spark.

Once all three have been brought to the receptacle, the next door will open. Head on through to reach a side-scroll area.

As you enter, you will see a ledge above with a Spark circling it. Create a Platboom to the left of this and ride it up. Defeat the Spark, or avoid it and continue right from here to find a **Treasure Chest** with a Red Rupee.

Continue to the right, past another Spark to reach the door leading to the next room. In this area you will have a pool of water with three Sparks in it, and a receptacle on a central island. Again, you can chase down the Sparks if you like, or simply spawn **Echo**es directly into the receptacle.

Head through the next room and in the subsequent, larger area you will find yourself in a boss fight.

❖ Boss: Smog (Second Encounter)

The large, sentient electrical cloud is back! Fortunately, it will behave in a similar fashion to how it did in the Let's Play a Game side quest, so you should know the basic gist of the fight. Its going to split apart and we need to corral the various pieces of the cloud so that they recombine into the bass so that we can attack it.

To start the fight, it will split itself into three small clouds. These will stick to walls and blocks and patrol around them. Whilst they are relatively harmless, watch for them to start charging electricity – after doing so they will shoot an electrical projectile your way, which we will want to avoid where possible.

Our goal is, as mentioned above, to recombine the boss. A good method to do so is to trap the clouds in the lower area and then use an **Echo** to block the path upward (beds are good for this). This can be a bit tricky as they all have a mind of their own but try and focus on getting two together to start with (and then go for the third after they combine), rather than trying to get all three together at once.

Once you have merged all the clouds back into one, Smog will reappear and will attack as he did in our previous encounter - zipping around the room and launching electrical projectiles. He moves a bit faster this time around, and can charge himself electrically, so if he is sparking, do not touch him. It is a good idea to spawn a high-level **Echo** such as a Lizalfos Lv.3 / Darknut Lv.3 to have them attack it, and use swordfighter mode to slash away and dish out further damage of your own.

After damaging him a few times, he will split up into four smaller clouds. These will then take off and act independently of one another as they move around the room. Again, round them all up and get Smog to re-form and then take down Smog once he has returned. Defeating him this time will end the fight.

For defeating this boss, you will be rewarded with a bunch of **Rupees** and a **Piece of Heart**. A portal will appear as well, allowing you to teleport back to the start of the area. With all that done, exit the temple and chat with the Deku Scrub back in Scrubton. Report your success to him to complete the side quest.

Reward/s: Accessory - Curious Charm

Looking for Bempu

- Location: Speak with a Deku scrub in the southern part of Scrubton after completing Dungeon - Faron Temple.

After starting this quest, we will essentially be playing a game of Hide and Seek with Bempu. He will give us a clue and we need to go to the location indicated and look for him. Pluck him from the ground to find him. Each time you find him, he will run off and give you a clue to the next hiding spot. We will need to do this four times.

He can be found in the following locations:

The first clue is 'near the trendiest shop in town' which is, of course the Smoothie Shop.

The second clue is 'a lake that's a symbol of love'. This is the Heart Lake in the southwestern corner of the Faron Wetlands. You can find Bempu to the west of the lake.

The third clue is 'between four stone siblings'. This is located in the northern part of the region on the path between the initial entry point into Faron Wetlands to the Sweet Spot.

The fourth and final clue is 'a home that used to be covered in thorns'. This is of course Blossu's house which we cleared of the rift during the main quest. It is in the southeastern corner of Faron Wetlands.

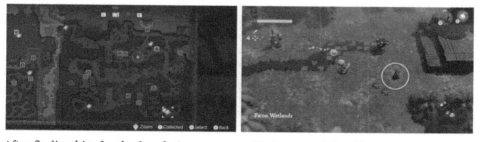

After finding him for the fourth time, a scene will play to end the side quest.

Reward/s: Accessory - Fairy Fragrance

Mobbing Mothulas!

- Location: Pluck and talk to a Deku scrub just outside of the lockup on the western side of Scrubton after completing Dungeon - Faron Temple.

Upon starting this side quest, we will be tasked with hunting down and destroying a group of Mothulas that are terrorizing our friends here. To find the monsters, you want to head out of Scrubton to the east and follow the path to the south.

Eventually you will reach a small, wooded area where you will encounter the monsters that we need to vanquish. We will need to kill two Mothulas and a Mothula Lv. 2 here. Defeating them all will update your objective.

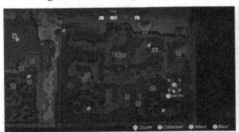 

Return to the quest giver and report your success to complete the side quest.

Reward/s: **Might Crystal**

The Mythical Deku Snake

- Location: Speak with a Deku scrub outside of the Smoothie Shop in Scrubton after completing Dungeon - Faron Temple.

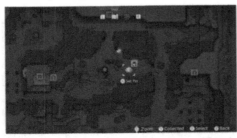 

This quest has us assisting this particular Deku Scrub locating a Deku Snake. However, our role is simply to provide the bait. In order to do so we need to give this fellow Electro Apple x3. If you have some on hand we can simply hand them over, if not we can grab some in a few locations:

- The short side quest - The Rain-Making Monster in Scrubton will reward you with Electro Apples.

- Electro Apples can be purchased from Hyrule Castle Twon General Store for 30 **Rupees**.

- Electro Apples can occasionally drop from grass, smashing rocks, **Treasure Chests** and by defeating enemies in the Faron Wetlands.

Once you have found Electro Apple x3, return it to the quest giver in order to complete this short Side-Quest.

Reward/s: Monster Stone x2

The Rain-Making Monster

- Location: Speak with the Deku scrub in the centre of Scrubton.

This fellow wants us to retrieve a rain making monster from somewhere in the Faron Wetlands. Now if you were following our walkthrough, we will have picked this up already and is in fact the Drippitune. Simply pull out a Drippitune **Echo** in front of him.

If you do not have the Drippitune, we can make a quick detour to go grab one. From the **Waypoint Stone** at the start of the Faron Wetlands area, you can follow the main path to find one after a short walk. Additionally, the watery area just east of the entrance to the Sweet Spot, north of Scrubton also has a Drippitune about.

Once you have the Drippitune, simply summon an **Echo** of it in front of the quest giver to complete the side quest.

Reward/s: Electro Apple x8

HEBRA MOUNTAIN & MOUNT LANAYRU

Getting it Twisted

- Location: Speak with the Business Scrub on Lower Hebra Mountain to the northwest of Conde's house.

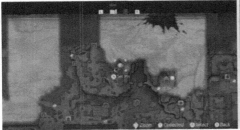 

This side quest is a fairly short and simple one. Our role is simply to provide the Smoothie crafter with a Twisted Pumpkin. If you have some on hand we can simply hand them over, if not we can grab some in a few locations:

Twisted Pumpkins can occasionally drop from grass, smashing rocks and boxes, looting **Treasure Chest**s, melting ice columns and by defeating enemies in the Hebra Mountain and Mount Lanayru areas.

Once you have found a Twisted Pumpkin, return it to the quest giver in order to complete this short Side-Quest.

Reward/s: Warm Pepper x10

Stamp Stand Swallowed!

❖ How to Start Stamp Stand Swallowed!

Visit Northeastern Hebra Mountain:

Players will likely encounter "Stamp Stand Swallowed!" late into their Hebra Mountain experience. It is somewhat out of the way, so it is possible for players to miss it. When you reach the final Waypoint at the top of Hebra Mountain, you'll have the choice to head north, towards the Lanaryu Temple dungeon, or head east, along the small snowball-filled passage. To find the quest, you'll want to head east.

As you approach the end of the passage, you'll find the Stamp Guy standing in front of a rift. You will discover that one of the Stamp Rally stands was supposed to be found here, but it was swallowed by the rift. As you speak with Stamp Guy, it is made clear that you must close the rift to gain access to the Stamp Stand. Tri will inform Zelda that he can make an opening. Use the opening and enter the rift.

❖ *Where to Find Tri's Friends in Stilled Hebra Mountain Passage*

Tri has three friends stuck within this rift. Below, we will list the locations of every friend. Collect them all to close the rift.

◦   *Tri's Friend 1:*

When you first enter the rift, turn right and make your way across the first two gaps. Even though it's cold, you can still use Water Blocks to cross. At this point, you will encounter Ice Keese. These enemies can freeze Zelda solid, so a potion is useful if you have them. Use a Piping-Hot Potion (Monster Guts + Warm Pepper) to become Ice-proof.

This potion will help when you reach the final platform on the right. You'll encounter a large platform with a Freezard and a Dark Freezard. These enemies spew a freezing mist. Fire can take them out very fast. The Dark Freezard will drop the first Tri's Friend.

◦   *Tri's Friend 2:*

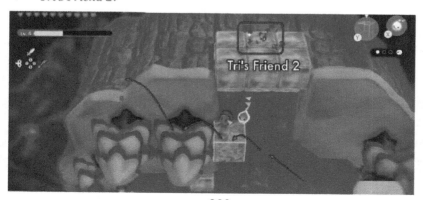

Return to the starting platform, and head straight ahead to the large vertical wall with the large pool. Jump into the pool and make your way to the top. You'll notice the exit at the very top is blocked by ice. Use a Water Block to extend the pool horizontally, then jump to the top of the tree on the left. From here, you can reach the top of the platform.

From the top, use any Fire **Echo** to melt the ice that was blocking the exit from the water. Tri's second friend is in the center of the melted ice.

> ⁃ *Tri's Friend 3:*

From the start, head left and use Water Blocks to cross the gap to the last platform. You'll notice a large number of Ice Blocks sitting around the entire final platform. Watch out for the Snomaul launching snowballs at Zelda.

After getting rid of the enemies, melt the ice blocks sitting at the far right edge. There, you'll find Tri's Friend 3 within the Ice Blocks.

❖ *Completing Stamp Stand Swallowed!:*

When you collect the final orb containing Tri's Friend, the rift will automatically begin to close. Tri will earn about 20% of the bar towards his next level. Zelda will earn Two **Might Crystals**.

When Zelda returns to the Stamp Guy, the Stamp Rally Stand will now be back, and be available for Zelda to use. This will conclude "Stamp Stand Swallowed!".

Snowball Magic

- Location: Speak with Conde in his house on Hebra mountain after completing Dungeon - Lanayru Temple.

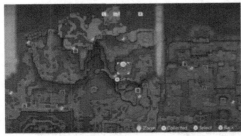 

After chatting with Conde to start this quest, he will whisk you away to the to p of the mountain. Remember how there were side paths leading away to the left and the right from the main slope? We will end up on the right-hand path.

In this location, Conde will mention the nearby snowballs. He wants us to grab one of these and take it across the top of the mountain to the top of the left-hand path. As you would know by now the snowballs are quite fragile, so you will need to be careful and keep it away from the other snowballs rolling around the area.

When grabbing the snowball, try and do so from behind. That way when you get to the far end of the mountaintop, we will be hiding it over the cliff, rather than in the centre of the path. Carefully make your way past the snowballs here to the top of the path.

Place the snowball on the small, raised ledge at the top of the path for a brief scene with conde to complete the side quest.

Reward/s: **Piece of Heart**

OPTIONAL RIFTS

STILLED LOWER SUTHORN FOREST RIFT

Location: Found in the southeastern part of Suthorn Forest after completing Dungeon - Hyrule Castle.

After you enter the rift to reach the Still World, we will need to find and rescue Tri's friends. There are four glowing orbs hidden around this area and we will need to find and collect them all to complete the area.

As soon as you gain control of Zelda, hop across the trees on the right. Defeat the Rift monsters here and then look atop the trees in the northeast corner of this platform to find a glowing orb atop one of them.

Return to the starting platform and this time make your way all the way left to find a Moblin camp. The Spear Moblin atop the wooden platform at the centre of this area will drop the second glowing orb when slain. Watch out for the Ropes hiding in the grass here!

Head back to the starting platform once more and this time head north until you reach a vertical platform that you can climb using the trees growing from it. As you ascend, watch out for the Peahat here.

As you climb, you will want to jump over to another floating island to the right midway up the platform to find a stack of crates we can break to find the third glowing orb. At the very top of the previous vertical platform, you will find the final glowing orb.

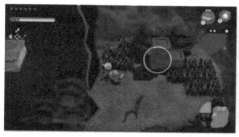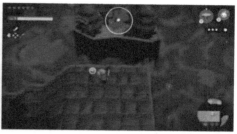

Finding all four orbs will have Tri and her friends cleanse the rift. Tri will also gain a bit of XP, and will hand over **Might Crystal** x2. We will also find ourselves back outside in the 'real' world and the rift will vanish.

STILLED LAKE HYLIA RIFT

Location: On a small island in Lake Hylia to the southwest of the Great Fairy Island.

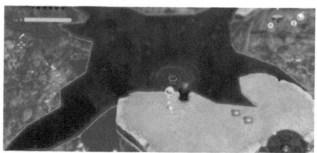

After you enter the rift to reach the Still World, we will need to find and rescue Tri's friends. There are three glowing orbs hidden around this area and we will need to find and collect them all to complete the area.

Upon entering the area, move across to the next platform to the left and then for the head northern end of the platform. From this location, you can see another area to the left filled with water (and a bunch of Rift Tanglers). Take them all out using some water **Echo**es and then claim the glowing orb they had been guarding.

297

After claiming thew orb, swim to the top of this platform and jump across to the next to the north. This platform is another water one and we can swim either to the north (and then jump over to another to the left) or to the right. Both of the paths leading off this platform will take you to the remaining two orbs.

Head to the left first. We will arrive in a large, open water area. There are boulders on the seabed here, but if you move them, you will either find nothing or Rift Tanglers. Look for a sneaky hard to spot tunnel, in the back, left of the area. The rock on the far side of this can be moved to find the second glowing orb.

 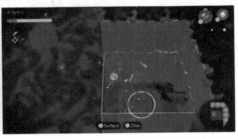

Return to the previous large watery platform and this time take the path to the right.

Swim to the top of the first watery block here and use some flying **Echo**es to deal with the Rift Spear Moblin across the gap. Climb up onto the tree here and then to the top of the ledge above. From here, we can create a staircase to a second water-filled platform to the right. You will find the third glowing orb behind a boulder here.

Finding all three orbs will have Tri and her friends cleanse the rift. Tri will also gain a bit of XP, and will hand over **Might Crystal** x2. We will also find ourselves back outside in the 'real' world and the rift will vanish.

STILLED NORTHERN GERUDO DESERT RIFT

Location: Found in the far northwestern part of Gerudo Desert after completing Dungeon - Hyrule Castle.

After you enter the rift to reach the Still World, we will need to find and rescue Tri's friends. There are four glowing orbs hidden around this area and we will need to find and collect them all to complete the area.

As you enter the rift, you will see a cave ahead. Proceed inside. There are some Flying Tiles and a Rift Redead in here. Avoid the tiles and defeat the Redead for the first glowing orb.

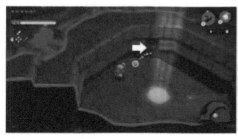 

Head outside. We will now need to climb up onto the raised ledge above the cave. Once up, you can find floating islands nearby both to the left and right of the initial platform.

First, head left and create a bridge off to the floating island nearby. Once across, use a Platboom to reach the ledge high above. Continue north to find a group of Boarboblins. Defeat them all, one of these fellows is carrying a glowing orb.

 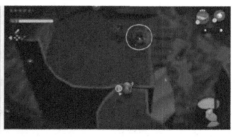

Drop down to the lower ledge on the right and create another bridge out of **Echo**es to the next floating island to your right. Here, there is another, higher island that we can Platboom/Waterblock up to. Atop this higher platform, you will find the third glowing orb.

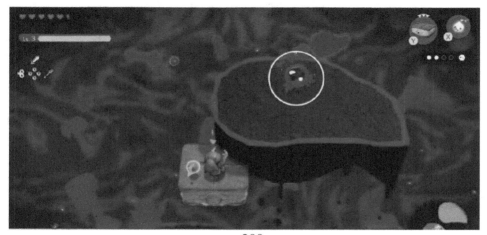

From the platforms below, again make your way over to the right. You will reach a collection of sandy floating islands with piles of sand scattered about. The island in the top, right corner has a sand pile hiding a glowing orb. Make your way over and use the wind cannon to blow it away for your prize.

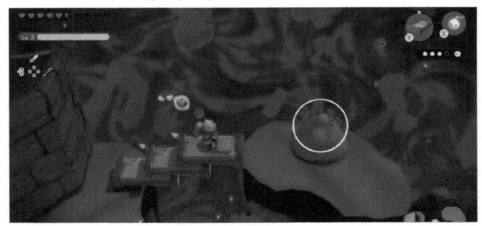

Finding all four orbs will have Tri and her friends cleanse the rift. Tri will also gain a bit of XP, and will hand over **Might Crystal** x2. We will also find ourselves back outside in the 'real' world and the rift will vanish.

STILLED EASTERN ZORA RIVER RIFT

Location: Found in the northeastern part of the Zora River after completing Dungeon - Hyrule Castle. It can be found by entering the cave behind the second tier of buildings in River Zora Village and then heading all the way to the right.

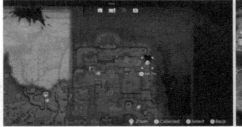

After you enter the rift to reach the Still World, we will need to find and rescue Tri's friends. There are three glowing orbs hidden around this area and we will need to find and collect them all to complete the area.

Once you are inside the rift, hop across the first gap to the north to reach a vertical platform with a pool of water on it. Defeat the Rift Tangler here. From this platform we can head to the left or the right.

Head to the left first. Continue across the next pair of floating islands until you reach one with a tree tat its centre. The tree will have the first glowing orb sitting atop it. Go ahead and grab that bad boy.

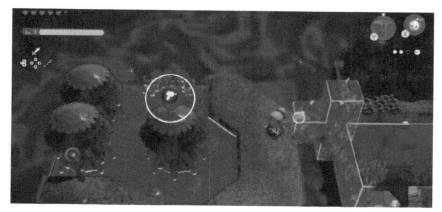

Return to the vertical water platform and this time, lets head right. On the next island over, you should be able to see a higher island above. Use a Platboom or waterblocks to climb up to it. Here, you will find a cave entrance. Continue inside.

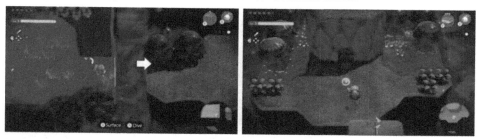

We will arrive in a side scrolling area. There is a bottomless pit below and a number of floating platforms above it, many pf which are completely covered in water, so navigating can be a bit tough – hopefully, you have the waterblocks by now! We will be able to explore both the left and the right of the initial entry point.

Check out the eft side first to reach a large, watery platform with a path leading upwards. There are several Rift Biri here, so be sure to send some **Echo**es to deal with them. At the top of this watery platform, there is a glowing orb.

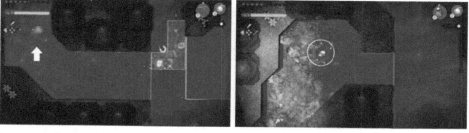

Return to the entrance and this time, make your way to the right. In the watery platform furthest to the right, you will find some Rift Tanglers. Defeat them all and you will discover that one is holding a final glowing orb.

Finding all three orbs will have Tri and her friends cleanse the rift. Tri will also gain a bit of XP, and will hand over **Might Crystal** x2. We will also find ourselves back outside in the 'real' world and the rift will vanish.

STILLED WESTERN ELDIN VOLCANO RIFT

Location: Found west of the entrance to Goron City. Drop down from the first bridge you come across to find it.

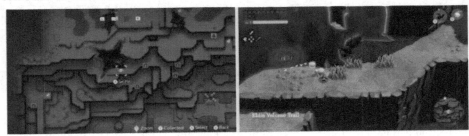

After you enter the rift to reach the Still World, we will need to find and rescue Tri's friends. There are five (!) glowing orbs hidden around this area, and we will need to find and collect them all to complete the rift.

Use the wind gusts here in tandem with a Ghirro **Echo** to continue to the right. We then want to boost up to the smaller islands above and Ghirro dash between these back to the left. On a small island with wind gusts on either side, you will find the first glowing orb.

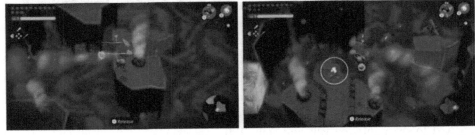

The next platform has a large lava pool on it. Be careful here as there is also a Fire Wizzrobe lurking about! Use A Ghirro to reach the ledges to the northeast of the lava pool to find a ladder we can use to descend into a side-scrolly area.

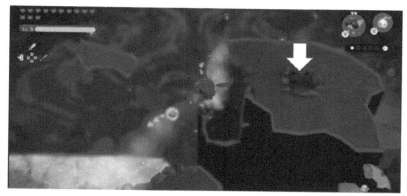

Once you arrive, drop down the gap on the right. Defeat the Fire Octo here and then drop down once again. Here on the left, you will find a Rift Spear Moblin. Defeating this will net you another glowing orb.

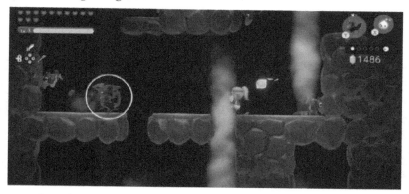

Continue to drop down and you will find another pair of glowing orbs. Once you reach the bottom, you will see a glowing orb in the middle of three wind gusts. Spawn a boulder or two here to block them and grab it. Jump onto the wind gust on the far right and as you ride it up, hop off onto the small ledge on the left with another glowing orb.

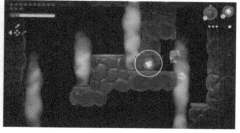

With all that looting done, climb back out of the side-scroll area.

When you are back outside, we now want to use a Ghirro to traverse the large pool of lava. On the western (left) side of this lava pool, there is a platform housing the final glowing orb.

Finding all five orbs will have Tri and her friends cleanse the rift. Tri will also gain a bit of XP, and will hand over **Might Crystal** x2. We will also find ourselves back outside in the 'real' world and the rift will vanish.

STILLED NORTHERN SANCTUARY RIFT

- Location: Found west of the graveyard across the moat to the north of Hyrule Castle.

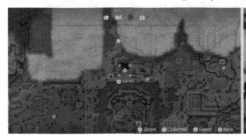

After you enter the rift to reach the Still World, we will need to find and rescue Tri's friends. There are three glowing orbs hidden around this area, and we will need to find and collect them all to complete the rift.

Upon arriving in this rift, the first thing you want to do is enter the church building ahead. Inside there are some Boarboblins. Defeat them all, one of them will be holding the first glowing orb.

Exit the church and take the path leading off to the right behind the church, using the trees to climb up into a graveyard area (watch out for the Rift Keese as you go). In the graveyard you will find some new ghost-like enemies. Kill these to learn an **Echo** - Ghini.

Head south from the main graveyard platform to find an island below with a smaller graveyard. Defeat the Ghini here and then bind and move the central gravestone to find the second glowing orb. On the platform to the west, we will find the final glowing orb, again below a gravestone we have to bind and pull. This time you will need to climb up to the ledge above and pull it from there.

Finding all three orbs will have Tri and her friends cleanse the rift. Tri will also gain a bit of XP, and will hand over **Might Crystal** x2. We will also find ourselves back outside in the 'real' world and the rift will vanish.

COLLECTIBLE & OTHER USEFUL ITEM LOCATIONS

PIECES OF HEART

Suthorn Prairie (5 Pieces of Heart)

❖ Piece of Heart #1

In the southeastern part of Suthorn Beach, climb up onto the central island here. From this location, use some beds to the left to reach a ledge with a **Piece of Heart**.

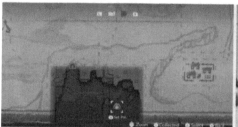 

❖ Piece of Heart #2

In the Beach Cave, continue to the right until you see a climbing wall with a stack of wooden crates beneath it and a **Piece of Heart** below. Climb the wall and hop onto the ledge on the right. Stand on the edge of this and spawn boulders. These will drop down and break the crates below. Repeat this until you can grab the **Piece of Heart**.

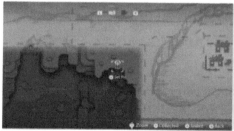 

❖ Piece of Heart #3

A **Piece of Heart** can be purchased from the General Store in Suthorn Village.

❖ *Piece of Heart #4*

Inside a cave in the northeastern part of Suthorn Forest. Inside, proceed to the right and grab **Echo** - Caromadillo. We can then send out a Caromadillo to burst through the line of crates ahead. Climb the climbable walls at the end, whilst avoiding the second Caromadillo. At the top you will find a **Piece of Heart**.

❖ *Piece of Heart #5*

There is a square pool of water at the centre of the columns in the field north of Suthorn Village with a large stone column at its centre. Atop this, there is a **Piece of Heart**. To grab this, you can place a bed/table bridge at its base and then summon a Crawltula. Bind yourself to this and have it carry you up to the top of the pillar to claim your prize.

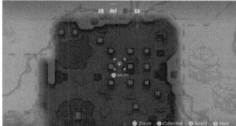

Gerudo Desert (5 Pieces of Heart)

❖ *Piece of Heart #1*

To the east of the Boarblin camp in the northern part of Gerudo Desert, you can find a pool of quicksand with a number of stone pillars in it. The large, central stone pillar has a **Piece of Heart** atop it. There are a couple of different ways to get to this. Initially, I used a collection of beds to keep making higher ledges until I could jump to it, however you can also use the stone pillars to the north of the quicksand to reach the large ledge facing the heart piece. From here you can simply create a bridge across. Much easier!

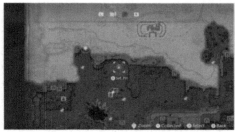

❖ *Piece of Heart #2*

Head south from the entrance to Gerudo Town until you find a small recess in the ground with a pile of sand in it. On some ledges just south of this, you will find a collection of sand piles. Use your wind cannon here to blow them away. There are several Arurodas hiding here along with a **Piece of Heart**.

 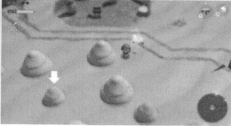

❖ *Piece of Heart #3*

After completing Dungeon - Gerudo Sanctum we can access the upper level of the Gerudo palace. Use a Platboom against the back wall and ride it up to the ledge above to find a set of stairs we can descend.

In the side-scroll area move past the first Platboom here and then use the second as a lift to reach a ledge above. You will see some stacks of crates in the next vertical shaft. Spawn a Platboom on top to crush them all. Jump down after it. You will find a giant boulder blocking the path. We want to bind this and then jump back onto the previous Platboom. Ride this up and carry the boulder with you. At the top, walk to the right to place it on an upper ledge. Return down the shaft and continue to the right to find a **Piece of Heart**.

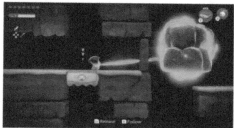 

❖ *Piece of Heart #4*

After completing the Still Missing main quest we can pick up the Side Quest: Wild Sandstorms. Defeat the Lanmola as part of this quest for a **Piece of Heart**.

❖ *Piece of Heart #5*

Complete the Ultimate Seed difficulty level of the Mango Rush mini-game with a perfect score to earn a **Piece of Heart**.

Hyrule Field (9 Pieces of Heart)

❖ *Piece of Heart #1*

Just north of the Moblin Camp in the southern part of Hyrule Field. Continue through the wooded area here, avoiding the Rope enemies in the grass. You will eventually reach a clearing with a **Piece of Heart** on a stump at its centre. Clear the nearby Peahat and then claim your prize.

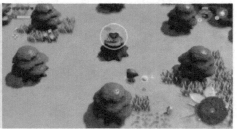

❖ *Piece of Heart #2*

Proceed to the west from the Hyrule Ranch until you find a lake with a tall stone pillar at its centre with a **Piece of Heart** on top. Spawn a bed by the base of the pillar and then a Crawltula. Bind yourself to this and have it carry you up to the top to claim the **Piece of Heart**.

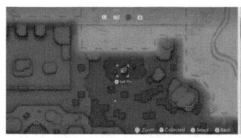

❖ *Piece of Heart #3*

There are some ruins in the northern part of Hyrule Field. In the northern part of these ruins, there are quite a few Caromadillos around. So go ahead and take them out. Afterwards, you will find a **Piece of Heart** atop a pillar on the eastern side of this area (use a Platboom or water blocks).

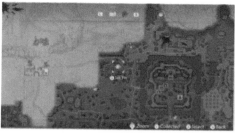 

❖ *Piece of Heart #4*

Just east of the entrance to Kakariko Village there is a cave to explore. Whilst you can head in here, you will not be able to find its ultimate prize from this entry point. Instead, climb to the ledge above the cave entrance and use a Holmill on the patch of dirt here. This will create a tunnel, and we can drop down inside for a **Piece of Heart**.

❖ *Piece of Heart #5*

Just north of the eastern gate to Kakariko Village you will find the fellow who starts the Acorn Gathering mini-game. If you can do this course in less than 20 seconds, you will be rewarded with a **Piece of Heart**.

❖ *Piece of Heart #6*

Just west of Kakariko Village, you will come across a large boulder. Approach from above, bind this and then summon a Platboom (or create some stairs or use water blocks). To lift the boulder up and out of its position. Place it somewhere nearby. Drop down to where the boulder had been to find a **Piece of Heart**.

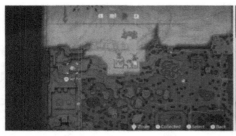 

❖ *Piece of Heart #7*

West of Kakariko Village, you will find a cave entrance. If you head inside, you will find that there are some boulders in place preventing us from exploring. To do so, outside the cave, look for a patch of dirt above it. Use a Holmill to create an opening and drop down inside. There is a **Piece of Heart** here. Use your bind to pull the boulders out of the way so that you can escape.

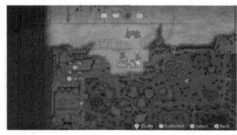 

❖ *Piece of Heart #8*

Complete the Side Quest: Let's Play a Game from Sago at the Eastern ruins in the Eastern Hyrule Field. Defeat Smog as part of this quest for a **Piece of Heart**.

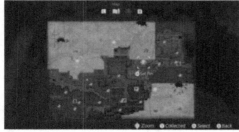 

❖ *Piece of Heart #9*

After completing the Side Quest: Impa's Gift you will unlock the Flag Races mini-game at Hyrule Ranch. Complete the middle Course under 20 seconds to earn a **Piece of Heart**.

Kakariko Village (2 Pieces of Heart)

❖ *Piece of Heart #1*

Complete 2 Training Challenges in the Slumber Dojo mini-game in Kakariko Village.

❖ *Piece of Heart #3*

Complete 11 Training Challenges in the Slumber Dojo mini-game in Kakariko Village.

Hyrule Castle Town (2 Pieces of Heart)

❖ *Piece of Heart #1*

After crossing the bridge, before entering the town itself, follow the narrow strip of land around the outside of the walls. When you reach the area north of the castle, you will find a **Piece of Heart** to snaffle. Nice!

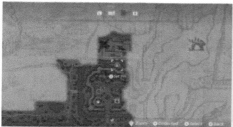 

❖ *Piece of Heart #2*

Complete the Side Quest: An Out-There Zol in Hyrule Castle Town for a **Piece of Heart** You will need to complete both Side Quest: A Curious Child and Side Quest: Performance Artist! to get this quest.

Jabul Waters (5 Pieces of Heart)

❖ *Piece of Heart #1*

On the seabed near the Stamp platform in Zora Cove, you will find a large, cracked boulder. Swim down and blow this up with a Bombfish for a sneakily placed **Piece of Heart**.

❖ *Piece of Heart #2*

Upon entering this cave, you will find the first area is occupied with Zols. You will find both regular Zols and Ignizols, and a Hydrozol. Be sure to learn **Echo** – Hydrozol here. These are useful for putting out fires!

After moving through the side-scroll area to the next room, clear it of enemies. Once the room is safe, note the four braziers around the room. We need to summon a Hydrozol and throw it into each of the lit braziers to douse the flames. Once they are all out, both doors will open. The left-hand door leads back to the cave entrance, but the northern door leads to a **Piece of Heart**.

❖ *Piece of Heart #3*

After completing the Dungeon - Jabul Ruins return to Jabu-Jabu's Den to find that it is free of the rift that covered it earlier. Head around to the right side of the building and you will spot a **Piece of Heart** sitting on a pillar. Use some water blocks to swim right up to it.

❖ *Piece of Heart #4*

After completing the Dungeon - Jabul Ruins head to River Zora Village. Climb to the top of the waterfall behind Dradd's hut. Here we can use water blocks to climb the eastern wall. At the top, head to the east until you see another waterfall. Again, use water clocks to climb this. At the top, you will find a Fairy and a **Piece of Heart**.

 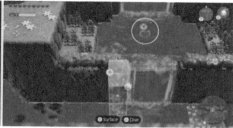

❖ *Piece of Heart #5*

After completing the Still Missing main quest we can pick up the Side Quest: The Zappy Shipwreck in Seesyde Village. Defeat the giant Biri boss as part of this quest for a **Piece of Heart**.

Eldin Volcano (4 Pieces of Heart)

❖ *Piece of Heart #1*

From the first **Waypoint Stone** on Eldin Volcano, head north. At the top of the first climbing wall, you will see a second dead ahead. Climb this too. At the top, there is a longer horizontal climbing wall with a Torch Slug, so use some flying critters to deal with it. Hop up to the wall above and climb all the way to the right to find a ledge with a **Piece of Heart**.

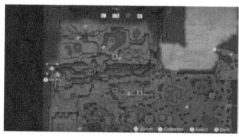 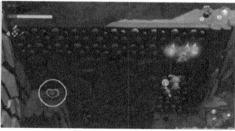

❖ *Piece of Heart #2*

On an island in the lava pit just northeast of the Lizalfos Burrow. To reach this, use a Lava Rock or Tweelus **Echo** to hop across to a small island with a **Piece of Heart**.

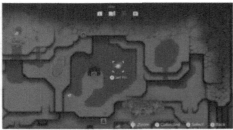

❖ *Piece of Heart #3*

This can be found at the very end of a narrow ledge sticking out above the **Waypoint Stone** near the entrance to the Lizalfos Burrow. Follow the path here south to find a **Piece of Heart**.

❖ *Piece of Heart #4*

After completing the Dungeon - Eldin Temple we can pick up the Side Quest: A Mountainous Mystery in Goron City. Defeat the giant Igneo Talus boss as part of this quest for a **Piece of Heart**.

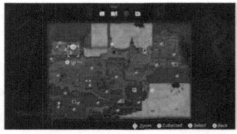

Faron Wetlands (4 Pieces of Heart)

❖ *Piece of Heart #1*

On the far, western side of the Faron Westland region as you head south, you will see a cave entrance. Whilst you can explore this, you will find it is blocked. Fortunately, there is an alternate entrance nearby. Climb up onto the ledge above the cave entrance and locate the pool of water here. We can dive down inside this to reach the very same cave.

Enter the cave to reach an underwater side-scroll area. As soon as you arrive, defeat the monster for **Echo** - Lizalfos Lv. 3 and a **Treasure Chest** that contains a Purple Rupee. Continue to the left and you will find the path forwards is blocked by a pair of boulders.

Pull the first one back and out of the opening, then swim down and push the second forwards. Swim up the vertical passage here, using a Bombfish to access the bubbles on the left if needed. We will come across another passage blocked by a boulder. Bind this from below and push it all the way to the right. After it sinks, grab it again and pull it out of the opening. We can now swim up to the top.

A short swim to the east, we can surface into a room with a pair of Needleflies. Summon some aerial critters to eliminate them. In this room, use water blocks to create a vertical path. At the top, jump to a ledge on the left. At the top there is a platform with an Armos guarding a **Piece of Heart**.

Run over to activate the enemy. It will hop along the length of this passage back and forth. In the middle of this passage, you will see a section of roof that is slightly higher. We need to use this location to jump over the Armos I used a Trampoline (but water blocks will probably work too). Once you are behind it, defeat the Armos and claim your prize.

❖ Piece of Heart #2

In the cave between the Heart Lake and Blossu's House in the southern part of Faron Wetlands. Just before exiting the cave, look across the gap to the left and you should be

315

able to spot a **Piece of Heart**. Build a bridge over to this to grab it.

❖ *Piece of Heart #3*

In the Scrubton Lockup, after the first stealth section, check out the three decorative shrubs on the back wall of the next room. Pull away the middle one to find they are hiding a door. Inside you will find a **Piece of Heart** atop a collection of pillars. We need to create a set of successively higher platforms to reach the top of the pillars. This setup worked for me – bed > torch > torch on bed > tree > tree on table. From here you can jump to the top.

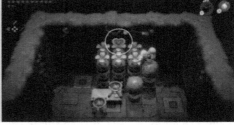

❖ *Piece of Heart #4*

After completing the Dungeon - Faron Temple we can pick up the Cotton-Candy Hunt in Scrubton. Defeat the Smog boss as part of this quest for a **Piece of Heart**.

Hebra Mountain and Mount Lanayru (4 Pieces of Heart)

❖ *Piece of Heart #1*

In the middle section of Hebra Mountain, there is a large frozen lake. In the southwest corner of this lake, you will find a **Piece of Heart** on an island. Melt away the ice on the island and work your way up to the prize at the top.

❖ *Piece of Heart #2*

In the upper section of Hebra Mountain, follow main path until you climb a wall. From the top of this wall, you will see the obvious path to the right, but also a lower path on the left.

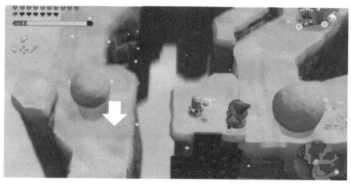

Jump down to this lower area and work your way up the hill, dodging snowballs (or using a boulder as a blocker). As you go, you will spot a rock pillar on the right side of the path with a **Piece of Heart**. Climb up to grab this.

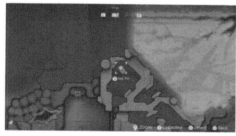 

❖ *Piece of Heart #3*

After completing the Dungeon - Lanayru Temple, return to the middle section of Hebra Mountain, to where we crossed the large icy pool. In this location, head to the east to where the Ice Wizzrobe was located. Here we can climb up onto the ledges overlooking his area to find a **Piece of Heart**.

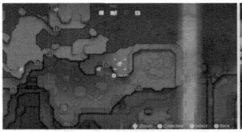

❖ *Piece of Heart #4*

After completing the Dungeon - Lanayru Temple we can pick up the Snowball Magic from Conde at his House. Complete this quest for a **Piece of Heart**.

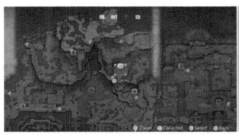

ACCESSORIES

Accessories are extremely useful pieces of armour that can be equipped from the inventory menu to provide Zelda with a number of passive bonus. Players can initially equip a single Accessory, but by finding the Great Fairy in Lake Hylia, you can purchase additional Accessory Slots allowing you to equip up to five Accessories. Finding and experimenting with combinations of Accessories can greatly enhance your gameplay experience.

Accessories can be found in several different places and are usually obtained from chests purchased from merchants, dropped by bosses or from completing NPC side-quests. Below you'll find a list of Accessories, their effects and where you can find them organized alphabetically.

Accessory	Effect	Region	Location
Ancient Charm	Damage Reduction	Hyrule Field	Complete Side Quest: Let's Play a Game
Charging Horn	Increase Horse Attack Damage	Hyrule Field	Complete the Long Course of the Flag Races mini-game in under 40 seconds.
Climbing Band	Increase Climbing Speed	Kakariko Village	Purchase from General Store in Kakariko Village for 400 **Rupees**.

Accessory	Effect	Region	Location
Clockwork Bangle	Increase windup speed	Hyrule Field	Complete Side Quest: Get Rich Quick! and speak with Dampe.
Curious Charm	Damage Reduction Lv.2	Faron Wetlands	Complete Side Quest: Cotton-Candy Hunt
Energy Belt	Increased Energy Appearance Lv.2	Hebra Mountain	Found in a **Treasure Chest** in the cave past the Moblin Camp by Conde's house on Hebra Mountain.
Energy Glove	Increased Energy Appearance	Gerudo Desert	Found in a **Treasure Chest** in the Boarboblin Camp in northwest Gerudo Desert.
Fairy Flower	Increased Fairy Appearance	Eldin Volcano	Found in a **Treasure Chest** behind a weak wall just below and west of the westernmost **Waypoint Stone** on Eldin Volcano.
Fairy Fragrance	Increased Fairy Appearance Lv.2	Faron Wetlands	Complete Side Quest: Looking for Bempu
Final Mastery	Energy Consumption Reduced Lv.3	Kakariko Village	Complete 14 Challenges in the Slumber Dojo mini-game.
First Mastery	Energy Consumption Reduced	Kakariko Village	Complete 4 Challenges in the Slumber Dojo mini-game.
Frog Ring	Increase jump height	Hyrule Castle Town	Found in a **Treasure Chest** in Dungeon - Hyrule Castle.
Gerudo Sandals	Quicksand Proof	Gerudo Desert	Purchase from General Store in Gerudo Town for 400 **Rupees**.
Gold Brooch	Increased Rupee Appearance Lv.2	Jabul Waters	Complete Side Quest: Secret Chief Talks.

Accessory	Effect	Region	Location
Gold Sash	Wind Proof	Gerudo Desert	Complete Side Quest: Wild Sandstorms.
Goron's Bracelet	Increase movement speed whilst carrying	Eldin Volcano	Complete Side Quest: A Mountainous Mystery.
Heart Barrette	Increased Heart Appearance Lv.2	Gerudo Desert	Complete Side Quest: Beetle Ballyhoo.
Heart Pin	Increased Heart Appearance	Suthorn Forest	Found in a **Treasure Chest** in Dungeon - Suthorn Ruins.
Ice Spikes	Reduce slip when walking on ice	Hebra Mountain	Found in a **Treasure Chest** in a cave on the middle section of Hebra Mountain.
Might Bell	Detects nearby **Might Crystals**	Lake Hylia	Complete Side Quest: The Great Fairy's Request .
Second Mastery	Energy Consumption Reduced Lv.2	Kakariko Village	Complete 8 Challenges in the Slumber Dojo mini-game.
Silver Brooch	Increased Rupee Appearance	Jabul Waters	Found in a **Treasure Chest** behind a weak wall just west of the River Zora Village.
Spin Brace	Spin attacks cause knockback	Faron Wetlands	Found in a **Treasure Chest** in the ruins east of Scrubton.
Stone Anklet	Reduce knockback	Hyrule Castle Town	Purchase from General Store in Hyrule Castle Town for 400 **Rupees**.
Survey Binoculars	Increased Material Appearance Lv.2	Business Scrubs	Complete 30 recipes during Side Quest: Recipes, Please!

Accessory	Effect	Region	Location
Survey Scope	Increased Material Appearance	Business Scrubs	Complete 10 recipes during Side Quest: Recipes, Please!
Zora Scale	Slightly increases Dive Time	Jabul Waters	Complete Side Quest: The Zora Child's Fate.
Zora's Flippers	Increase Swim Speed	Jabul Waters	Purchase from General Store in River Zora Village for 400 **Rupees**.

FAIRY BOTTLES

The Fairy Bottles are a useful item to obtain because having bottles allows you to, well, capture Fairies. These are useful as they act as essentially extra lives - when Zelda dies whilst carrying a Fairy in a bottle, the Fairy will pop out of a bottle and bring her back to life along with a few hearts.

There are four Fairy Bottles to be found around the world map. Below you'll find a list of where you can find them organized chronologically as they appear in our walkthrough.

Accessory	Region	Location
Fairy Bottle #1	Suthorn Forest	This is located in a **Treasure Chest** in a cave in Suthorn Forest, just east of the **Waypoint Stone** By Suthorn Village.
Fairy Bottle #2	Jabul Waters	Complete Side Quest: The Zappy Shipwreck.
Fairy Bottle #3	Kakariko Village	Complete Side Quest: Cuccos on the Loose.
Fairy Bottle #3	Stamp Guy	Find 15 Stamps to complete the Stamp Guy's third Stamp Rally.

OUTFITS

Outfits can change the look of Zelda and although these are mostly cosmetic, a few of them to have some specific effects when equipped. Players can only equip a single **Outfit** at a time. These can be obtained from chests, or from completing NPC side-quests. Several of these can also be obtained by using Amiibos.

Below you'll find a list of **Outfits**, their effects and where you can find them organized alphabetically.

Unlockable Outfits

Accessory	Effect	Region	Location
Cat Clothes	Allows Zelda to speak with cats.	Kakariko Village	Complete Side Quest: Questioning the Local Cats.
Customary Attire	N/A	Hyrule Castle Town	Complete Side Quest: From the Heart.
Dancing Outfit	Increases range of Zelda's spin.	Gerudo Desert	Complete the 'Ultimate' difficulty of the Mango Rush mini-game.
Disguise	People do not recognize Zelda, changing dialogue	Hyrule Castle Town	Acquired during Main Quest: The Mysterious Rifts.
Green Tunic	N/A	Kakariko Village	Complete all 15 challenges in the Slumber Dojo mini-game.
Royal Travel Attire	N/A	Hyrule Castle Town	Acquired after completing Dungeon - Hyrule Castle.
Silk Pajamas	Recover Hearts more quickly when sleeping.	Gerudo Desert	Complete Side Quest: Dohna's Challenge.
Stamp Suit	N/A	Stamp Guy	Find and collect all 25 Stamps.

Amiibo Outfits

Accessory	Effect	Region	Location
Black Cat Clothes	Allows Zelda to speak with cats.	Amiibo	Scan any Ganon Amiibo to be awarded this **Outfit**.
Blue Attire	N/A	Amiibo	Scan any Zelda Amiibo to be awarded this **Outfit**.
Red Tunic	N/A	Amiibo	Scan any Link Amiibo to be awarded this **Outfit**.

STAMPS

Hyrule Field (6 Stamps)

❖ *Stamp #1*

By the entrance to Hyrule Ranch, you will find a Stamp platform.

❖ *Stamp #2*

Swim to the southeastern corner of Lake Hylia to find a ledge that we can climb out on. Here there is another Stamp platform to keep your Stamp Rally going.

❖ *Stamp #3*

To the far left of Kakariko Village climb up to the high ledge at the end. There is a Stamp platform here we can use to progress our latest Stamp Rally. Nice!

❖ *Stamp #4*

By the entrance to Kakariko Village, you will find a Stamp platform.

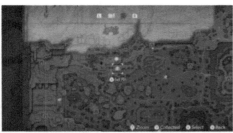

❖ *Stamp #5*

By the entrance to the Eastern Ruins in Eastern Hyrule Field there is a large set of stairs leading upwards. Along the wall to the right of this, there is a Stamp platform. Go ahead and use this to keep that Stamp Rally going.

❖ *Stamp #6*

In the lake just northeast of Hyrule Castle fight off the Tektites and Spear Moblin on and around the small islands here. At the northern end of this water, there is a taller platform we can water block our way up to with a Stamp platform. Use this to continue our latest Stamp Rally.

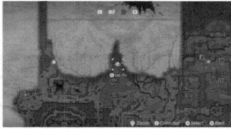
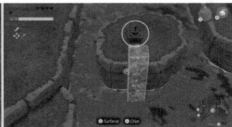

Gerudo Desert (4 Stamps)

❖ *Stamp #1*

On a ledge to the east of the ruins south of the Oasis. Climb up here using a trampoline and continue north to find a Stamp stand.

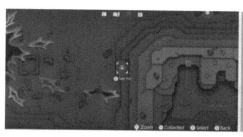 

❖ *Stamp #2*

From the pink tent at the Oasis, we can travel directly west to reach Gerudo Town. However, around halfway to Gerudo Town, you will come across a pair of rocky pillars. There is another Stamp to collect here for your Stamp Rally.

❖ *Stamp #3*

Head to the western side of Gerudo Town. On the cliff overlooking the settlement, you should be able to spot another Stamp platform. Spawn and ride a Platboom up to it to add it to your Stamp Rally.

❖ *Stamp #4*

Fight through to the end of the Boarboblin Camp north of Gerudo Town. At the end, use a Platboom to reach the ledges to the north overlooking this area. Once up, head a short distance to the east. You will see another Stamp platform above. Use a Platboom to reach it and add it to your Stamp Rally collection.

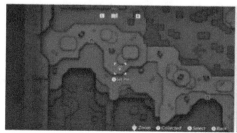 

Jabul Waters (4 Stamps)

❖ *Stamp #1*

On the beach by the entrance to Seesyde Village, you will find a Stamp platform.

❖ *Stamp #2*

Swim out your way all the way to the eastern side of the water in Zora Cove to find a small island with a Stamp platform. Go ahead and activate this to add another stamp to your collection.

❖ *Stamp #3*

Continue to the west from the entrance to Jabu-Jabu's Den to reach the next section of water. Before following it to the north, look on the far, eastern side of this stretch of river to find a Stamp platform to notch another entry in your Stamp Rally.

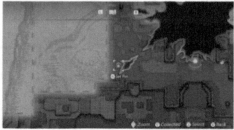 

❖ *Stamp #4*

In the River Zora Village climb up to Dradd's hut. There is a Stamp platform on the ledge above and to the west of this. You can use water blocks to climb the nearby waterfall and then follow the path on top around to reach it. Add to that Stamp Rally!

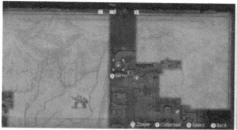

Eldin Volcano (4 Stamps)

❖ *Stamp #1*

By the entrance to Goron City, you will find a Stamp platform.

❖ *Stamp #2*

From the entrance to Goron City, we want to head to the right (east). Look for a stone ramp leading upwards. Before climbing this, head to the edge of the nearby cliff and look below. You should be able to make out a **Treasure Chest** and a Stamp platform.

We can simply drop down to the ledge with the **Treasure Chest** and loot it for **Might Crystal** x2. The Stamp platform below can be reached using a Ghirro and its wind gust to propel you over. Activate this to continue with your latest Stamp rally.

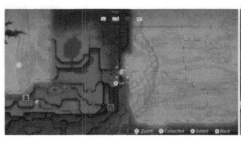
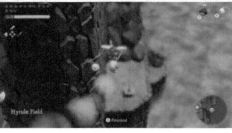

❖ *Stamp #3*

Just south of the entrance to the Rock-Roast Quarry, head down a ramp. On the right side of this area, you will find a small island surrounded by lava with a Stamp platform. Build a bridge over to collect it for your Stamp Rally!

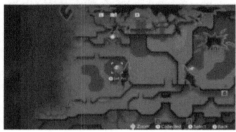

❖ *Stamp #4*

After completing Dungeon - Eldin Temple, fast travel to the **Waypoint Stone** outside the Rock-Roast Quarry. Without the rift here, you can climb up to the ledges above the entrance. Continuing climbing upwards and head all the way to the right to find a Stamp platform. Go ahead and use this to continue your current Stamp Rally.

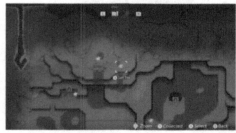

Faron Wetlands (4 Stamps)

❖ *Stamp #1*

Head to the east from the entrance to the Sweet Spot. Defeat the enemies and then climb up above the waterfall to deal with the Drippitune here. In the pool above the waterfall there is a small island with a Stamp platform.

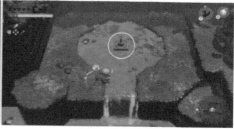

❖ *Stamp #2*

Head directly south from the prison area in the western part of Scrubton, you can find a Stamp platform.

❖ *Stamp #3*

Just north of Heart Lake in the southwestern part of Faron Wetlands, the path will split. Between the two paths, you will find a raised ledge with another Stamp platform for your Stamp Rally. Go ahead and activate that.

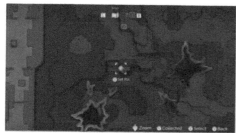

❖ *Stamp #4*

Head west from Blossu's House, and fight the Electric Wizzrobe. Head north from its location. At the northern end of this area, you will find a pair of lit braziers. Head past these and it will start raining. Defeat the pair of Ribbitunes here to stop the rain. You can then light the two tall braziers in the water here to have the statue ahead move, revealing a secret staircase. Look behind the statue for a raised ledge we can climb up to. Do so and head left to find a Stamp platform. Activate this to continue your Stamp Rally.

Hebra Mountain and Mount Lanayru (3 Stamps)

❖ *Stamp #1*

From the start of the cold area in the lower part of Hebra Mountain, you can climb the ledges on the left to find a Stamp Platform.

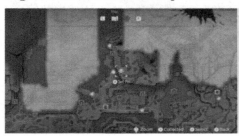

❖ *Stamp #2*

In the Moblin Camp northeast of Conde's house, head for the guard tower on the western side of the camp. Climb on top of this and you should be able to spot a Stamp platform in a small clearing in the trees nearby. Jump up onto the tress and down into the clearing to grab the Stamp for your Stamp Rally.

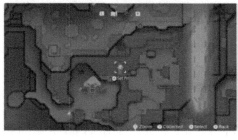

❖ *Stamp #3*

At the very top of Hebra Mountain, head to the path leading right. At the end of this path you will find the Stamp Guy. Speak with him here for a side quest - Stamp Stand Swallowed!. Complete this side quest to remove the nearby rift and reveal the Stamp platform.

ALL MIGHT CRYSTAL LOCATIONS

Might Crystals are the most prevalent form of collectible hidden around the world map in The Legend of Zelda: **Echo**es of Wisdom. They can be found hidden under rocks, grass plants, in dirt patches that can be dug up, ice crystals that can be melted down and a few are just sitting out in the open. Additionally, they can be earned by sealing rifts, finishing dungeons and completing various side quests throughout the game... what we are trying to get at is, that there is a lot of them!

Might Crystals are important as we can use the machine at Lueberry's house to upgrade the damage dealt by the Sword of Might, Bow of Might, Bombs of Might and Zelda's energy meter (upgrading this allows you to stay in swordfighter mode for longer) To fully upgrade your sword, Bow and Bombs, you require 30 **Might Crystals** for each and to max out Zelda's Energy meter, you require 35 **Might Crystals**.

Note: All these upgrades will require 125 of the 150 **Might Crystals**. If you can collect the remaining 25, Lueberry can use them to create an energy recharge station outside of his house!

Of the 150 **Might Crystals** available, we will get several for completing a few different activities and can be unlocked in the following ways:

- 35x **Might Crystal** can be earned for completing each of the first seven dungeons.

- 26x **Might Crystal** can be earned for closing Rifts (including both mandatory and optional)

- **Might Crystal** can be earned through side quests. These include:
    - Side Quest: Finding the Flying Plant
    - Side Quest: Elusive Tumbleweeds
    - Side Quest: A Curious Child
    - Side Quest: A Treat for My Person
    - Side Quest: Glide Path Trailblazer
    - Side Quest: The Flames of Fortune
    - Side Quest: Mobbing Mothulas!
    - Side Quest: Impa's Gift
    - Side Quest: From the Heart
    - Side Quest: Stamp Stand Swallowed!

- 9x **Might Crystals** can be earned by participating in mini-games (3x **Might**

Crystal from each of Acorn Gathering, Flag Races and Mango Rush)

- Additional **Might Crystals** can be found hidden around the world map. Read on below to find them all!

Suthorn Prairie & Suthorn Forest (4 Might Crystals)

❖ *Might Crystal #1*

Dive down and perform a spin on the central piece of seaweed in the lake in the northwest part of Suthorn Prairie to receive a Might Stone.

❖ *Might Crystal #2*

On the ridge to the north at the very start of the path leading from Suthorn Prairie to Gerudo Desert, you can find a rock that we can pick up for a **Might Crystal**.

❖ *Might Crystal #3*

Just north of the **Waypoint Stone** at the entrance to Gerudo Desert there is a tree stump with a rock on top of it. Trampoline up and bind the rock to move it. Beneath the rock there is a **Might Crystal**.

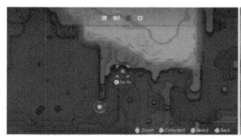 

❖ *Might Crystal #4*

After climbing the waterfall on the east side of Lake Hylia, you will reach a narrow ridge that borders the Faron Wetlands and Suthorn Forest. Continue south and you will reach a rocky area with a number of Mini-Moldorms. Clear all of these out. Once it is safe to do so, look for a raised ledge in the northern part of this area. Climb up here and slash the lone plant here for a **Might Crystal**.

Gerudo Desert (7 Might Crystals)

❖ *Might Crystal #1-2*

Found in a **Treasure Chest** at the end of the cave in the ruins south of the Oasis.

❖ *Might Crystal #3*

Climb up onto the ledge to the east of the ruins that are south of the Oasis. Follow this ledge to the south to find a pile of sand. Summon a wind cannon to blow this away to reveal a **Might Crystal**.

❖ *Might Crystal #4*

Work your way through the cave by the Boarblin Camp in the northern part of the central desert (east of the **Waypoint Stone** by the Ancestor's Cave of Rest) after reaching the end of the cave, exit to find a **Treasure Chest** with a **Might Crystal**.

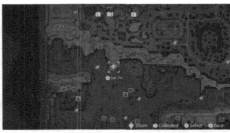

❖ *Might Crystal #5*

On a ridge overlooking the large Boarboblin Camp north of Gerudo Town. Once up, follow the top of the ridge south until you find a small patch of dirt on the ground. You can deploy a Holmill here and it will dig up another **Might Crystal** to add to our growing collection.

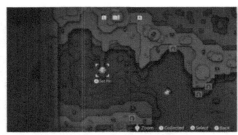

❖ *Might Crystal #6*

Check out the ridge above the northern Boarboblin camp (roughly northwest from the Oasis), you can find another stone to pick up here that hides a **Might Crystal**.

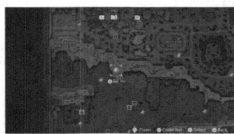

❖ *Might Crystal #7*

Climb up onto the ridge to the west of the Oasis using a Platboom. On top, there is a rock that we can lift up to find a **Might Crystal**.

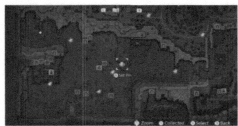

Hyrule Field (23 Might Crystals)

❖ Might Crystal #1

From Hyrule Ranch, head southwest to find a small, raised ledge with a single shrub on top. Suspicious, no? Spin through the shrub to find a **Might Crystal**.

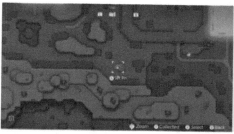 

❖ Might Crystal #2-4

To the west of Hyrule Ranch there is a small pool of water. Just northwest of here there is a cave we can explore. Inside are three Sword Moblins guarding a **Treasure Chest**. We can loot this for **Might Crystal** x3.

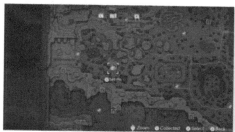 

❖ Might Crystal #5

To the west of Hyrule Ranch there is a small pool of water. West of the pool there is a collection of tall grass on the ground in the shape of an arrow. Spin through the shrub that this is pointing to in order to find another **Might Crystal**.

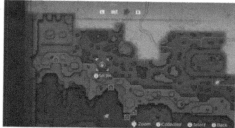 

❖ Might Crystal #6

Just southwest of the bridge leading to Hyrule Castle Town is a raised ledge we can jump up to with a rock hiding a **Might Crystal**.

❖ *Might Crystal #7*

From the southern end of the bridge to Hyrule Castle Town, follow the moat to the west and after passing a collection of trees look in behind it for a single grass plant that doesn't really below. Spin through this to find a **Might Crystal**.

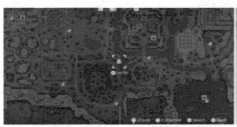 

❖ *Might Crystal #8*

After crossing the bridge north of Lake Hylia, immediately run to the left to find a boulder nearby. Bind this and move it to the side to reveal a hidden **Might Crystal**. Nice!

❖ *Might Crystal #9*

After crossing the bridge north of Lake Hylia, head east. As you go, watch out for a Crow that will likely attack. Defeat it. Before continuing, look by the tree the Crow had been on initially to find a boulder. Move this with bind to reveal a **Might Crystal**.

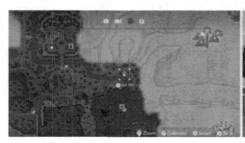 

❖ *Might Crystal #10*

After crossing the bridge north of Lake Hylia, head east. The path will soon come to a four-way intersection with roads leading off in all four cardinal directions. Continue to the east. You will proceed through a fairly lengthy canyon like area occupied by several Ropes and Caromadillos. By the entrance to this canyon, if you climb up to the ledges to the north, you can find a stone we can pick up that is hiding a **Might Crystal**.

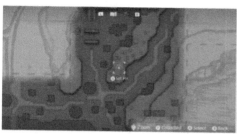 

❖ *Might Crystal #11*

Just southeast from the entrance to the Eastern Ruins where Sago is waiting, you can find a ledge with a single rock on it that we can climb up to. Pick this up to find another **Might Crystal**.

❖ *Might Crystal #12-14*

Outside of Dampe's house, climb the ledge on the right to find a cave. Inside, there is a fence with a **Treasure Chest** on the left and a pressure plate on the right. Summon an **Echo** through the bars on the right (I used a Caromadillo) and have it move onto the pressure plate to lower the fence. Loot the chest for **Might Crystal** x3.

❖ *Might Crystal #15*

Outside of Dampe's house, climb the ledge on the right to find a cave. Follow the ledge to the south of the cave to find a small dirt patch that we can excavate with a Holmill. Doing so will earn you a **Might Crystal**.

337

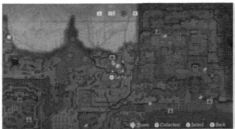

❖ *Might Crystal #16*

Just west of Dampe's hut, we can climb up to a ledge above with a collection of suspicious looking rocks. We can pick up the rock at the centre to find a **Might Crystal**.

❖ *Might Crystal #17*

Southwest from Hyrule Castle is a pit in the ground by the main road. There will be several Ignizols and regular Zols in here. Cut down the plant on the rocky pillar at the centre of this pit for a **Might Crystal**.

❖ *Might Crystal #18*

Look for a set of stairs in a ruin in northern Hyrule Field. This will take you to a small underground area that we visited briefly during the prologue. There is a **Might Crystal** here... don't jump into the water or you will end up back on Suthorn Beach!

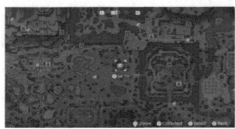

❖ Might Crystal #19

Look for a ruin in northern Hyrule Field. Make your way to the southwest from the ruins In the grassy field, you should spot a Peahat by a suspicious collection of stones. Defeat the critter and then pick up the rocks, the middle one is hiding a **Might Crystal**. Just west of this location, you will also find a **Waypoint Stone**.

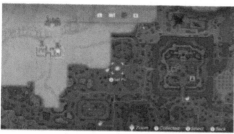 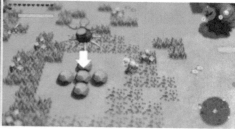

❖ Might Crystal #20

On one of the stone pillars south from Kakariko Village there is a collection of stones, one of which we can pick up for a **Might Crystal**.

❖ Might Crystal #21

Head south from the stamp platform on the far, western side of Hyrule Field to find a rock on its own... pick this up to find a **Might Crystal**.

❖ Might Crystal #22

From the Waypoint Marker east of Hyrule Ranch, by the path leading to Suthorn Prairie head northwest. There is a circular clearing in the middle of the forest (we snagged a **Piece of Heart** here earlier) occupied by a Peahat and some Ropes. In the northwest corner of this clearing, there is a patch of dirt we can dig up using a Holmill. Doing so will net you another **Might Crystal**.

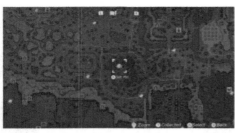

❖ *Might Crystal #23*

Check out the graveyard in the northwest part of Kakariko Village for a small patch of dirt that a Holmill can dig up for a **Might Crystal**.

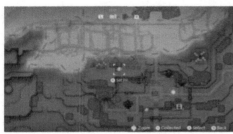

Hyrule Castle Town (3 Might Crystals)

❖ *Might Crystal #1-2*

In Hyrule Castle Town there is a bird-shaped statue. Bind this and pull it to the side to reveal a set of stairs leading downwards. There is a **Treasure Chest** here with **Might Crystal** x2.

❖ *Might Crystal #3*

Climb up to the roof of Hyrule Castle to find a **Might Crystal**.

Lake Hylia (2 Might Crystals)

❖ *Might Crystal #1*

To the west of the Great Fairy's Island is an optional rift. South of here, beneath the water there is a large boulder on the lakebed. Grab this with bind and move it to find a **Might Crystal** beneath it.

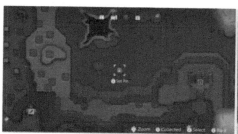
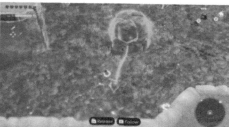

❖ *Might Crystal #2*

Found inside the Great Fairy's Island after purchasing 4 accessory slots is a **Treasure Chest** we can loot for a **Might Crystal**.

Jabul Waters (10 Might Crystals)

❖ *Might Crystal #1*

Climb the ledge behind the **Waypoint Stone** and continue north until you reach another raised ledge. Atop this, you can find a small patch of dirt that we can dig up with a Holmill. Doing so will net you a **Might Crystal**.

❖ *Might Crystal #2*

At the very southern end of the docks in Seesyde Village, you can find a **Might Crystal** below.

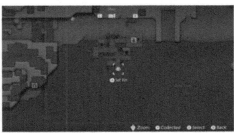

❖ Might Crystal #3

To the west of the Sea Zora island, you can find a cracked rock on the seabed. Use a Bombfish to blow this up to find a recess beneath it housing a **Might Crystal**.

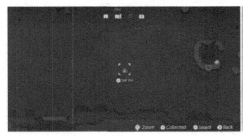

❖ Might Crystal #4

Northeast of the Zora island, there is a circular clump of seaweed on the seabed. Dive down and twirl through the plant at its centre to find a **Might Crystal**.

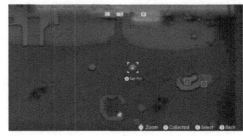

❖ Might Crystal #5-7

Head to the west from Jabu-Jabu's Den until you reach the Stamp platform nearby. From here, head south until you reach a section of shallow river with trees surrounding it. Use a trampoline to jump onto the trees here and then follow the treetop path to the west until you can drop down.

We will be in a relatively large open area that is in essence a large Moblin camp. Slowly work your way north, dispatching the Needleflies, Spear Moblins and Sword Moblins as you go. Defeating them all will unlock the **Treasure Chest** here which holds **Might Crystal** x3.

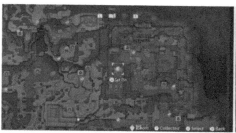

❖ *Might Crystal #8-10*

Head for the destroyed huts midway up the River Zora Village and head east from them and then follow the ledge here south and then around the corner to the east. Along the eastern wall you can create a stack of water blocks to reach the area above.

We will land in another large, open Moblin camp occupied by Spear Moblins, Sword Moblins and Needleflies. In the lower, left section of this area you will find a **Treasure Chest** with **Might Crystal** x3, and for defeating all the enemies, you can unlock the **Treasure Chest** they were guarding for Golden Egg.

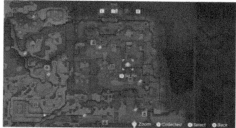

Eldin Volcano (7 Might Crystals)

❖ *Might Crystal #1-3*

As you ascend the mountain, you will proceed through a Lizalfos camp. Clear these out and be sure to learn **Echo** - Lizalfos here. Defeating them will also unlock a nearby

Treasure Chest we can loot for **Might Crystal** x3.

❖ *Might Crystal #4-5*

From the entrance to Goron City, we want to head to the right (east). Look for a stone ramp leading upwards. Before climbing this, head to the edge of the nearby cliff and look below. You should be able to make out a **Treasure Chest** and a Stamp platform.

We can simply drop down to the ledge with the **Treasure Chest** and loot it for **Might Crystal** x2.

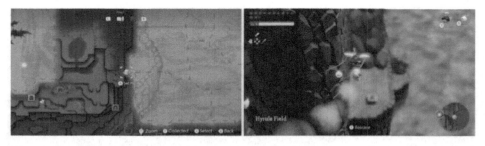

❖ *Might Crystal #6*

From the entrance to Goron City, we want to head to the right (east). Look for a stone ramp leading upwards. Before climbing this, head to the edge of the nearby cliff and look below. You should be able to make out a **Treasure Chest** and a Stamp platform. 730px-TLoZEOW_CH11-01.jpg

From the Stamp platform, you will see a third, lower platform off to the right. Again, use a Ghirro to fly over to this. Pick up the rock here to find a **Might Crystal**.

344

❖ *Might Crystal #7*

From the entrance to the Rock-Roast Quarry. Use a Platboom/Water Block to climb up to the left of the entrance to find a Lizalfos Lv.2 guarding a **Treasure Chest** with a **Might Crystal**.

Faron Wetlands (4 Might Crystals)

❖ *Might Crystal #1*

From the entrance to the Sweet Spot, head to the east until you reach a waterfall. Climb up to the top of this. On the left side of this upper area, you should be able to see a webbed opening on the cliff wall. Create a bridge up to this and use a fire-based **Echo** to burn away the web. Behind it you will find a **Might Crystal**.

❖ *Might Crystal #2*

On the far, western part of the Faron Wastelands, follow the main path south. As you go, look for a smaller path on the left side of the main path. This leads to a small clearing with a suspicious arrangement of plants. Spin attack the central plant for a **Might Crystal**.

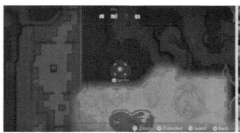

❖ *Might Crystal #3*

Above the cave entrance to the west of Blossu's house. Use waterblocks or a Platboom, to get up there. Here you will find another suspicious collection of shrubs. Cut down the middle one for a **Might Crystal**.

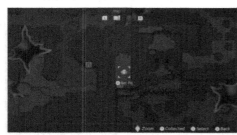

❖ *Might Crystal #4*

As you escape the Deku Scrub Lockup, you will go through a side-scrolling underwater area. In the last part of this, there are two downwards currents here that we can navigate upwards. The first leads to the exit, whereas the right current leads up to a **Might Crystal**. There are two solutions to getting up each. The first involves using a box in the vertical path between the two currents – bind this and drag it to the bottom of the wall. Swim off to the sides that you are in the current and then hold ZR to follow the box's movement upwards through the current. The other, simpler method is to just use a Platboom!

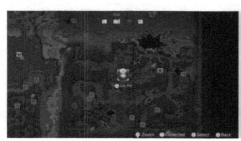
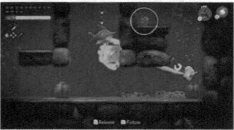

Hebra Mountain & Mount Lanayru (5 Might Crystals)

❖ *Might Crystal #1*

On Hebra Mountain, lower make your way north from where you find Conde sleeping initially to find a cave. Spawn a Platboom and use it to reach a ledge above the cave. There is an ice column here surrounded by grass that we can melt for a **Might Crystal**.

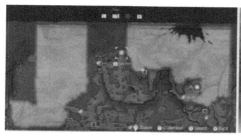 

❖ Might Crystal #2

On Hebra Mountain, lower proceed to the west from the broken bridge (the one Conde jumps us over) and when the path turns a corner, hop up on the ledge to the left. Defeat the Wolfos and Ice Keese here. In the southwestern corner of this ledge, you will find a patch of grass with a rock at its centre. Pick up the rock to find **Might Crystal**.

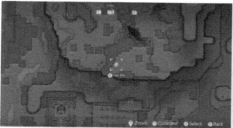 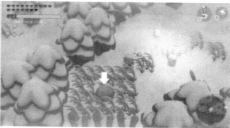

❖ Might Crystal #3

Head to the cave behind Conde's house. Before entering, spawn a Platboom and use it to reach a ledge above the cave. There is a block of ice here we can melt for a **Might Crystal**.

❖ Might Crystal #4

On Hebra Mountain, middle use the small section of land on the left side of the waterfall to the northwest of the main lake here to create a stairway of beds jutting out from the waterfall. From this, summon a Ghirro (or another flying beasty) and glide down to the sneaky out of sight ledge on the left.

In this area, melt the ice column in the grass here for a **Might Crystal**.

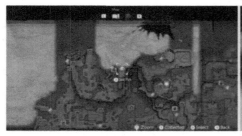

❖ *Might Crystal #5*

On Hebra Mountain, upper follow the set path here maneuvering around snowballs. As you go look for a ledge to the side of the path with an ice crystal. Melt this to find a **Might Crystal**.

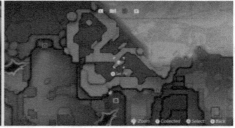

Eternal Forest (1 Might Crystal)

❖ *Might Crystal #1*

In the northwest corner of the area with the Lynel, you can climb up on top of the trees to find a raised ledge nearby with a suspicious looking collection of shrubs. Spin through the middle one to find a **Might Crystal**.

ALL ECHO LOCATIONS

Echoes are one of the most important collectibles that we can find in legend of Zelda: **Echo**es of Wisdom. Some are used for solving environmental puzzles, others are used for combat, more can be used to complete specific side-quests and still more can be just plain fun to play around with.

Each **Echo** requires a certain number of Tri Points (TP) to summon. The amount of TP available is represented by the number of Triangles following Tri about. By completing dungeons and optional rifts, you can level Tri up. Upon doing so you can reduce the amount of TP required to summon certain **Echo**es, as well as increase the TP that Tri has available. When maxed out, Tri will have 6TP available for use.

Below you'll find a list of all 127 **Echo**es, and where you can find them in our walkthrough organized by the order in which they appear in Zelda's Notebook.

Echo	TP	Location
001. Table	1 TP	Hyrule Castle - During Prologue.
002. Old Bed	1 TP	Hyrule Castle - During The Mysterious Rifts.
003. Soft Bed	2 TP	Gerudo Desert (Oasis) - During A Rift in the Gerudo Desert.
004. Zelda's Bed	3 TP	Hyrule Castle - After completing Dungeon - Hyrule Castle.
005. Decorative Shrub	1 TP	Hyrule Castle - During The Mysterious Rifts.
006. Wooden Box	1 TP	Hyrule Castle - During Prologue.
007. Pot	1 TP	Suthorn Village - During The Mysterious Rifts.
008. Hyrule Castle Pot	1 TP	Hyrule Castle - During Prologue.
009. Gerudo Pot	1 TP	Gerudo Desert - During A Rift in the Gerudo Desert.
010. Boulder	1 TP	Hyrule Castle - During The Mysterious Rifts.
011. Rock	1 TP	Suthorn Beach - During The Mysterious Rifts.
012. Lava Rock	4 TP	Eldin Volcano - During Lizalfos Burrow.
013. Ice Block	1 TP	Hebra Mountain - During Rift on Holy Mount Lanayru.
014. Snowball	2 TP	Hebra Mountain - During Rift on Holy Mount Lanayru.
015. Sign	1 TP	East of Suthorn Village - During The Mysterious Rifts.
016. Grilled Fish	1 TP	Jabul Waters (Seesyde Village) - During The Jabul Waters Rift.
017. Meat	1 TP	Suthorn Village - During The Mysterious Rifts.
018. Rock Roast	1 TP	Eldin Volcano (Rock-Roast Quarry) -

Echo	TP	Location
		During Rock-Roast Quarry.
019. Stuffed Toy	1 TP	Hyrule Field (Graveyard Cave) - During Lands of the Goddesses - Mount Lanayru.
020. Carrot	1 TP	Hyrule Field - Complete Side Quest: Impa's Gift.
021. Water Block	1 TP	Jabul Waters (Stilled Jabul Waters) - During The Jabul Waters Rift - Part 2.
022. Elephant Statue	1 TP	Dungeon - Gerudo Sanctum.
023. Hawk Statue	1 TP	Dungeon - Gerudo Sanctum.
024. Cat Statue	1 TP	Dungeon - Gerudo Sanctum.
025. Snake Statue	1 TP	Dungeon - Gerudo Sanctum.
026. Ancient Orb	1 TP	Eternal Forest - During The Prime Energy and Null.
027. Trampoline	1 TP	Suthorn Village - During The Mysterious Rifts.
028. Wind Cannon	2 TP	Gerudo Desert - During A Rift in the Gerudo Desert.
029. Flying Tile	3 TP	Dungeon - Gerudo Sanctum.
030. Cloud	2 TP	Hebra Mountain (Stilled Hebra Mountain) - During Rift on Holy Mount Lanayru.
031. Spiked Roller	4 TP	Hyrule Field (cave east of Kakariko Village) - During Hyrule Field Exploration.
032. Beetle Mound	3 TP	Gerudo Desert - During A Rift in the Gerudo Desert.
033. Firework	2 TP	Complete Side Quest: The Fireworks Artist.
034. Brazier	2 TP	Suthorn Forest - During The Mysterious Rifts.
035. Zol	1 TP	Suthorn Beach - During The Mysterious Rifts.
036. Ignizol	2 TP	Suthorn Forest (Middle Cave) - During The Mysterious Rifts.
037. Hydrozol	2 TP	Jabul Waters (Zora Cove West Cave) - During The Jabul Waters Rift.
038. Buzz Blob	3 TP	Faron Wetlands - During A Rift in the

Echo	TP	Location
		Faron Wetlands.
039. Spear Moblin	2 TP	Suthorn Forest - During The Mysterious Rifts.
040. Spear Moblin Lv.2	4 TP	Jabul Waters (Zora River) - During Jabul Waters Exploration.
041. Sword Moblin	2 TP	Hyrule Field - During Searching for Everyone - Jabul Waters.
042. Sword Moblin Lv.2	4 TP	Hyrule Field East - During Hyrule Field Exploration.
043. Sword Moblin Lv.3	2 TP	Hebra Mountain (Cave by Moblin Camp east of Conde's house) - During Rift on Holy Mount Lanayru.
044. Club Boarboblin	2 TP	Gerudo Desert - During A Rift in the Gerudo Desert.
045. Club Boarboblin Lv.2	4 TP	Gerudo Desert - During Gerudo Desert Exploration.
046. Boomerang Boarbolin	2 TP	Gerudo Desert - During A Rift in the Gerudo Desert.
047. Boomerang Boarbolin Lv.2	4 TP	Gerudo Desert - During Gerudo Desert Exploration.
048. Lynel	6 TP	Eternal Forest - During The Prime Energy and Null.
049. Lizalfos	3 TP	Eldin Volcano - During The Rift on Eldin Volcano.
050. Lizalfos Lv.2	4 TP	Eldin Volcano (Lizalfos Burrow) - During Lizalfos Burrow.
051. Lizalfos Lv.3	5 TP	Faron Wetlands (West Cave) - During A Rift in the Faron Wetlands.
052. Darknut	3 TP	Dungeon - Suthorn Ruins.
053. Darknut Lv.2	4 TP	Dungeon - Hyrule Castle.
054. Darknut Lv.3	5 TP	Faron Wetlands (East Ruins Cave) - During A Rift in the Faron Wetlands.
055. Armos	2 TP	Faron Wetlands (East Ruins Cave) - During A Rift in the Faron Wetlands.
056. Ball-and-Chain Trooper	4 TP	Dungeon - Hyrule Castle.
057. Gibdo	3 TP	Gerudo Desert (Cryptic Cavern) - During A Rift in the Gerudo Desert -

Echo	TP	Location
		Part 2.
058. Gibdo Lv.2	4 TP	Gerudo Desert (Cryptic Cavern) - During A Rift in the Gerudo Desert - Part 2.
059. ReDead	3 TP	Gerudo Desert - During A Rift in the Gerudo Desert.
060. Fire Wizzrobe	5 TP	Eldin Volcano - During Lizalfos Burrow.
061. Ice Wizzrobe	5 TP	Hebra Mountain (Middle) - During Rift on Holy Mount Lanayru.
062. Electric Wizzrobe	5 TP	Faron Wetlands - During A Rift in the Faron Wetlands.
063. Caromadillo	2 TP	Suthorn Forest (West Cave) - During The Mysterious Rifts.
064. Caromadillo Lv.2	3 TP	Gerudo Desert - During A Rift in the Gerudo Desert.
065. Rope	1 TP	Suthorn Forest - During The Mysterious Rifts.
066. Tornando	2 TP	Gerudo Desert - During A Rift in the Gerudo Desert.
067. Ribbitune	2 TP	Hyrule Field - During Lands of the Goddesses - Mount Lanayru.
068. Drippitune	3 TP	Faron Wetlands - During A Rift in the Faron Wetlands.
069. Torch Slug	3 TP	Eldin Volcano - During The Rift on Eldin Volcano.
070. Freeze Slug	3 TP	Hebra Mountain (Stilled Hebra Mountain) - During Rift on Holy Mount Lanayru.
071. Holmill	3 TP	Gerudo Desert - During Ancestor's Cave of Rest Rift.
072. Wolfos	3 TP	Hebra Mountain (Stilled Hebra Mountain) - During Rift on Holy Mount Lanayru.
073. White Wolfos	5 TP	Dungeon - Lanayru Temple.
074. Keese	1 TP	Beach Cave - During The Mysterious Rifts.
075. Fire Keese	4 TP	Eldin Volcano (Lizalfos Burrow) - During Lizalfos Burrow.

Echo	TP	Location
076. Ice Keese	4 TP	Hebra Mountain - During Rift on Holy Mount Lanayru.
077. Electric Keese	4 TP	Faron Wetlands (Stilled Faron Wetlands) - During A Rift in the Faron Wetlands.
078. Mothula	3 TP	Dungeon - Gerudo Sanctum.
079. Mothula Lv.2	5 TP	Faron Wetlands - During A Rift in the Faron Wetlands.
080. Needlefly	2 TP	Jabul Waters (Zora River) - During The Jabul Waters Rift.
081. Albatrawl	2 TP	Jabul Waters (Zora Cove) - During The Jabul Waters Rift.
082. Crow	2 TP	Suthorn Prairie - During Searching for Everyone - Gerudo Desert.
083. Beakon	3 TP	Faron Wetlands - During A Rift in the Faron Wetlands.
084. Guay	3 TP	Hyrule Field - During Searching for Everyone - Jabul Waters.
085. Octorok	1 TP	Suthorn Prairie - During Searching for Everyone.
086. Fire Octo	2 TP	Eldin Volcano - During Lizalfos Burrow.
087. Ice Octo	2 TP	Hebra Mountain (Middle) - During Rift on Holy Mount Lanayru.
088. Sea Urchin	1 TP	Suthorn Beach - During The Mysterious Rifts.
089. Sand Crab	1 TP	Hyrule Field East - During Searching for Everyone - Jabul Waters.
090. Biri	2 TP	Jabul Waters (Zora Cove) - During The Jabul Waters Rift.
091. Tangler	1 TP	Hyrule Field - During Searching for Everyone - Jabul Waters.
092. Tangler Lv.2	2 TP	Jabul Waters (Zora Cove East Cave) - During The Jabul Waters Rift.
093. Bombfish	4 TP	Jabul Waters (Middle Cave) - During The Jabul Waters Rift.
094. Chompfin	4 TP	Dungeon - Jabul Ruins.
095. Piranha	2 TP	Faron Wetlands - During A Rift in the Faron Wetlands.
096. Sand Piranha	2 TP	Gerudo Desert - During A Rift in the

Echo	TP	Location
		Gerudo Desert.
097. Deku Baba	2 TP	Dungeon - Suthorn Ruins.
098. Bio Deku Baba	3 TP	Dungeon - Jabul Ruins.
099. Deku Baba Lv.2	3 TP	Faron Wetlands - During A Rift in the Faron Wetlands.
100. Peahat	3 TP	Suthorn Forest (West Cave) - During The Mysterious Rifts.
101. Giant Goponga Flower	4 TP	Faron Wetlands - During A Rift in the Faron Wetlands.
102. Zirro	3 TP	Eldin Volcano (Stilled Goron City) - During The Rift on Eldin Volcano.
103. Ghirro	3 TP	Eldin Volcano (Cave) - During The Rift on Eldin Volcano.
104. Mini-Moldorm	2 TP	Hyrule Field West - During Hyrule Field Exploration.
105. Strandtula	2 TP	Dungeon - Suthorn Ruins.
106. Crawltula	3 TP	Suthorn Prairie - During Searching for Everyone.
107. Baby Gohma	2 TP	Faron Wetlands - During A Rift in the Faron Wetlands.
108. Beetle	1 TP	Gerudo Desert - During A Rift in the Gerudo Desert.
109. Aruroda	2 TP	Gerudo Desert - During A Rift in the Gerudo Desert.
110. Tektite	2 TP	Lake Hylia - During Searching for Everyone - Jabul Waters.
111. Tektite Lv.2	3 TP	Hebra Mountain (Middle, West Cave) - During Rift on Holy Mount Lanayru.
112. Hoarder	3 TP	Faron Wetlands - During A Rift in the Faron Wetlands.
113. Poe	4 TP	Dungeon - Gerudo Sanctum.
114. Moa	3 TP	Hebra Mountain (Upper) - During Rift on Holy Mount Lanayru.
115. Goo Specter	3 TP	Faron Wetlands - During A Rift in the Faron Wetlands.
116. Ghini	1 TP	Hyrule Field (Graveyard Cave) - During Lands of the Goddesses - Mount Lanayru.
117. Ghini Lv.2	1 TP	Hyrule Field (Graveyard Cave) -

Echo	TP	Location
		During Lands of the Goddesses - Mount Lanayru.
118. Leever	2 TP	Hebra Mountain - During Rift on Holy Mount Lanayru.
119. Pathblade	1 TP	Gerudo Desert (Cryptic Cavern) - During A Rift in the Gerudo Desert - Part 2.
120. Gustmaster	4 TP	Dungeon - Hyrule Castle.
121. Tweelus	2 TP	Eldin Volcano - During Lizalfos Burrow.
122. Temper Tweelus	3 TP	Hebra Mountain (Upper) - During Rift on Holy Mount Lanayru.
123. Freezard	3 TP	Hebra Mountain - During Rift on Holy Mount Lanayru.
124. Snomaul	3 TP	Hebra Mountain - During Rift on Holy Mount Lanayru.
125. Spark	2 TP	Hyrule Field East (East Ruins) - During Side Quest: Let's Play a Game.
126. Platboom	3 TP	Gerudo Desert - During A Rift in the Gerudo Desert - Part 2.
127. Beamos	3 TP	Faron Wetlands (East Ruins Cave) - During A Rift in the Faron Wetlands.

Made in United States
North Haven, CT
18 December 2024

62990018R00196